Employment Tribunals

SECOND EDITION

Related titles from Law Society Publishing:

Age Discrimination
General Editor: Shaman Kapoor

Discrimination in Employment
General Editor: Jenny Mulvaney

Employment Law Handbook (3rd Edition)
Daniel Barnett and Henry Scrope

Titles from Law Society Publishing can be ordered from all good bookshops
or direct (telephone 0870 850 1422, email **law.society@prolog.uk.com** or visit
our online shop at **www.lawsociety.org.uk/bookshop**).

EMPLOYMENT TRIBUNALS

A Practical Guide

SECOND EDITION

Isabel Manley and Elaine Heslop

The Law Society

© Law Society 2008

ISBN 978-1-85328-633-9

First edition published in 2004
This second edition published in 2008 by the Law Society
113 Chancery Lane, London WC2A 1PL

Typeset by IDSUK (DataConnection) Ltd
Printed by CPI Antony Rowe, Chippenham, Wilts

FSC
Mixed Sources
Product group from well-managed
forests and other controlled sources

Cert no. SGS-COC-2953
www.fsc.org
© 1996 Forest Stewardship Council

The paper used for the text pages of this book is FSC certified. FSC (The Forest Stewardship Council) is an international network to promote responsible management of the world's forests.

Contents

Preface and acknowledgements

A book on employment tribunal procedures will always present its own challenges and rewards. There were substantial changes to legislation and rules which govern the process of taking claims through the tribunal system in 2004 and these were all tackled in our first edition. We aimed then, as we do now, to try to explain how these changes operated in the context of taking and defending claims in the employment tribunal.

We hope that this second edition reflects a more analytical approach to the changes which were all new at the time of the first edition. It certainly reflects the fact that during the past three or so years since the 2004 Dispute Resolution Regulations were introduced practitioners and tribunals have had to do some hard thinking about the workings of these Regulations, the relevant parts of the Employment Act 2002 and the revised 2004 employment tribunal rules. The Employment Appeal Tribunal has been required on a number of occasions to come to our aid and it has provided some highly useful and insightful guidance to many puzzling aspects of the changes, much of which we are grateful to be able to refer to in this edition.

Although there are more changes on the horizon we believe it is still relevant to revisit the processes which are now embedded firmly into the way that tribunal claims are conducted. We can look back at the early days of the new processes and see how they now impact on our conduct of employment tribunal claims.

Many of the processes introduced in late 2004 will be substantially revised in the not-too-distant future, but those processes have meant that, in the context of an employment dispute, both employers and employees have been required to focus more on dispute resolution, and tribunals have been able to use more active powers of case management to assist in the efficient processing of claims. This legacy and much of the good practice associated with careful preparation of employment tribunal claims is likely to continue.

We have tried to use this second edition to guide both employees and employers and their advisers through the process of conducting and defending a claim, to assist them in getting over preliminary hurdles, and to help them prepare for a tribunal case. We have tried, as before, to sprinkle the guidance with hints and tips from our experience where we think it might be of assistance. We have, as ever, been grateful to a number of people whose writing and thoughts have assisted us in revisiting this book, including colleagues at Watford Employment Tribunal, Kent Law Clinic and Daniel Barnett.

We are also conscious of the support and encouragement of our families and friends who have generously given their time in a number of ways to allow us to revisit this book in recent months.

The law is stated as on 1 March 2008.

Abbreviations

ACAS	Advisory, Conciliation and Arbitration Service
DDA 1995	Disability Discrimination Act 1995
DDP	disciplinary and dismissal procedures
EA 2002	Employment Act 2002
EAT	Employment Appeal Tribunal
EAT Rules 1993	Employment Appeal Tribunal Rules 1993, SI 1993/2854
ECJ	European Court of Justice
EDT	effective date of termination (of employment)
EHRC	Equality and Human Rights Commission
ERA 1996	Employment Rights Act 1996
ET	employment tribunal
ETA 1996	Employment Tribunals Act 1996
GP	grievance procedures
HRA 1998	Human Rights Act 1998
SDA 1975	Sex Discrimination Act 1975
'the 2001 Rules'	Schedule 1 to the Employment Tribunals (Constitution and Rules of Procedure) Regulations 2001, SI 2001/1171
'the Dispute Resolution Regulations'	Employment Act 2002 (Dispute Resolution) Regulations 2004, SI 2004/752
'the Recoupment Regulations'	Employment Protection (Recoupment of Jobseeker's Allowance and Income Support) Regulations 1996, SI 1996/2349
'the Regulations'	Employment Tribunals (Constitution and Rules of Procedure) Regulations 2004, SI 2004/1861
'the Rules', 'the 2004 Rules' or 'the Employment Tribunal Rules'	Schedule 1 to the Employment Tribunals (Constitution and Rules of Procedure) Regulations 2004, SI 2004/1861
UD	unfair dismissal

Glossary

Appeal A party's right, once an employment tribunal has made a decision, to appeal against it on a point of law to the employment appeal tribunal. An appeal can be made against a preliminary or a final decision or judgment.

Application A party may make an application to an employment tribunal in the circumstances set out in the 2004 Rules (see **Rules** below). Applications must be in writing but there is no set form or precedent for how to set them out. What they must refer to will be inherent in the Rule under which the application is made.

Bundle The collated documents which both parties to an employment tribunal claim have agreed which will be used as part of the evidence to try the issues.

Case management The employment tribunals are required to manage the preparation of a case to ensure that it is heard promptly and fairly, and that the issues are made clear and the parties are properly prepared. They will issue orders and/or hold a case management discussion with the parties to assist in this process, prior to the main Hearing. This concept came into being in the 2004 Rules (see **Rules** below), but employment tribunals have always had the capacity to take an active part in preparing cases for a hearing.

Chronology A summary of the main events in the employment tribunal claim. Prepared by the claimant and agreed between the parties in advance of the Hearing date.

Claimant The person that brings the claim in the employment tribunal – employee/worker.

Claim form ET1 The form that the claimant in an employment tribunal case is required to use to start the proceedings.

Counsel A barrister in practice in their own right who will be instructed to advise or draft aspects of the claim and/or briefed to attend the employment tribunal hearing and represent a party.

Cross-examination   The process employed by an opponent to a party to establish his own party's case, by means of adversarial questioning designed to draw from a witness any admissions which will help the opponent's case. A barrister advocate will have been taught cross-examination techniques.

Disclosure   Where a party informs the other of their relevant documents.

Discovery   Where the parties in the tribunal claim give each other the titles/descriptions of the documents they have in their possession which are relevant to the claim – they may also be ordered or directed to provide this by the employment tribunal.

Evidence-in-chief   The oral or written evidence given by a witness, usually contained in a typed statement, not including that given when they are asked questions by the other party's representative.

Exchange   Parties to a tribunal claim are usually ordered or directed by an employment tribunal to exchange witness statements so many days before a hearing date. Exchange is normally simultaneous (as agreed between the parties) either by post or by fax.

Expert   Someone who is called upon to give an opinion, either in writing or as a witness to assist the tribunal in making a decision, based on their expert knowledge in a particular (non-legal) area.

Hearing   This may be a hearing to deal with issues during a case – either a pre-hearing review or case management discussion. Where it has a capital 'H' it is the main or full Hearing.

Inspection   Where the parties let each other have sight of or copies of their documents prior to the Hearing date. This is usually as agreed or as required by a timetable set out by the employment tribunal.

Issues   The main areas of factual dispute and employment law which the claimant has raised and which need to be decided for or against the claimant by the employment tribunal.

Judgment   A final tribunal decision on the case.

Judicial review   An application to the divisional court of the High Court to challenge a decision made by a public body including decisions made by employment tribunals which are not capable of being challenged by review or appeal.

Jurisdiction   The powers which are given to an employment tribunal as set out in various Acts or regulations. A tribunal may not act outside the jurisdiction given to it. Its jurisdiction to hear claims is also defined by various employment law statutes which state, for example, who can bring what claims or within what time period.

Order   Can be made by an employment tribunal in the circumstances set out in the 2004 Rules (see **Rules** below). The tribunal can either order or direct.

Practice Directions   Powers are given to the President of the employment tribunals under the 2004 Rules to make Practice Directions. As in the civil court system these are to ensure uniformity and efficiency in how parties use the system.

Pre-hearing review   A hearing prior to a main Hearing in order to decide a particular point. An example is to decide if the claimant has the correct legal status to bring a claim.

Questionnaires   Usually means the statutory questions relating to claims of discrimination. See Chapter 4 for further details.

Remedy or **remedies**   What may be awarded to a successful claimant by the employment tribunal. Includes money awards (compensation and damages) and declarations, recommendations and reinstatement orders to be complied with by the respondent.

Respondent   Defends the claim in the employment tribunal – usually the employer and in some discrimination cases may be the alleged individual discriminator.

Response form   ET3 – the form which the respondent to an employment tribunal claim is required to use to defend an employment tribunal claim.

Review   The employment tribunal's power to revisit Decisions on application by a party, in certain circumstances.

Rules   These govern the powers of the employment tribunal – the Rules are contained in the Employment Tribunals (Constitution and Rules of Procedures) Regulations 2004 – the Rules of Procedure are contained in the Schedules to the Regulations.

Skeleton argument   A summary of the main issues and the legal basis and arguments from the standpoint of a party to the tribunal claim. Each party's representative (usually a barrister or solicitor) will prepare one which highlights their arguments, as supported by law and case law, for succeeding in the claim.

Statutory procedures   The grievance and/or disciplinary or dismissal procedures which employees/employers are required to use under the Dispute Resolution Regulations.

Strike out   The phrase which is used where a chairman or a tribunal decides to bring to an end part or all of a claim or response. It is final except for the possibility of review or appeal.

Submissions   The summing up and legal argument which each side will present to summarise and support their case at the end of the tribunal hearing. Will usually be prepared in advance (and may be called the skeleton argument) and revised as necessary once the evidence has been heard.

Witness statements   All witnesses to be called by a party to an employment tribunal claim will be required to set out their evidence in advance in writing by way of a witness statement. The statement should be signed and dated (but there is currently no Practice Direction which requires this).

Table of cases

Table of statutes

Table of statutory instruments and European legislation

European legislation

Introduction to employment tribunals

1.1 INTRODUCTION

When the first edition of this book was published in October 2004, the Employment Tribunals (Constitution and Rules of Procedure) Regulations 2004, SI 2004/1861 had just come into force. At the same time the provisions of the Employment Act (EA) 2002 and the Employment Act 2002 (Dispute Resolution) Regulations 2002, SI 2004/752 ('the Dispute Resolution Regulations'), dealing with the statutory dismissal and disciplinary and grievance procedures, also took effect, leading to enormous changes in access to and process at employment tribunals for both workers/employees and employers.

In writing the first edition we had to make some assumptions about how the new Rules and requirements of the statutory procedures would be interpreted and how they would work in practice. The experience of the majority of users has been added complications and complexities, more hearings and delays in getting to the full Hearing. In 2006/07, of the over 10,000 claims initially rejected only 3,891 were resubmitted and accepted, although we have no idea how many may have been resolved between the parties. Some improvements have been seen in the workings of the online communication system and, to a certain extent, case management.

In December 2006 the Secretary of State at the DTI appointed Michael Gibbons to carry out a review of 'options for simplifying and improving all aspects of employment dispute resolution, to make the system work better for employees and employees'. The report *Better Dispute Resolution* was published in March 2007 and, to the considerable relief of many people, suggested abolition of the procedures. A total of 17 recommendations under three main headings were made. Under the first heading 'Support employers and employees to resolve more disputes in the workplace', the very first recommendation was 'Repeal the statutory dispute resolution procedures set out in the Dispute Resolution Regulations', with suggestions then made for guidelines and incentives to encourage early resolution. Under the next heading 'Actively assist employers and employees to resolve disputes that have not been resolved in the workplace', the recommendations include introducing a simple process for settling monetary disputes without a hearing, providing advice through a helpline, providing advice on alternatives, and offering incentives to early reso-lution. Under the third heading 'Make the employment tribunal system simpler and cheaper for users and government' (a call we have heard consistently for many years), seven recommendations were made, including simplifying employment law, simplifying the claim and response forms, unifying time limits, encouraging active, early case management, judges sitting alone, and consideration of whether tribunals have appropriate powers for dealing with weak and vexatious claims.

In March 2007 a consultation document incorporating most of Gibbons' recommendations was published, with a closing date of 20 June 2007. The Employment Simplification Bill was announced in the draft legislative pro-gramme for 2007/08, with key benefits being that it would 'Simplify, clarify and build a stronger enforcement regime for key aspects of employment law' and provide administration savings through 'legislation to implement the Gibbons review'. In early December 2007 it was published as the 'Employment Bill' and contains provisions abolishing the statutory procedures, giving tribunals a dis-cretion to increase awards by 25 per cent for a failure to comply with the ACAS code, and removing fixed conciliation periods. At the time of writing it is unclear when the Bill is likely to take effect but it is believed that it will not be before April 2009, with current rumours that it may be October 2009. One of the questions which has not yet been answered is how much of the Rules will need to be changed. What is clear is that the changes will all take some time, partly because primary legislation is required for some aspects, and no major changes would thus be expected until 2009 at the earliest.

We have therefore decided that this is an appropriate time to prepare a second edition of this book, as the system has bedded down and thus we can now be clearer about certain aspects. We also now have some clarification and guidance from the Employment Appeal Tribunal (EAT), particularly on what constitutes a grievance, what considerations apply when reviewing default judgments and accepting late claims and responses, and on the application of the Rules.

This book is aimed mainly at those who prepare cases on behalf of people involved in employment tribunal proceedings. Whilst the primary readership may be solicitors or others who are legally qualified, it is hoped that human resources departments, lay advisers and trade unionists will also find it useful. If you are not legally qualified and you are making a charge, including under a conditional fee arrangement, you must be authorised by the Ministry of Justice. Failure to gain authorisation or an exemption could lead to criminal proceed-ings and increase the possibility of a wasted costs order under r.48 (see **13.2**). See also *Miller* v. *Community Links Trust* (unreported, UKEAT/0486/07) where the papers in an EAT case were referred to Jack Straw as the regulator. Those who are embarking on their own representation, either through choice or lack of it, should also be able to find the information they need within this book.

Where we discuss rules and procedure they will apply, as a general rule, across the most common jurisdictions of the employment tribunals. Many references will be made to the Employment Tribunals (Constitution and Rules of Procedure) Regulations 2004, SI 2004/1861 which will be referred to in this book as 'the Regulations'. In particular, we will also refer regularly to Sched.1 to those Regulations which contains the Employment Tribunals Rules of Procedure, which will be referred to throughout this book as 'the Rules' or 'the 2004 Rules'. Where a rule number is referred to with no further information, the reference is to the 2004 Rules. Schedule 1 covers claims involving unfair dismissal, discrimination, unpaid wages and most other matters that constitute by far the largest number of cases. Readers should also be aware that there are separate schedules to the Regulations which relate to some of the less common jurisdictions, training levy appeals and national security. The Regulations were re-written after consultation and are a little more user-friendly and in plain(er) English than their predecessor 2001 Rules. The Rules themselves are divided into sections, making it somewhat easier to find the relevant part.

Employment Tribunals (Constitution and Rules of Procedure) Regulations 2004

Regulations 1–20

Rules contained in Schedules as follows:
Schedule 1 – Everything except those below (rules 1–61)
Schedule 2 – National security
Schedule 3 – Levy appeals
Schedule 4 – Health and safety, improvement and prohibition notice appeals
Schedule 5 – Non-discrimination notices
Schedule 6 – Equal value

Whilst this book concentrates on employment tribunals, it is important to consider any and all alternatives before getting involved in the often long and stressful business of a tribunal case. Early dispute resolution has much to commend it. Consideration should always be given to mediation, conciliation and settlement at all stages (see also **Chapter 3**). Since August 2006 a pilot scheme for judicial mediation has been running in three tribunal regions: London Central, Newcastle and Birmingham. Early indications are that it has met with a measure of success and may be rolled out across other regions, but much depends on funding and training.

There have been significant changes in employment tribunals over the last six years. These include the recommendations of the Leggatt report with respect to tribunals generally (see **1.5**), the recommendations of the Employment Tribunal System Taskforce which reported in July 2002, and the provisions of EA 2002. Most of these changes came into effect in October 2004 and with the absorption of the employment tribunals into the Tribunals Service (now a part of the Ministry of Justice). The implementation of the Dispute

Resolution Regulations, new Rules and considerable administrative and technological changes have seen some big changes to how cases run in employment tribunals. When the changes were relatively new much had to be tested over time, and we now have some clarification from the EAT, particularly on the flexibility which should be applied to acceptance of claims and responses. There remains, though, considerable doubt around some other areas, for instance the uplift or reduction for failing to follow the relevant procedure.

There has also been an increasing concentration by the employment tribunal system to improve the processes in accordance with the 'overriding objective' (below) and the human rights aspects of a fair trial. Continuing attempts to achieve a greater degree of consistency across the regions are being made, and this can be expected to continue. There is increasing use of case management (see **Chapters 7** and **8**) which means that files are looked at regularly by a tribunal judge and matters progressed in an appropriate manner. The introduction of a 'track' system allows cases to be allocated to a 'short track' if they are of a certain type, usually low value money claims. This system largely accords with the fixed periods introduced by EA 2002 for Advisory, Conciliation and Arbitration Service (ACAS) conciliation: seven weeks, 13 weeks and no fixed period.

Case study: *Molly Martin* v. *Just in Time Catering Ltd*

Throughout the book we make reference to a fictional case (*Molly Martin* v. *Just in Time*) as an example of the sort of case that may go through the employment tribunal system. This is for demonstrative purposes only, illustrating the process and what might happen from the institution of proceedings, through case management, hearings and the final judgment. The facts of the case are set out briefly below.

Molly Martin v. *Just in Time Catering Ltd*

Molly Martin has been working as a 'casual' waitress for Just in Time for five years, starting some time in 2002. The company is a firm of external caterers for events such as weddings, birthday parties and corporate functions of various kinds. They have a large number of staff whom they refer to as 'casual', who are called on as required from time to time. Some preferred staff have longer service with the company and are considered to be more reliable, and Molly falls into this category. She has worked for them, on average, for three days per week. She has two children of school age. The company provides transport to each event and staff are required to wear a uniform.

Molly has become pregnant and when she told the Events Manager in November, he asked her how long she would continue working for them. Molly answered that she wished to take maternity leave just before the baby was due in June and then for a few weeks before returning to work but that she would need more notice for events as she would have to arrange childcare. He advised her that this would be difficult because of the nature of

---

4

the business. He said that he had had some bad experiences with pregnant staff before as they had to take lots of time off for medical appointments and had morning sickness. He said 'We'll see how it goes'. The Events Manager also made comments about how pregnant staff look in the uniform. Molly was upset and wrote to Just in Time on 26 November complaining about his treatment of her, which she believed was connected to her pregnancy. After that there were a number of last minute changes to Molly's shifts which were particularly difficult for her to cope with because of her children.

On 6 December the Events Manager asked her when her maternity leave was starting as 'it was already beginning to show'. He said she should think about leaving straight away. Molly understood that she was being dismissed. She has heard nothing from the company since.

There are a number of possibilities and likely outcomes that arise from these imaginary but not completely fantastic facts. We will use the progress of this claim to illustrate how representatives may choose to approach different issues and how the employment tribunal may deal with such issues. However, it should always be remembered that a slight difference in facts can make an enormous difference to any outcome and it may well be that similar cases would not be decided in the same way.

1.2   TERMINOLOGY

A glossary of terms is included at the beginning of this book, containing words and phrases commonly used in employment tribunals. As far as possible, plain language has been used in this book, but it is inevitable that some technical legal words have to be used from time to time. It is also important to point out that some of the terminology changed in 2004 so that, from time to time, you may come across some of the 'old' terminology of the tribunal system. For example, the claim form (IT1 or ET1) was formerly known as the 'Originating Application', and the respondent's reply as the 'Notice of Appearance' (IT3 or ET3). They are now the claim form (or the ET1) and the response (or ET3). In 2007, the Tribunals, Courts and Enforcement Act changed the title of 'chairman' to 'employment judge' from 1 December 2007. This may well take some time to get used to and much of the legislation, both primary and secondary, still refers to the 'chairman'. We have used 'judge' throughout this edition.

Throughout the book we refer to advisers, parties or representatives to describe those involved in proceedings and those acting on behalf of both sides. In fact, in the majority of hearings one or both parties represent themselves. The person making the claim (almost always the employee/worker) is referred to as the 'claimant' (formerly known as the 'applicant') and the person defending the claim (almost always the employer) is referred to as the 'respondent'. This reflects usage in the tribunal system itself. There remain some cases for which the employment tribunal has jurisdiction where the claimant may be an employer – for instance, in a claim as between transferee and transferor under the 2006 TUPE Regulations, appeals against national minimum wage enforcement orders and training levies – but these cases are really quite rare.

Abbreviations will also be used in the book, especially where these are used commonly within the employment tribunal system itself. For instance, we refer to the claim form and the response form as the ET1 and ET3. Many Acts of Parliament are also abbreviated; for example the Employment Rights Act 1996 will be referred to as ERA 1996, the Sex Discrimination Act 1975 is abbreviated to SDA 1975, and so on. If you are in any doubt, a full list of these abbreviations appears at the beginning of this book.

1.3 HISTORY OF EMPLOYMENT TRIBUNALS

Employment tribunals were known as 'industrial tribunals' up until 1998. They were created by the Industrial Training Act 1964, initially to hear appeals regarding industrial training levies. During the 1960s, their jurisdiction was extended to include contracts of employment and redundancy payments, with unfair dismissal first being added by the Industrial Relations Act 1971. With a number of discrimination jurisdictions given to employment tribunals during the 1970s, and disability discrimination, minimum wage and working time added during the 1990s, the number of areas currently covered amount to over 80. Employment tribunals are not courts of record but are inferior courts, so that they are covered by the rules on contempt of court and vexatious litigants. It also means that, where an employment tribunal has decided a point, other courts cannot hear a case arising out of the same facts. This is known as the principle of 'res judicata' or 'estoppel' and will be applied where any court, including a previous employment tribunal, has made a determination on a point, it cannot be re-opened. It will prevent a person trying to raise new points that could have been raised before (known as the rule in *Henderson* v. *Henderson* and see, for its application to employment tribunal proceedings, *Barber* v. *Staffs County Council* [1996] IRLR 209).

Whilst the number of jurisdictions and the complexity of matters coming before employment tribunals have changed considerably since their inception, tribunals continue to aspire to be what Lord Donovan first identified as 'easily accessible, speedy, informal' (in the Donovan Report in 1968). It remains the case that employment tribunals are less formal than most courtrooms with the parties, representatives, witnesses and members of the tribunal remaining seated, no wigs or gowns being worn and a degree of flexibility in the hearings. Indeed, the Rules specifically provide for this within r.14:

> (2) So far as it appears to it appropriate to do so, the judge or tribunal shall seek to avoid formality in his or its proceedings and shall not be bound by any

enactment or rule of law relating to the admissibility of evidence in proceedings before the courts.

(3) The judge or tribunal (as the case may be) shall make such enquiries of persons appearing before him or it and of witnesses as he or it considers appropriate and shall otherwise conduct the hearing in such manner as he or it considers most appropriate for the clarification of the issues and generally to the just handling of the proceedings.

What this informality means in practice can vary considerably, depending on a number of factors. These can include the nature of the case, the value of the claim, its legal complexity, whether the parties are represented and by whom, and the preference of the judge and tribunal dealing with the case at any given time. What it does mean, in broad terms, is that there are no 'pleadings' (the legal documents which set out the case in the ordinary civil courts). After the initial claim form, response and any further particulars, most matters can be dealt with by letter, or, indeed, in some cases telephone and there is a degree of flexibility in how the case proceeds. Hearings should be conducted in a polite manner, but the formal rules of evidence do not apply and the language used should be accessible to those present. While employment tribunals and the Tribunals Service are continuing to strive to achieve this accessibility, it is important that those who use the system should also ensure that they avoid unnecessary legal language or formality – remembering, of course, that respect should be shown at all times to the other party and/or representative, any witnesses, the tribunal and its staff.

One of the most important aspects of the employment tribunals is what is known as the 'overriding objective'. This was first introduced into tribunal procedure in the 2001 Rules and is a concept borrowed from the Civil Procedure Rules 1998, SI 1998/3132, which apply in the ordinary civil courts. It is worth setting out the 2004 version of the regulation in full here.

The overriding objective

(1) The overriding objective of these regulations and the rules in Schedules 1, 2, 3, 4, and 6 is to enable tribunals and judges to deal with cases justly.

(2) Dealing with a case justly includes, so far as practicable:

  (a) ensuring that the parties are on an equal footing;
  (b) dealing with the case in ways which are proportionate to the complexity or importance of the issues;
  (c) ensuring that it is dealt with expeditiously and fairly; and
  (d) saving expense.

(3) A tribunal or judge shall seek to give effect to the overriding objective when it or he:

  (a) exercises any power given to it or him by these regulations or the rules in Schedules 1, 2, 3, 4 and 5; or
  (b) interprets these regulations or any rule in Schedules 1, 2, 3, 4 and 5.

(4) The parties shall assist the tribunal or judge to further the overriding objective.

It should particularly be noted from reg.3(4) that the parties are also required to assist the overriding objective and that it is part of the whole process. This will particularly include case management matters (see **Chapters 7** and **8**) and the Hearing (**Chapter 10**).

1.4 JURISDICTION OF EMPLOYMENT TRIBUNALS

A list of all the current jurisdictions appears at **Appendix 5**. The main ones, which make up the vast majority of claims and cases heard, are as follows:

The claim	Statutory provision	Number of claims 2006/07
Unfair dismissal	Employment Rights Act 1996	44,491
Unpaid wages	Employment Rights Act 1996	34,857
Breach of contract	Employment Tribunals Extension of Jurisdiction Order 1994	27,298
Sex discrimination	Sex Discrimination Act 1975	28,153
Redundancy pay	Employment Rights Act 1996	7,692
Equal pay	Equal Pay Act 1970	44,013
Race discrimination	Race Relations Act 1976	3,780
Disability discrimination	Disability Discrimination Act 1995	5,533
Working time	Working Time Regulations 1998	21,127
With 'others', total claims registered		238,546

Apart from the equal pay figure above, which is largely accounted for by mass equal pay litigation involving public sector NHS and local authority employees, it can be seen that it remains the case that unfair dismissal claims, which can be brought under the Employment Rights Act (ERA) 1996, form by far the largest single proportion of employment tribunal work. There has also been an increase in 'multi-action' claims where the application is for determination under more than one statutory authority: for example, very commonly a discrimination claim will be brought along with an unfair dismissal and/or a breach of contract claim at the end of employment.

The work of employment tribunals continues to increase, with newer jurisdictions being added in the years since the publication of the first edition of this book. These included the addition of matters contained within EA 2002 on flexible working and paternity leave (from April 2003), fixed-term employees, discrimination on the grounds of sexual orientation and religion or belief and, from 2006, age discrimination. The figures for claims in these areas are still comparatively low but growing: for instance, there were 972 age discrimination claims, 648 religious discrimination claims and 470 sexual orientation discrimination claims during 2006/7.

It is very important to remember that employment tribunals, as creatures of statute, can only deal with matters where jurisdiction has been given to them. For example, in spite of regularly being asked to do so by unrepresented parties, employment tribunals cannot hear a claim for defamation, personal injury (unless it arises from the dismissal or discrimination), or breach of contract where employment is continuing.

1.5   STRUCTURE AND CONSTITUTION OF EMPLOYMENT TRIBUNALS

The constitution of employment tribunals and their appellate body, the EAT, is governed by the Employment Tribunals Act (ETA) 1996. Within the UK, England, Wales and Scotland are administratively connected whilst Northern Ireland has a separate structure. They are overseen by the Administrative Justice & Tribunals Council (which has replaced the former Council on Tribunals) which provides an annual report to Parliament. A report by Sir Andrew Leggatt on all tribunals including employment tribunals (*One System, One Service*), was published in March 2001 and the Employment Tribunal System Taskforce published its report *Moving Forward* in July 2002. The government announced a single Tribunal Service to be made up of 21 tribunals. Employment tribunals joined the Tribunals Service in 2006 and are part of the recently re-named Ministry of Justice. There is now a senior judicial office held by Lord Justice Carnwath who, as Senior President of Tribunals, has a role which includes representing tribunals to ministers and parliament and considering some policy matters arising from the functioning of the Tribunals Service. Further changes are expected as a result of the Tribunal Service strategic plan 2007/08, which envisages hearing centres with more than one type of tribunal and for some resources to start to be shared. We will have to wait and see what happens in the next few years, and whether these changes will provide a better service.

The President of the Employment Tribunals in England and Wales, at the time of writing, is His Honour Judge Goolam Meeran, who has been in post since 2002. There are 10 regions, including Scotland. Scotland has a vice president whilst the regions in England and Wales have a regional judge within each regional office.

Regulation 13 of the Regulations gave the President a new power to make practice directions and although it was expected that this power would be used to bring more consistency across the regions, this has not happened, at least, not on a formal level. To date the President has issued a limited number of practice directions, usually to stay cases, such as age discrimination and agency worker cases, pending clarification from higher courts. Some regions have a number of hearing centres and other offices. A full list of offices appears on the employment tribunals website (**www.employmenttribunals.gov.uk**).

Employment judges and lay members

Under ETA 1996, s.4 the tribunal is to be composed of a judge and two other members, or with the consent of the parties, one other member in accordance with the Regulations. Under regs.8 and 9 the three members must be drawn one from each panel of:

1. *a chairman* (now judge) who has been appointed by the Lord Chancellor;
2. *representatives of employees* appointed by the Secretary of State for Trade and Industry (now Secretary of State for Business, Enterprise and Regulatory Reform);
3. *representatives of employers* appointed by the Secretary of State for Trade and Industry (now Secretary of State for Business, Enterprise and Regulatory Reform).

The purpose of the employee and employer representatives, often known as 'lay members' is to give balance, and to bring to the decision-making process an element of industrial relations knowledge which a legally qualified person might not have. The role of the lay members has been emphasised in a number of decisions and it is recognised that they can be of great assistance to the process. At the time of writing there is a review of the role of lay members and, although their involvement is very much valued, it is likely that there may be a reduction in the number of occasions when they will be used. Although the two members are selected to represent both 'sides' of industry, it is explicit that they are not there to be partisan and they and the judge are expected and trained to be unbiased in their deliberations. Parties are not entitled to know from which panel a lay member is drawn, and it ought not to be obvious from their conduct. The fact that the majority of hearings will be before a panel of three people who will all have an equal say in the judgment is central to employment tribunal procedure. Although many of the matters that are dealt with before the full Hearing may be decided by a judge alone, when they go to a Hearing, in the vast majority of cases a full tribunal will be deciding the case and should all be addressed.

With the consent of the parties, it is possible for the tribunal to be composed of two members. In limited cases, a judge may sit alone (see below). Where there is a full tribunal the judgment will almost always be a unanimous one but it is possible for the decision to be by a majority. Where the tribunal has two members, the judge has the casting vote if needs be.

Independence and conflicts of interest

It is of central importance to the justice system that decisions are taken by independent people. Indeed, it will be a breach of Art.6 of the European Convention on Human Rights for that not to be the case. This means that for all members of the tribunal consideration has to be given to situations where a conflict of interest might arise. This includes not only where there would be such a conflict, but also where there might be the appearance of bias. The case of *Lawal* v. *Northern Spirit* [2003] IRLR 538 in the House of Lords illustrates this point. It was stated that the test was:

> whether a fair-minded and informed observer, having considered the given facts, would conclude that there was a real possibility that the tribunal was biased. The key to this test is public perception of the possibility of unconscious bias.

For instance, it is often the case that a lay member may have a connection to a particular trade union or company where that organisation may be appearing in the case. In a recent case before the EAT, *Hamilton* v. *GMB (Northern Region)* [2007] IRLR 391, very clear guidance was given on this issue by the EAT President. It was said that, even where there was no interest but apparent bias, the lay member in that case being a member in a trade union with a similar policy to that challenged, the request for her to stand down should have been considered, and the case was remitted to a differently constituted tribunal. If such involvement would lead that member's independence to be questioned, the lay member should consider withdrawing from the case or drawing the attention of both parties to the involvement. Exactly the same principles apply to the judge.

This was clarified in the cases of *Jones* v. *DAS Legal Expenses Insurance Co Ltd* [2004] IRLR 218 and *Lodwick* v. *Southwark Borough Council* [2004] IRLR 554 in which the Court of Appeal considered situations where appellants argued that the chairman (as they were then called) had been biased. In *Jones*, the appellant argued that the fact that the chairman's husband was a barrister who was occasionally instructed by the respondent indicated bias. In rejecting that argument, the court laid down guidelines when dealing with suggestions of bias. First, it should be ascertained if any other person could hear the case and a careful note made of the interest of the chairman. Secondly, the party should be informed of the right to make an application for the chairman to stand down, and the party should be given time to reflect before deciding whether to object. In the *Lodwick* case, the issue was whether the chairman was biased because the applicant had previously appeared as a representative before the chairman, who had made adverse comments about his conduct. This was said not of itself to give rise to an appearance of bias and the circumstances in which a chairman would need to stand down because of previous comments would be rare. However, *Lodwick* emphasises the need to test any allegations of bias carefully.

If representatives or parties appearing in the tribunal feel there may be a conflict of interest, the matter should first be raised with the clerk. If the matter proceeds, it should be raised again with the tribunal. In order for the tribunal to deal with this issue, it should be raised no later than at the commencement of the Hearing.

The judge

The judge will be a solicitor or barrister having at least seven years' experience in practice, in accordance with s.71 of the Courts and Legal Services Act 1990. All employment judges are initially appointed on a part-time fee-paid basis and sit between 20 and 70 (sometimes increased to a maximum of 100) days per year. They may then be appointed on a salaried basis, either full or part time. Most interim or interlocutory matters (that is, matters that have to be dealt with before the main and final Hearing, including extensive case management) are dealt with by a salaried judge, but the Hearing may be with either a salaried or fee-paid judge. Multi-day Hearings will usually be heard by either a salaried or a more experienced fee-paid judge.

The judge's role is to ensure the smooth running of the proceedings (including matters before the final Hearing in case management), to preside at the Hearing, to give the tribunal's judgment, and put that into writing. Whilst most cases are before the full tribunal mentioned above, there are some limited circumstances in which the judge may sit alone.

Judge or full tribunal?

There are some circumstances in which a judge may 'sit alone'. These have increased over the years and can broadly be categorised as falling under the following main areas.

In some cases the legislation states that a judge *shall* sit alone. A detailed and very tortuous explanation for the composition of the tribunal is set out in ETA 1996, s.4(3). First, it specifies the three-person tribunal mentioned above and then goes on to say when the judge shall sit alone by specifying the sections of the relevant Acts of Parliament. These are as follows:

(a) some matters under the Trade Union and Labour Relations (Consolidation) Act 1992 concerning subscriptions and applications for interim relief;

(b) complaints under the Pension Schemes Act 1993;

(c) unlawful deductions of wages under Part 11 of ERA 1996, complaints under ERA 1996, s.11 (written statements), guarantee payments and insolvency payments by the Secretary of State, suspension on medical grounds and application to take over a tribunal case where the applicant has died, reg.11(5) of the Transfer of Undertakings (Protection of

Employment) Regulations 1981, SI 1981/1794 (as amended) (TUPE) (on consultation), access to records, and enforcement appeals under the National Minimum Wage Act 1998;

(d) breach of contract claims;
(e) where parties have given written consent; and
(f) where proceedings are no longer contested.

In day-to-day terms the most common claims where this is relevant are unlawful deduction of wages, breach of contract claims and where there has been no response.

However, although the wording is that these matters shall be heard by a judge sitting alone, s.4(5) provides further explanation on whether the tribunal will be a three-person tribunal (as in s.4(1)) or a judge alone (as in s.4(2)). The decision on whether there should be a full tribunal is for the judge, who should have regard to:

(a) whether there is a likelihood of a dispute arising on the facts which makes it desirable for the proceedings to be heard in accordance with subsection (1),
(b) whether there is a likelihood of an issue of law arising which would make it desirable for the proceedings to be heard in accordance with subsection (2),
(c) any views of any of the parties as to whether or not the proceedings ought to be heard in accordance with either of those subsections, and
(d) whether there are any other proceedings which might be heard concurrently but which are not proceedings specified in subsection (3)

There has been some judicial guidance, some of which is arguably conflicting, on how the judge's discretion in relation to the question of whether to sit alone should be exercised. It was suggested in *Sogbetun* v. *Hackney Borough Council* [1998] IRLR 676 that it was mandatory for the judge to exercise discretion before sitting alone. Other cases suggest, however, that the failure to show that the discretion had been exercised would not make the decision wrong (see *Morgan* v. *Brith Gov Cyf* [2001] ICR 978. The most recent pronouncement on this issue was that of the President of the EAT, Elias J, in *Gladwell* v. *Secretary of State for Trade and Industry* [2007] ICR 264, where it was said that the tribunal's standard practice of listing the sorts of cases above, breach of contract, unpaid wages and holiday pay etc., before a judge alone is appropriate as long as there is an opportunity for either party to raise the issue and ask for a full tribunal. In short, the judge need not actively consider how to exercise his or her discretion or give any reasons for it unless it has been raised by either party. Suffice it to say that if a party objects to the case being heard by a judge alone, this should be raised at the first opportunity, even if that is the morning of the Hearing, although that may well lead to delay.

Since the introduction of the 2004 Rules there are also circumstances where it is specified that a judge will deal with matters alone. Other rules make it clear it that the matter will be conducted by a judge alone as follows:

(a) case management discussions, r.17;

(b) pre-hearing review, r.18 (unless there is a full tribunal under r.18(3));

(c) review against default judgment;

(d) preliminary consideration of review applications and full consideration of reviews where initial decision was by judge alone, rr.34–7.

There will also be a number of times throughout the progress of the claim that judges will take decisions without a full tribunal. There is the general power contained within r.10 to manage proceedings and under r.12 to act on their own initiative. There is also under r.60 the stipulation that the judge or tribunal may regulate its own procedure. In practice, virtually all interim and case management matters are dealt with by a judge alone. These include decisions on adjournment requests, jurisdictional questions, dismissals on withdrawal or with written agreement, striking out and orders. This will be discussed in more detail in the following chapters.

1.6 ADMINISTRATION

The administrative responsibility for employment tribunals rests with the Tribunals Service which is an executive agency and also publishes an annual report. At the time of writing, the Chief Executive of the Tribunals Service is Peter Handcock. The Ministry of Justice is responsible, through the Tribunals Service, for the running of the tribunal service. All tribunals, including employment tribunals, are overseen by the Administrative Justice and Tribunals Council which makes recommendations to the appropriate government departments and is concerned with accessibility and workability (see www.ajtc.gov.uk). The Council is consulted on changes and recommendations. Resources and facilities will in future be shared but how much crossover there will be for staff and the tribunal members is unclear at the moment. There is also a strong move towards a more coherent IT strategy within the Tribunals Service. A project board will manage a process which should allow the internal arrangements to be less paper dependent over the next few years. It is hoped that this will make for efficiencies both for the service and for users.

The Tribunals Service employs staff in all its offices to receive applications and deal with them within the rules. Initial contact will generally be with the regional office and remain there for the duration of the case. A clerk will be assigned to the case at the Hearing. Most employment tribunal cases will have a clerk assigned to that file so that queries can be directed to that person. Often, the clerk will check the position with a judge if a particular query needs judicial consideration. It can be difficult to decide when a matter requires a judge or the regional judge's involvement but the clerks will give assistance where they can. There is a regional secretary in charge of the administration in each regional office.

The Tribunals Service also produces very good booklets to assist the parties and has a website for employment tribunals (**www.employmenttribunals.gov.uk**). Steps are being taken to modernise the system so that more use is being made of IT. Claim forms and response forms are available online and communication with the office can be by email.

The judicial and administrative lines of responsibility work together to run a service which continues to thrive and deals with a high volume of cases in a relatively efficient and speedy way. During the customer survey in March 2006, 96 per cent expressed their satisfaction, either 'very satisfied' (55 per cent) or 'fairly satisfied' (41 per cent) with the service.

1.7 WHERE TO GET ADVICE AND ASSISTANCE

As we have indicated, this book aims to give practical advice where a relatively straightforward matter is to be dealt with in the employment tribunal. For more complicated cases, it may be necessary to seek the advice of a specialist agency, such as the new Equality and Human Rights Commission (EHRC) which absorbed the Equal Opportunities Commission, the Commission for Racial Equality and the Disability Rights Commission in October 2007.

Information on solicitors specialising in employment matters can be obtained through the Law Society (**www.lawsociety.org.uk**) or through the Employment Lawyers Association (**www.elaweb.org.uk**). Community Legal Advice has a website (**www.clsdirect.org.uk**) and some free assistance may be available from Citizens Advice Bureaux (**www.nacab.org.uk**) or law centres (**www.lawcentres.org.uk**).

There are a number of publications in the field of employment law and it is useful to make sure you keep up to date. It may be useful to take out a subscription to a regular bulletin with the Employment Lawyers Association (above), Incomes Data Services (**www.incomesdata.co.uk**) or Industrial Relations Law Bulletin (**www.irsonline.co.uk**).

Finally, the website for the Department for Business, Enterprise and Regulatory Reform (BERR) (formerly the Department for Trade and Industry) (**www.berr.gov.uk**) is excellent and readily accessible. Although much of the control of employment tribunals is now with the Tribunals Service and the Ministry of Justice, BERR is still involved in some policy aspects of workplace legal development.

CHAPTER 2

Claims and time limits

2.1 PRE-CLAIM STEPS AND TIME LIMITS

Before a claim is commenced in the employment tribunal, claimants or their advisers will need to be aware of the time limits within which claims must be commenced. In addition there are statutory steps which must be taken by a claimant before certain claims are commenced. It will be necessary to be aware of how the taking of the statutory steps will have an impact on how the time limit for commencing those claims is calculated.

There is also a requirement for employers responding to some claims to have taken certain pre-action steps in order to avoid penalties in the tribunal. The statutory steps to be taken by an employer to deal with a disciplinary or dismissal matter or by an employee to raise a grievance will be referred to as the statutory procedures. The employer's statutory disciplinary and dismissal procedures will be referred to as the 'DDP' and the employee's use of the statutory grievance procedure as the 'GP'.

These procedures apply only to claimants who are employees and not those who are workers. There are statutory definitions of an 'employee' and a 'worker' and the status of a worker, as defined, can attract rights to pursue certain claims in the employment tribunals. A worker with a tribunal claim will have no requirement to show that he or she has complied with the statutory procedures. It is therefore important to check not only the type of claim being made to see if it requires the use of the statutory procedures, but also the legal status of the person who wishes to bring it.

Employees with complaints or grievances about certain matters which may later form the subject of a claim in the employment tribunal must satisfy the tribunal on their claim form that they have first raised that matter using their pre-action steps – the statutory grievance procedure or GP. If they cannot do so their claim will not be accepted as the tribunal will have no jurisdiction to hear the claim.

Employers involved in a tribunal claim must demonstrate to the tribunal that they have used the DDP prior to certain types of dismissal, otherwise they will face a finding of automatically unfair dismissal. The failure to use a DDP will not impact on the employer's ability to proceed with defending a claim or the time frame for responding to a claim. Its impact is on the fairness of the dismissal.

In addition both employee and employer can be penalised for a failure to complete the statutory procedures in terms of an increase of the compensatory award to be paid by the employer or a decrease to be received by the employee depending on where the fault lies.

Statutory procedures: the legislation

There are two key pieces of legislation which advisers for both employees and employers will need to be familiar with when checking the pre-action steps which need to have taken place and calculating whether the time limits for starting claims have been properly complied with.

The Dispute Resolution Regulations provide a statutory framework for both the DDP and the GP. The Regulations explain the circumstances in which each procedure should be used and provide for some exceptions for use or completion. The Regulations also provide for the time extensions referred to above and deal with a number of miscellaneous points including the proviso that the use of a statutory discrimination questionnaire (discussed at **4.10**) is not a substitute for using the statutory procedures where their use is required.

The substantive legislation which requires the statutory procedures to be used prior to an employment tribunal claim and which provides for an adjustment of awards where procedures have not been completed is EA 2002. The relevant provisions of EA 2002 are as follows:

- s.29 – introduces the process ('the Steps') of the statutory procedures, as set out in Sched.2;
- s.30 – refers to the procedures being contractual (this has *not* been enacted, and is unlikely to be: see **Chapter 1** for a discussion of the possible future changes to these procedures);
- s.31 – the regime for adjustment of awards to penalise for incomplete use of the procedures;
- s.32 – refers to the tribunal's jurisdiction (it cannot hear claims where the employee has failed to utilise a grievance relevant to that type of claim; this is discussed in more detail below);
- s.34 – inserts ERA 1996, s.98A (which states that in a claim for unfair dismissal, where the tribunal finds that the employer has failed to use a disciplinary and dismissal procedure, the finding will be of an automatically unfair dismissal for that reason);
- Sched.2 to EA 2002 sets out the steps that the parties are required to follow to comply with the statutory procedures. These are discussed in more detail below.

Section 32(3) of EA 2002 also requires employees to show that they have waited 28 days after putting in an internal grievance before sending a claim to the employment tribunal. Under the 2004 Rules (r.3(2)(c)) the tribunal will not accept a claim where it appears that the employee has not complied with s.32(3).

The employment tribunal can reject a claim form which omits to state that the employee has waited 28 days after putting in the grievance (see later). The tribunal will be able to refer it back to the claimant, who must then resubmit the claim form, but this must be done no later than a month after the original time limit (of three months) has expired (see EA 2002, s.32(4)(b)).

As well as being aware of the right time to commence a tribunal claim after starting the GP, the claimant must also remember the required time limit for the particular claim submitted (usually three months) and how that is affected by the use of a GP. The claimant should be aware of the automatic three-month extension granted under reg.15 of the Dispute Resolution Regulations where the statutory grievance procedure has been begun within the required time limit. So the claimant should start neither too soon nor too late!

The aim of requiring both parties to use these procedures is to encourage the employer and employee to resolve disputes internally, without resorting to employment tribunal proceedings. As a result, as we shall see, the tribunal may take action to penalise parties who have not followed the requirements for using these procedures in the workplace.

2.2   THE STATUTORY PROCEDURES

This chapter will look at the steps under the statutory procedures which the employee must take (the GP) prior to presenting a claim, as well as how these affect the time limits for commencing a claim.

Later, in **Chapter 5**, we will look at the employer's obligations to use a DDP where there has been a dismissal. Employers and their representative should nevertheless note the importance of the employer being aware of the employee/claimant's obligations, as:

(a)   it will be incumbent on the employer to allow access to a statutory griev-ance procedure and to show that the procedure has been properly com-plied with and operated in accordance with the statutory requirements in order to avoid the penalty uplift on the compensatory award; and

(b)   the employer will check to see if an employee who has started a claim in the employment tribunal has used a GP and has properly followed the procedures and adhered to the appropriate time limit, and therefore has a right to pursue a tribunal claim against the employer.

How the statutory grievance procedure operates

Under the Dispute Resolution Regulations, where an existing employee wishes to complain about any action which the employer has taken or is contemplating taking in relation to the employee (other than to discipline or dismiss the employee), the employee must follow either a standard or a modified grievance procedure. These procedures are set out in EA 2002, Sched.2, which will be discussed in further detail below (see also **Appendix 2**).

The employee must use these procedures in relation to any claim that the employee wishes to raise or enforce against the employer as provided for in EA 2002, Sched.4. Claimant advisers should regularly remind themselves of the contents of Sched.4 to check if they apply to a claim which the employee wishes to make to a tribunal.

Schedule 4 – Tribunal jurisdictions to which section 32 applies

- Section 2 of the Equal Pay Act 1970 (c.41) (equality clauses).
- Section 63 of the Sex Discrimination Act 1975 (c.65) (discrimination in the employment field).
- Section 54 of the Race Relations Act 1976 (c.74) (discrimination in the employment field).
- Section 146 of the Trade Union and Labour Relations (Consolidation) Act 1992 (c.52) (detriment in relation to trade union membership and activities).
- Paragraph 156 of Sched.A1 to the Trade Union and Labour Relations (Consolidation) Act 1992 (detriment in relation to union recognition rights).
- Section 8 of the Disability Discrimination Act 1995 (c.50) (discrimination in the employment field).
- Section 23, ERA 1996 (c.18) (unauthorised deductions and payments).
- Section 48, ERA 1996 (detriment in employment).
- Section 111, ERA 1996 (unfair dismissal).
- Section 163, ERA 1996 (redundancy payments).
- Section 24 of the National Minimum Wage Act 1998 (c.39) (detriment in relation to national minimum wage).
- Schedule 3 to the Tax Credits Act 1999 (c.10) (detriment in relation to tax credits).
- Regulation 30 of the Working Time Regulations 1998, SI 1998/1833 (breach of regulations).
- Regulation 32 of the Transnational Information and Consultation of Employees Regulations 1999, SI 1999/3323 (detriment relating to European Works Councils).

It will be seen that Sched.4 refers to an employee's money claims, and all discrimination claims, including an equal pay claim. It does not refer to a dismissal claim and this includes a discriminatory dismissal (see *Lawrence* v. *HM Prison Service* [2007] IRLR 468). Nor does it refer to wrongful dismissal.

Note however that there is one type of dismissal for which a grievance *must* be used and that is a claim for constructive dismissal. This type of dismissal as defined in ERA 1996, s.95(1)(c) is not covered in the interpretation section (s.2) of the Dispute Resolution Regulations as being a dismissal covered by the use of the DDP and so the employee needs to use a grievance prior to commencing such a claim.

To decide which procedure is the correct one to use, see **Figure 2.1**. The standard procedure is used where the employee is/was employed at the time that the complaint was raised. The modified procedure will be used where the employee has left the job without telling the employer about the complaint. Alternatively, where the employee has left the job and told the employer about the complaint and the standard procedure was neither started nor completed, the modified procedure will be used. Both parties must agree to its use in writing.

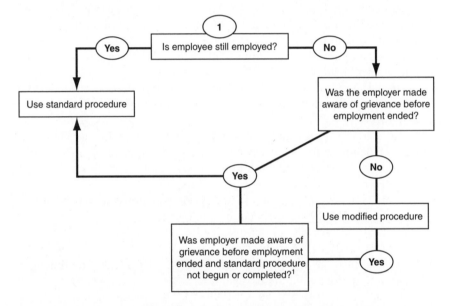

[1]Both parties must have agreed in writing to use modified procedure.

Figure 2.1   Which procedure?

Steps in the standard procedure

For the standard grievance procedure, there are three steps as set out in paras.6–9 of EA 2002, Sched.2:

Step 1 – Statement

The employee must write to the employer stating what his or her grievance is in writing. Examples might be discriminatory treatment, a deduction of wages or a failure to pay holiday pay.

Case law has confirmed that at this stage there are no formal requirements as to what constitutes a Step 1 statement (see *Shergold* v. *Fieldway Medical Centre* [2006] IRLR 76). The EAT in that case indicated that it would be a matter of commonsense for the employer to grasp that the employee was complaining about an action of the employer's. Furthermore the format of the grievance statement is not specified and the following communications have been held to be Step 1 statements:

- a solicitor's letter, including a letter written 'without prejudice' (see *Arnold Clark Automobiles* v. *Stewart* (unreported, EAT 0052/05));
- an employee's resignation letter (see *Thorpe and Soleil* v. *Poat and Lake* (unreported, EAT 0503/05) or a threat of resignation (see *Galaxy Showers* v. *Wilson* [2006] IRLR 83);
- letters written both by the employee and his or her solicitor – both combining to form a Step 1 statement (see *Martin* v. *Class Installations* (unreported, EAT 0188/06));
- a memo written by a manager after the employee spoke to him about his grievance (see *Kennedy Scott Ltd* v. *Francis* (unreported, EAT 0204/07)).

Note that in claims for discrimination the EAT has taken a more exacting view. See *Canary Wharf Management* v. *Edebi* [2006] IRLR 416, where the employee failed to use the word 'discrimination' when complaining of his treatment in the Step 1 statement.

Step 2 – Meeting

The next step is for the employer to invite the employee to a meeting. Prior to this meeting taking place the employee must have informed the employer what the *basis* of the grievance was when the Step 1 statement was made. The employer must also have had a reasonable opportunity to have responded to that information.

The word 'basis' has been held to mean that the employee will need to have provided the employer with sufficient information to understand the details of the grievance. Although employees do not have to set out their case in the sort of detail required for an employment tribunal claim form (see *Bradford MBC* v. *Pratt* (unreported, EAT 0391/06)), they will need to provide more detail of what they want the employer to decide on as part of the grievance. Again, as illustrated in the *Bradford* case, employees should be clear as to the basis of a discrimination claim so that the employer has the opportunity to respond to that information.

The tribunal claim can be accepted once the Step 1 stage has been under-taken by the employee who has then waited the required 28 days before put-ting in the claim. However the question of what will be regarded as a Step 1 statement and whether the employee has provided the employer with the basis for the grievance may be challenged by the employer in order to demonstrate that the procedures have not been used. For this reason the employee should provide as much detail as possible prior to Step 2.

There may be more than one meeting, but there must be at least one. The meeting should be at a reasonable time and place and the employee must show that he or she has made every reasonable effort to attend.

It should be noted that if the employee has not attended a meeting due to an inability to arrange to be accompanied (as entitled to do under s.10 of the Employment Relations Act 1999) for unforeseeable reasons, reg.13 of the Dispute Resolution Regulations states that the employer is not required to convene a meeting more than twice to show that the employer has complied with the requirement to hold a meeting.

After the meeting the employer will decide whether or not the complaint will be upheld and must put this decision to the employee in writing.

Step 3 – Appeal

If the decision was not favourable to the employee, the employer must hold an appeal meeting. The appeal meeting should be arranged by the employer in the same reasonable way as the original. After the appeal the employer will make a final decision about the employee's complaint and this will be 'communicated' to the employee (this means that it does not necessarily have to be in writing).

Steps in the modified procedure

There are two steps in this procedure, as set out in paras.9–10 of EA 2002, Sched.2:

Step 1

The employee writes to the employer setting out his or her grievance and also providing the employer with the basis for his or her complaint. This means that when the modified procedure is being used the employee needs to include the basis in the Step 1 statement. The case of *Bradford MBC* v. *Pratt* (above) was a case in which the employee had used the modified procedure and therefore had this additional requirement to provide more detail under Step 1 of that procedure. The court indicated that it was incumbent on the employee to give as much information as possible to assist the employer in dealing with the grievance under this mutually agreed procedure.

Step 2

The employer puts a response in writing and sends it to the employee.

Note that para.12 of EA 2002, Sched.2 states that each of these statutory steps and actions must be taken without unreasonable delay. Time scales are not provided for and the tribunal will look at each case on its facts to see if this proviso has been complied with. For example how long the employee has delayed in appealing might relate to the employee's state of mind at the time.

In *Codemasters Software Company* v. *Wong* (unreported, EAT 0639/06) the employee waited nearly six months to put in an appeal. The appeal was against dismissal rather than the decision on a grievance. However the principle remains the same: there are no statutory time limits for putting in an appeal under the statutory procedures and what amounts to a reasonable period of time will depend on the facts of the case.

Circumstances in which the parties will be regarded as having complied with the grievance procedure

There are some circumstances provided for in regs.7–10 of the Dispute Resolution Regulations in which the grievance procedure will not have been completed, but for the purposes of compliance with the requirements of the EA 2002, *both parties* will be deemed to have complied with the GP.

1. The overlapping procedure – the employee's written statement

This situation is referred to in reg.7 of the Dispute Resolution Regulations and will arise where the employer has begun the statutory disciplinary and dismissal procedure, and is contemplating taking disciplinary action against the employee. It refers to actions short of dismissal.

If the employee believes that this action of the employer's is unrelated to the grounds raised by the employer or is about unlawful discrimination, the employee may send in his or her grievance by way of a written statement to the employer. If the employee sends in a written statement to the employer either prior to the statutory appeal meeting or prior to beginning employment tribunal proceedings, the grievance procedure is deemed to have been complied with. The employer's appeal hearing will therefore take the place of a grievance hearing. This means that employers should be allowing grievances sent in prior to the disciplinary appeal stage relying on these grounds to be heard at that appeal stage and not in a separate track, and this is sometimes referred to as the 'overlapping procedure'.

2. Not reasonably practicable to complete the procedure

If Step 1 of the standard grievance procedure has been complied with by the employee and the employee has subsequently left the job, the procedure will be deemed to have been complied with by both parties where it was not reasonably practicable to complete it. This notion of 'reasonably practicable' is likely to apply to situations where it is no longer practical for the parties to arrange to complete the procedures due to sickness or relocation.

3. Grievance raised by representative or alternative procedure available

The two other situations in which the grievance procedures are 'deemed' to have been complied with are where:

(a) the grievance has been raised on behalf of at least two employees by an 'appropriate representative' (a trade union official or elected or appointed workplace representative who has the authority under a workplace grievance procedure to represent the employees); or

(b) there has been an alternative procedure negotiated under a collective agreement which allows for employees to raise a grievance with their employer: see reg.10 of the Dispute Resolution Regulations.

Where the statutory procedures will not apply or are treated as having been complied with

Regulation 11 of the Dispute Resolution Regulations prescribes that in certain circumstances the statutory procedures need not be used or are deemed to have taken place for the purposes of being allowed to commence a claim in the employment tribunal.

The circumstances are where:

(a) the employee has a genuine fear of either a threat to their person or property if the employee starts or continues with the procedures;

(b) the employee states that he or she has been subject to harassment and believes it will occur again in the context of using a GP;

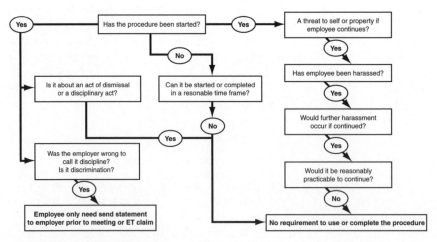

Figure 2.2 Statutory grievance procedure: exceptions to requirement for procedure to be used or completed

(c)   it would not be practicable for the employee (or the employer) to start or complete the procedure within a reasonable period; and

(d)   there is a threat to national security in using the statutory procedure.

Note that these provisions apply to *both* parties and to both the GP *and* the DDP. The word 'employee' has been used here to clarify the position for an claimant; the wording of the Regulations refers to 'a party' and so refers to both types of statutory procedures.

The definition of harassment is also set out in reg.11 and it is the same as the definition of harassment in the discrimination legislation. The employee must be able to relate the use of the procedures to a recurrence of harassment and so may be saying that he or she suffered discriminatory or other types of harassment at the hands of a manager or supervisor who the employee will need to face in a Step 2 meeting. See *Harris* v. *Hodgsons and Mortimer* (unreported, ET 2502865/05) where a cancer sufferer was put under severe pressure by her manager due to her levels of sick leave and where his brother would have been sitting in on the Step 2 meeting.

If employees are using the modified procedure they will not be required to attend a meeting and so will be less likely to rely on this exception. They will need to show a real likelihood of the harassment recurring as well as some evidence of the original acts of harassment.

The 'not practicable' provision under reg.11(3)(c) therefore applies to both the DDP and the GP. In *Bainbridge* v. *Cleveland and Redcar Borough Council* [2006] 1 All ER 197, a case about equal pay, the employer, a local authority, stated that it would not be practicable for it to hold Step 2 grievance meetings within a reasonable period at all their scattered sites for the large number of employees who had put in their grievances about equal pay claims. The EAT indicated that the word 'practicable' means only 'feasible', and so found that the employers could have held these meetings.

Failure to comply with the statutory procedures

If the employee has failed to comply with the statutory procedures in relation to a relevant tribunal claim, and then proceeds to make the claim in the tribunal, there are a number of possible outcomes.

The first is to note that a tribunal claim raising the same matters cannot be accepted. This relates to the tribunal's jurisdiction to hear claims. Section 32(4) of EA 2002 states that employees cannot present a claim to the tribunal unless they have complied with the required pre-action step of embarking on the statutory GP. As we have seen this inability to entertain claims is reflected in the 2004 Rules (r.3(2)(c)).

If the tribunal finds that either there has been no GP commenced (by using Step 1) or that the employee has not waited 28 days after starting the procedure before putting in the tribunal claim, it will return the claim with an explanatory letter telling the claimant what the pre-claim requirements and time limits are. This will give the claimant an opportunity to comply and to re-submit the claim. If the omission relates to a failure to wait the required 28 days following the commencement of the GP, the employee may re-submit the claim once the 28 days have elapsed (see *Mackays Newsagent* v. *Blake* (unreported, EAT 0181/07)).

Where it is clear to the tribunal that the claimant will not be able to commence Step 1 and wait the required 28 days within the extended six-month time period, the tribunal will not invite the claimant to re-start the claim but will instead reject it. A decision to reject a claim is capable of appeal or review and the claimant will be informed of these procedures (see further below and **Chapters 7** and **13**).

Finally, if a claim is allowed to go ahead and the tribunal subsequently finds that the claimant has failed properly to complete the GP, the claimant must be prepared, if successful, for the tribunal to reduce compensation by between 10 per cent and 50 per cent when exercising its discretion to award such sums as are just and equitable under ERA 1996. This is the power given to it under EA 2002, s.31. The reduction will be made after any possible reductions for contributory fault made under s.118.

2.3 CALCULATING THE TIME LIMITS BY REFERENCE TO THE STATUTORY PROCEDURES

The Dispute Resolution Regulations allow for an extension of the normal time limits for sending in claims in certain circumstances involving the use of the statutory procedures. The employee's time limit of three months, which applies to most employment claims, will be extended to six months in those circumstances, which relate to both the use of the DDP and the GP.

Regulation 15 of the Dispute Resolution Regulations provides that the normal time limit for presenting a claim to an employment tribunal is extended by three months where an employer has begun but not concluded its DDP and the employee reasonably believes that a DDP is still being followed. Note that the procedure referred to here could be *either* the statutory procedure *or* a contractual procedure (as long as it complies with the statutory procedure).

The question of the employee's belief that a procedure is being followed was looked at in *Harris* v. *Towergate London Market Ltd* (unreported, EAT 0090/07) where an employee made redundant later received information that the process may have been unfair and so wrote to her employer to query it. Her letter was regarded as being her appeal in the DDP standard procedure and she was found to have reasonably believed that the DDP was still being followed and so could take advantage of the three-month extension for claiming unfair dismissal.

An employee who commences Step 1 of a GP is under the same regulation granted a three-month extension from the date of the act being complained about in which to file a claim in the tribunal.

The employee claimants will need to ensure that, within this time frame of six months, they have started their grievance no later than four months following on from the action complained of and have waited 28 days from that date as required by EA 2002, s.32(3) before commencing the tribunal claim. This requirement is also set out in r.1(4)(h) of the 2004 Rules. As outlined above, this four-month period is referred to in EA 2002, s.32(4)(b) which states that where the employee is required to use a grievance in order for a claim to be accepted by the tribunal, the employee needs to demonstrate that he or she started that GP no later than one month after the employee's original time limit (of, say, three months) for putting in such a claim expired.

Employees may put in a grievance prior to the action they are complaining about, and if they do so their time limit will still run from the date of that action (see *HM Prison Service* v. *Barua* [2007] IRLR 4).

This time extension of up to six months runs from the day after the normal time limit for presenting the claim expires. The date is calculated to run three months from the relevant date. So if the action complained about took place on 20 June the claimant has until 20 December (not 19) to submit the claim (see *Singh t/a Rainbow International* v. *Taylor* (unreported, EAT 0183/06)). However, note that another branch of the EAT in *Joshi* v. *Manchester City Council* (unreported, UKEAT 0237/07) recently cast doubt on this calculation, and so to be safe advisers should calculate the six months as expiring within six months *less* a day.

How the 28-day waiting period operates

1. Section 32(3) of EA 2002 requires the employee to wait 28 days after initiating the GP prior to beginning a tribunal claim. Where the GP has begun but is not concluded, it will automatically trigger the three-month extension referred to above.
2. Rule 3 enforces this requirement by stating that if an employee has not waited the required 28 days, the claim will be scrutinised by a judge. Rule 3 allows the secretary of the tribunal to filter out a claim which does not comply with the requirements of Rule 1 and refer it to a judge.
3. A claim shall not be accepted by the tribunal after being referred to a judge where it shows that a 28-day period has not elapsed since the grievance was commenced, and it will be sent back to the claimant.
4. If time allows (i.e. if it can be done within the maximum time period allowed for such a claim), the employee can resubmit the claim after the 28-day period has elapsed. However, it may be resubmitted no more than three months after the original three-month time limit has passed (i.e. no later than the end of month six).

Working through the time limits

Employee's grievance	Employee's dismissal
Extended time limit six months	Extended time limit six months
Statutory grievance procedure begun within four months of date of action complained of	Statutory or contractual disciplinary and dismissal procedure begun
Start claim within six months of original incident	Employee has reasonable belief that a dismissal or disciplinary procedure is still being followed
Do not start claim without waiting at least 28 days following on from Step 1 of a statutory step grievance procedure	Start claim within six months of date of dismissal

2.4   CALCULATING THE DATE FOR PRESENTATION OF THE CLAIM

By reference to the statutory procedures

We have seen how carefully time limits need to be calculated by reference to the statutory disputes procedures and by reference to EA 2002 and the 2004 Rules.

We have also seen how time limits can be extended where dismissal and grievance procedures are being used. Regulation 15 of the Dispute Resolution Regulations refers to 'normal' time limits being extended from three to six months in the circumstances described above. The normal time limits refer to the time limits which are provided for by statute and not to any extensions of time allowable by various statutory provisions which are discussed below. So where an employee is relying, for example on the provision that it is just and equitable to extend time, any time extension being sought will not be limited by the six-month maximum provided for in reg.15 (see *BUPA Care Homes* v. *Cann* [2006] ICR 643).

By reference to the relevant date provided for by statute

Various statutes determine the time limits within which claims must be commenced in the employment tribunals. As a first step it will be important to understand how to calculate the normal time limits to ensure that the claim is received by the tribunal in time and that the tribunal will therefore have jurisdiction to hear the claim.

A Ready Reckoner to check what time limits apply to each type of claim can be found in **Appendix 4**. The most common exceptions to the three-month time limits are redundancy pay claims and equal pay claims (both six months).

The relevant date

The statute under which the claimant is making the claim will set out the time limit within which claims will need to be presented to the employment tribunal.

Unfair dismissal claims are governed by ERA 1996, s.111(2)(a) which states that the complaint 'shall be presented to the tribunal before the end of three months *beginning with* the effective date of termination' (our italics).

To calculate this, take the date upon which the act being complained of occurred as day 1. Count forward to the final date of the limitation period. In taking the first date as part of the three months, the deadline will be three months including that date, thus an employee dismissed on 8 March must present the claim by 7 June. Where there is no corresponding date on that month then the last date of that month is taken. This will mean that an employee dismissed on 30 November must present the claim by 28 February. This is because a month means a calendar month.

Claims for discrimination must be presented before the end of the three-month period *following* the occurrence of the act. See, for example, SDA 1975, s.76(1)(a). Here the first date for calculation is the day after the date upon which the act occurred.

Furthermore, the relevant date upon which the claim arose will need to be established in order to calculate the date from which time begins to run. For example, where a contract is terminable on notice it will be necessary to determine the effective date of termination (EDT). This will usually be the last day of work, whether the employee works out notice, is dismissed without being allowed to work out notice, or is paid notice pay in lieu. See ERA 1996, s.97. For discrimination claims it will be the date 'when the act complained of was done'.

2.5 THE MEANING OF 'PRESENTATION OF THE CLAIM'

The general rule is that 'presenting a claim' means that the claim has actually been received by the tribunal office (see *Hammond* v. *Haigh Castle and Co Ltd* [1973] 2 All ER 289). This concept of 'presentation' carries with it a more onerous responsibility on the claimant to ensure that it has arrived at the tribunal office within the relevant time period than that of relying on the postal system to deliver letters.

It will be for the claimant to show that the application was presented to the employment tribunal within the relevant time limit. If the claimant has an adviser who takes on this task, the adviser must ensure that the tribunal office has received the application otherwise the adviser may be liable in negligence to the client (see *Capital Foods Retail* v. *Corrigan* [1993] IRLR 430, EAT). This liability will also encompass advisers who are not legally qualified advisers (*Riley* v. *Tesco Stores* [1980] ICR 323, CA – adviser at Citizens Advice Bureau).

If at all possible, claims should be sent off well within the relevant time limits. If time is short, one approach will be to fax the application, keep the fax transmission reports and telephone the tribunal office to confirm that the application has arrived.

Employment tribunals will now accept applications submitted online and sent by email. However, it will still be important to seek confirmation by telephone that the application sent by email has arrived. Where the claim form is sent by email there is a presumption that it will have been received within an hour of being sent, as long as the sender does not receive a bounce-back message (see *Initial Electronic Security Systems* v. *Advic* [2005] IRLR 67). However it will still be more than prudent to ensure it has arrived by telephoning the tribunal office to check before the expiry of the relevant time limit. Most tribunal offices now have automated replies indicating that an email has been received but this will not specify that a claim form has been received by them.

Many problems occur (see *Corrigan* above) when advisers and claimants rely on the postal system to ensure that claims are presented in time. This can cause particular difficulties where the expiry date for presenting the claim falls on a weekend or a bank holiday. In the case of *Consignia* v. *Sealey* [2002] IRLR 624, the Court of Appeal set out some useful guidelines as to the days upon which a claimant can expect the claim to arrive if relying on the postal system (two days for first class post, excluding Sundays and bank holidays).

If the last date for presentation falls on a weekend the claimant still has an obligation to ensure the claim arrives in time, and there are some hard cases on this issue. Where a tribunal office had no letter box and the Post Office held the post back over a weekend the claimant could rely on the Post Office to hold it as his agent until it could be delivered on a Monday (see *Ford* v. *Stakis Hotels and Inns Ltd* [1988] IRLR 46).

2.6 LATE CLAIMS

Extending time

The employment tribunal has no power to hear a late claim. This is because it is a creature of statute and cannot exercise judicial discretion in the same way as a superior court. However, the tribunal has a statutory discretion to extend time. The test is different for unfair dismissal and for discrimination claims.

Unfair dismissal and the test of 'not reasonably practicable'

In the case of unfair dismissal, the employment tribunal can hold that it was not reasonably practicable for the claim to have been presented within the three-month time limit or within such further period as the tribunal considers reasonable in a case where it is satisfied that it was not reasonably practicable for the complaint to be presented before the end of that period of three months (ERA 1996, s.111(2)(b)).

The test of whether it was reasonably practicable to present the claim in time is largely a factual one. Guidelines in the Court of Appeal case of *Wall's Meat Co* v. *Khan* [1978] IRLR 499 suggest a number of circumstances (for instance ignorance, lack of advice, illness, postal strikes) in which the test may validly be applied in the claimant's favour.

Employment tribunals have the power to hold pre-hearing reviews under r.18 and one of the purposes of those will be to determine 'the entitlement of any party to bring or contest particular proceedings'.

Discrimination claims and the test of 'just and equitable'

In discrimination claims, the employment tribunal's discretion is wider. The tribunal can extend time if it is thought just and equitable to do so (see, for example, SDA 1975, s.76(5)).

This definition carries with it the notion of balancing the interests of justice to both parties and examining in detail the nature of the claim and any implications of a late claim as far as ensuring a fair hearing for the case is concerned. The tribunal will also weigh in the factual circumstances which led to the claimant presenting the claim out of time. See, for example, *British Coal Corporation* v. *Keeble* [1997] IRLR 336, EAT.

Ensuring claims are presented in time

As an adviser, it will be important for you to have systems in place for ensuring mishaps do not occur leading to missed deadlines.

Checklist

- Keep a central diary with all of the client's deadlines clearly marked.
- Note the caseworker responsible next to the client's details; add any supervisor's initials.
- Ensure that the individual caseworker has noted the deadline in their own diary.
- Ensure that the individual caseworker has a pre-deadline check in their diary.
- Ensure that the client is advised of the deadline in writing and is informed as to the actual date upon which the adviser needs to present the claim on the client's behalf and the method to be employed (post, fax or email).
- Have a system for the way in which claims are presented, for example always by fax or always by first class guaranteed post, at least five days before the deadline.
- Have a system of cover for a caseworker's unforeseen absences as well as holidays.
- Have a system for checking with the relevant tribunal office that the ET1 has been received in time.

2.7   OTHER RELEVANT TIME LIMITS

Respondents' time limits

As outlined in this chapter, time limits may be crucial to the employee as a failure to comply with them can be fatal to the claim. The statutory time limits of which the respondent/employer must be mindful are the requirement to reply to a statutory discrimination questionnaire within eight weeks of receiving it, and the requirement to present a response to the tribunal within 28 days of it being sent by the tribunal office. These procedures and time limits are discussed further in **Chapter 5**.

Reviews and appeals

There are also time limits for applying for a review or an appeal. The review and appeal processes are covered in **Chapter 14**. At this stage a note should be made of the relevant time limits as a review, in particular, may need to be considered at an early stage of the proceedings.

Rule 34 of the 2004 Rules sets out the circumstances in which a review of a judgment or decision may be applied for. They are a decision not to accept a claim or response, a final judgment, an award of costs, as well as a decision concerning an application to suspend a prohibition notice made under health and safety legislation. Rule 35(1) states that the time limit for requesting a review in all these circumstances is within 14 days of the date on which the decision was sent to the parties. See below for the meaning of 'within' in calculating time limits to comply with tribunal orders. Claimants who have had their claims rejected at the outset may consider they have grounds for a review of that decision. If so they should carefully check the time limits and note the relevant grounds upon which they may rely (see **Chapter 14**).

There is a separate rule, r.33, which allows for a review of a default judgment. As we shall see in **Chapter 7**, under r.8 a default judgment can be entered by the tribunal against a respondent who fails to enter a response in time or whose response is considered not to comply with the requirement to use the prescribed form. Either party can apply to have a default judgment set aside. A claimant may for example be unhappy with the calculation of the remedy in the default judgment and may wish for it to be set aside. Rule 33(1) states that this application must be made in writing within 14 days of the date the default judgment was sent to the parties.

The time limit for lodging an appeal in the EAT is 42 days from the date of the judgment or order as prescribed by the Employment Appeal Tribunal Rules 1993, r.3(3). This book is mainly concerned with employment tribunals, but if there is any need to appeal from a tribunal judgment it will be important to be aware of the relevant time limits. A judgment may be given out orally at the end of a Hearing or be sent to the parties.

The 42 days will run from that date or from the date of any reserved judgment or order. Appeals and time limits for appealing are discussed further in **Chapter 14**.

2.8   THE EMPLOYMENT TRIBUNAL RULES AND TIME LIMITS

Regulation 15 of the Regulations gives some examples of time limits, showing how time must be calculated in relation to any act required to be done by the Rules. This will include calculation of time for complying with anything promulgated by the tribunal, such as a decision or requiring compliance with an award.

Regulation 15(2) states that if an act must be done within a certain number of days then the day on which the requirement first arises is not counted. The example given is the requirement for a respondent to present a response to the employment tribunal within 28 days of the date on which a copy of the claim was sent to the respondent. If it was sent on 1 October, the respondent must present the response no later than 29 October.

Regulation 15(3) states that if an act must be done not less than a certain number of days 'before or after an event' then the date of the event is not included in the calculation. An example is given of a party required to submit representations in writing to the tribunal. If the party has been required to submit the representations not less than seven days before a hearing and the hearing is fixed for 8 October, then the representations must reach the tribunal no later than 1 October.

Regulation 15(5) also refers to the requirement for the tribunal to send a notice of hearing to parties 14 days before a hearing and states that this means that the notice of hearing only needs to be posted no less than 14 days before the hearing. The example given is of a hearing listed for 15 October. The notice does not need to be posted until 1 October. Dates in tribunal decisions will, as far as possible, be expressed as calendar dates.

CHAPTER 3

Alternatives to litigation

3.1   INTRODUCTION

It is always wise from the outset to keep in mind the alternatives for avoiding the issues in dispute going to a full tribunal Hearing. There are many risks associated with litigation. Notable in the case of employment tribunals is the uncertainty associated with the giving of evidence. Witness statements are now usually prepared in advance (see **9.3**); however a witness could fail to persuade the tribunal of their case, either on further examination by the tribunal or on cross-examination.

In addition, in spite of the existence of procedural rules governing the tribunals, the overriding objective to achieve fairness for all allows for some flexibility in the conduct of the case. This can mean last minute 'surprises' such as the production of documents at the Hearing hitherto not disclosed, which may damage a party's case at a late stage.

For the claimant there may be financial advantages in considering an alternative approach to settling the employment dispute. The employee may be able to receive some financial compensation from the employer without going to a Hearing. In addition, the Recoupment Regulations (discussed at **12.2**) will not apply on a settlement. These regulations operate by deducting state benefit payments paid to an unemployed claimant from the amount of compensation that the claimant receives from the employer as part of a tribunal award.

Furthermore an alternative approach to resolving the employment dispute may lead to outcomes which a tribunal cannot provide, such as the provision of a reference, or new arrangements for an employee in the workplace following discrimination complaints.

Employment tribunals are actively engaged in new approaches to resolving disputes. Mediation projects have been running in selected tribunals since 2006 and are discussed below.

Some of the larger employers are also engaging in professional mediation to try to resolve workplace disputes. Workers and employees who are in trade unions can seek the help of their union to try to negotiate issues with employers which might affect numbers of employees.

As in the main court service, employment tribunals will encourage parties to settle their differences if at all possible. In *Halsey* v. *Milton Keynes General NHS Trust* [2004] EWCA Civ 576 the Court of Appeal stated that all members of the legal profession who conduct litigation on behalf of clients should now 'routinely' consider if there is any alternative dispute forum they can pursue. Costs orders may be imposed on those who unreasonably decline to attempt to resolve their legal dispute. In the tribunal system costs are discretionary but can be ordered if parties behave unreasonably in the conduct of the proceedings.

There are now a number of options open to the parties as alternatives to going to a final Hearing in the tribunal, and both employee and employer should carefully consider these alternative options. Advisers should always be aware that alternative routes to settling differences apart from embarking on tribunal proceedings are available.

Parties who appear to be on course for a tribunal claim may be able to avoid litigation by the following routes:

1. *Internal dispute resolution.* The parties can resolve matters via an internal contractual or statutory dispute resolution procedure.
2. *Using ACAS.* The parties can, in some cases, utilise the ACAS arbitration scheme. Alternatively they may use the conciliation services of ACAS to achieve a settlement of their claims.
3. *Using mediation services.*
4. *Drawing up a compromise agreement* which has the effect of settling the claim.
5. *Withdrawing the claim.* The claimant can withdraw a claim once it has been commenced (and where the respondent has counterclaimed, the respondent can also withdraw).
6. *Settling at the Hearing* and obtaining a tribunal decision which reflects the terms.

It is important to be aware that if the employee has any complaint which could be the subject of tribunal proceedings, there are only two types of binding agreement as an alternative to the tribunal decision. These will either be the ACAS-conciliated settlement or the compromise agreement.

Any employer who attempts to persuade an employee or worker to sign a letter or to resolve any complaint capable of going to an employment tribunal by any other similar informal method, should be advised that the employee or worker will have no legal obligation to abide by any arrangement which is not incorporated into one of these prescribed routes.

3.2 INTERNAL RESOLUTION

The statutory procedures

We have already discussed the role of the statutory procedures in the context of ensuring that tribunal claims are properly started. The procedures can also be used to resolve a dispute effectively. In spite of that, the Government's decision referred to in **Chapter 1** to replace these procedures perhaps demonstrates that their efficacy in resolving disputes internally appears to be outweighed by their complexity and way in which they have been used by parties simply to protect their positions in the context of a tribunal claim.

Employer's contractual procedures

Many employers will have in place a contractual procedure for resolving disputes in the workplace. These should mirror the statutory procedures, or if in the form of a collective agreement, comply with the requirements under the disputes resolution regulations for such agreements. They may enhance the statutory disputes procedures and allow, for example, for informal resolution procedures prior to using the formal route.

Section 3 of ERA 1996 requires employers to provide information to employees about their disciplinary procedures and the person to whom they can go with any workplace grievance. If this information is not provided the employee will be awarded a minimum of two weeks' pay by a tribunal, as long as this claim is made in the context of other proceedings such as unfair dismissal claims. Even where no compensation is awarded to the employee, this award can be made (see EA 2002, s.38(2) and (4)). Employers are therefore encouraged by these provisions to make sure employees have access to a suitable procedure.

3.3 USING ACAS

The role of ACAS

The Advisory, Conciliation and Arbitration Service was established as a statutory body to improve industrial relations under the Employment Protection Act 1975.

ACAS has a number of statutory functions. Here we will discuss its role in running the ACAS arbitration scheme as well as how and when it can conciliate in employment tribunal claims. We will also make mention of the possible future role of ACAS if the statutory procedures are to be replaced.

The ACAS Arbitration Scheme

The ACAS arbitration procedure was introduced in May 2001 and revised in April 2004. It has had no significant take up. It is, however, designed to avoid some claims going to a tribunal Hearing and to offer arbitration as an alternative.

The scheme is governed by the ACAS Arbitration Scheme (Great Britain) Order 2004, SI 2004/753.

Under the scheme the ACAS arbitrator can only deal with unfair dismissal claims or claims arising out of disputes concerning the operation of the Flexible Working Regulations 2002, SI 2002/3207 (a right for some employees to request flexible working). Unfair dismissals include the unfair dismissal regime covered by s.98 of the ERA 1996 and also all the statutory unfair dismissals set out in ss.99–104 of the ERA 1996 (for example, pregnancy or health and safety related dismissals).

In applying to the arbitrator the parties must accept both that there was a dismissal and that the employee has a right to bring an unfair dismissal claim. The parties cannot ask the arbitrator to decide if there was a dismissal or to decide on any points of jurisdiction, such as whether the claimant was an employee or self-employed.

Furthermore the scheme states that 'complex' cases will not be referred. The arbitrator will not, for example, decide any questions of European law.

How to access the arbitration scheme

The parties must both indicate their willingness to enter into the scheme and each must sign an arbitration agreement. This document can be an ACAS agreement or a compromise agreement (see later). The parties will be required in writing to waive certain rights that they would otherwise have in the conduct of an employment tribunal claim, such as the right to a public hearing or to cross-examine witnesses.

Once the parties have agreed to arbitration they cannot revert back to a tribunal.

The arbitrator will list the matter for a hearing within 28 days of receiving the request for arbitration, although the arbitrator does have scope to allow adjournments. A 'statement of case' must be lodged with the arbitrator by the parties 14 days before the hearing.

The arbitrator must hear the case within two months of referral.

A hearing is held before the arbitrator, and this will be as informal as possible. It will be held in private. Hearings should be estimated to last no more than half a day. There is no allowance for any cross-examination (in contrast with many other forums for arbitration). Furthermore, the arbitrator will not be bound by case law.

Representatives of the parties may attend but no account is taken as to whether they are legally qualified or not. There may be circumstances, however, where the arbitrator is allowed to have legal assistance, for example where an issue arises in relation to the Human Rights Act 1998.

Award and remedies

The arbitrator will make an award which identifies the reason for the dismissal, states the decision, how it was reached and what the remedy is. The arbitrator can award compensation by way of basic and compensatory awards (see **Chapter 12** for calculations). These awards can be subject to deductions for failing to follow internal appeal procedures, or where the conduct of the employee is found to have contributed to the employee's dismissal. The arbitrator can also order reinstatement or re-engagement.

Arbitrators can enforce awards made and parties may appeal an ACAS arbitrator's decision in the courts.

For further details on how to use the scheme, see the ACAS website (**www.acas.org.uk**).

Settling a claim through ACAS conciliation

When ACAS may conciliate

An ACAS officer has the power to conciliate a settlement which is binding on the parties once either it is clear that the employee has a grievance capable of becoming a claim in the employment tribunal (for instance, the employee has been dismissed or has raised a grievance concerning discriminatory treatment) or once proceedings are actually issued. This is provided for in ETA 1996, s.18.

Under ETA 1996, ss.18(2A) and 19(2) and as provided for in the Rules, there are fixed periods for conciliation (see r.22). This means that ACAS has a statutory power to conciliate during those periods.

The fixed periods are either for seven weeks (the short conciliation period) or 13 weeks (the standard conciliation period). Note that claims under any employment discrimination legislation (which includes the Equal Pay Act 1970) can be settled by ACAS at any time and are not subject to any maximum conciliation period.

The claims subject to the seven-week or short conciliation period are set out in r.22(5). These include:

(a) breach of contract claims;
(b) redundancy payments;
(c) claims for unpaid wages or deduction from wages;
(d) claims for failure to pay a guarantee payment; and
(e) claims for failure to pay an employee who has had to be suspended on medical grounds.

Rule 22(5) also lists a number of less common claims subject to the short conciliation period, such as claims for time off to look for work, arrange training, or attend ante-natal appointments, and the money claims associated with a breach of those rights.

Rule 22(6) provides that all other claims will be subject to the 13-week conciliation period. This will cover unfair dismissal claims (including all the categories of automatically unfair dismissal) and various other statutory claims, such as those under the Working Time Regulations 1998, SI 1998/1833, bearing in mind always that claims for discrimination do not fall within the statutory conciliation period.

Under the Employment Bill 2007 it is provided that once the Bill becomes law these fixed conciliation periods will be repealed and the ACAS officer will be able to conciliate at all times leading up to the Hearing. This will require an amendment to the Rules, as will other changes in the Bill.

How the statutory conciliation procedures operate

STARTING THE PROCESS

Under r.21 the employment tribunal must send copies of the documents relevant to the claim to an ACAS officer. Under r.22(4) the conciliation period is deemed to commence on the date that the tribunal office sends a copy of the claimant's ET1 to the respondent. The tribunal should therefore send the claim form to the ACAS officer at the same time, as the clock will have started to run in a case subject to a fixed conciliation period.

DELAYING THE HEARING

Where there is a fixed conciliation period the employment tribunal must not hold a Hearing during that fixed period. A date for the Hearing may be arranged to take place after the fixed conciliation period. However, a pre-hearing review or a case management discussion may take place during a fixed conciliation period.

EXTENDING THE CONCILIATION PERIOD

If the claim is one subject to a standard conciliation period and the conciliation is underway, the 13-week period can be extended by a further two weeks as long as the ACAS officer notifies the employment tribunal and all the following circumstances apply (see r.22(7)(a)–(c)):

(a) all parties agree to the extension;
(b) there is a settlement proposal being considered; and
(c) ACAS considers it likely that the case will be settled in the additional two weeks applied for.

There is also a provision at r.22(8) for a judge to extend the short conciliation period into the standard period if the complexity of the proceedings makes that more appropriate.

EARLY TERMINATION OF THE PROCESS

The conciliation process can be ended early under r.23 if the following circumstances apply:

(a) there is a default judgment made determining liability and remedy;
(b) there is a default judgment made on liability (14 days after the default judgment signed);
(c) the claim, response or counterclaim is struck out;
(d) either party withdraws;
(e) a party has informed ACAS in writing that it does not wish to use the statutory conciliation proceedings;
(f) there has been a settlement by way of a compromise agreement (see **3.5** below);
(g) ACAS has settled the case early;
(h) the respondent has failed to put in a response within 14 days of the expiry of the time limit for doing so.

Note also that if the proceedings are stayed for any reason the conciliation period is frozen in time at that point and will be revived once the proceedings recommence.

The operation of ACAS conciliation

In 2006/07 ACAS reported that around a third of all tribunal claims are settled via ACAS conciliation and a further third are withdrawn. ACAS is also beginning to take a more pro-active role in mediation, which is referred to at **3.4**.

Under their powers in ETA 1996, s.18, ACAS officers are given professional freedom as to how exactly they achieve a conciliated settlement. The process will usually be as follows:

1. The officer will contact each party by letter and then follow up with a telephone call to introduce him or herself. Some information about the role of ACAS in conciliation accompanies the introductory letter. There is nothing to prevent a party contacting ACAS to discover if an officer has been assigned to the case in order to discuss conciliation.
2. In the initial letter and telephone call the ACAS officer will briefly explain the role of ACAS and its neutral approach in attempting to reach a conciliation. The officer will outline the best way of keeping in contact (usually by telephone). The officer will then ask both parties what, if any,

proposals they might have for settling the claim. Claimants will often be asked 'what are you looking for' and, similarly, respondents may be asked what they are prepared to offer to settle.

3. Thereafter the ACAS officer will maintain contact with both parties on a regular basis, usually by telephone, although a meeting can be arranged at a mutually convenient location if the parties think it might be helpful. The contact will be for the purpose of discussing with each party in turn what the other party's position is, in an effort to reach an agreement between them and achieve a settlement.

4. The officer will be willing to discuss the law and legislation which applies in the case. They can refer to case law (and often do!). The officer will discuss with each party the strengths of both their case and their opponent's. However, conciliation does not involve giving a party legal advice or advising on the merits of the case. They will 'test out' a party's case in discussion but not commit to advice on its merit.

5. Finally, the officer will advise each party how a settlement will operate, and the terms to be incorporated.

In the cases of *Clarke and ors* v. *Redcar and Cleveland Borough Council; Wilson and ors* v. *Stockton-on-Tees Borough Council* [2006] IRLR 324 the EAT gave guidelines on the function of ACAS with respect to conciliating settlements. It stated that:

*   there is no requirement on the part of ACAS to ensure that the terms of the settlement are fair in respect of either party;
*   'promoting a settlement' is a general term and related to the circumstances of a particular case;
*   ACAS officers must not advise on the merits of a case;
*   ACAS's duties to conciliate under ETA 1996, s.18 are not prescribed by that section;
*   if an ACAS officer were to act in bad faith (an unlikely circumstance) or adopt any unfair methods in the role as conciliator, a conciliated agreement might be set aside.

This claim had arisen due to a party alleging that ACAS had not acted properly in exercising its powers to conciliate under s.18, which led the EAT to restate the neutral and independent role of ACAS in this context.

How the claim is settled

Assuming that the negotiations are going well and are, where relevant, being conducted in the appropriate time frame, the ACAS officer will take the lead on settling the case. The settlement figure (the amount to be paid to the claimant) is usually agreed first and then any additional features of the settlement (wording, provision of a reference) follow on afterwards. Often the wording of a reference to be provided for future or prospective employers will be negotiated as part of the settlement and that form of wording will be attached to the signed agreement.

The COT3

The COT3 is the name given to the contract drawn up by the ACAS conciliation officer to reflect the settlement agreement.

Once the terms of the settlement are agreed, the ACAS officer will send draft wording of the proposed terms to the parties. It should be noted that:

1. the terms of the COT3 can lawfully exclude all claims or potential claims which the claimant has or may have against the respondent;
2. the agreement cannot lawfully exclude the employee's pension rights as against the employer or any personal injury claim;
3. the agreement is binding upon the parties once finalised and cannot be changed once the parties agree to be bound by it.

Because ACAS conciliation usually takes place almost entirely by telephone it is important for the parties to ensure that there is absolute clarity and agreement as to what the terms of settlement are prior to informing the ACAS officer that these terms are agreed. Furthermore, last minute negotiations often mean that the representatives are under pressure and may not always record every conversation and message left.

Prior to informing the ACAS officer that the terms are agreed, the representative must ensure that they have their client's consent to agree to these terms: see *Gloystarne* v. *Martin* [2001] IRLR 15 where a representative acted beyond his authority and the terms of the settlement were not therefore binding on his client.

Once agreement has been signalled to ACAS by both parties the ACAS officer will telephone the tribunal office to inform it that a binding settlement has been achieved. The Hearing will then be taken out of the list.

Thereafter the final COT3 is sent first to the claimant or the claimant's representative. The claimant must sign all copies and forward them to the respondent or the respondent's representative. The respondent will sign and keep a copy and send it to ACAS. ACAS will send a copy of the final agreement signed by both parties to the claimant.

The effect of an ACAS settlement

As indicated, once the tribunal office is told that the ACAS officer has negotiated a settlement, the matter is taken out of the list and no Hearing will take place. See also above for the situation where the case is settled in a time shorter than a statutory fixed period.

The effect of the agreement being concluded is most likely to be that the tribunal proceedings will be at an end. They are regarded as being dismissed or withdrawn, and the remedy for non-compliance with the terms of the agreement will be an action for breach of contract under the terms of the agreement in the county court or the High Court.

Occasionally the agreement may state that the tribunal Hearing is adjourned until all terms of the agreement have been put into effect. This is rare, but in this situation the claimant will have scope to reactivate the claim if the terms are not met. There is some scope for arguing that non-compliance will nullify the COT3 agreement and revive the tribunal claim automatically. However, there are no reported cases to this effect, although there are some tribunal decisions.

3.4 MEDIATION

Mediation is now beginning to play a more active role in civil court proceedings, with some district judges acting as mediators in their courts. The aim is to facilitate an outcome which the two parties agree between themselves. It is not legally binding on them but will offer an alternative solution to their legal dispute. The outcome may be similar or quite different to that which a court or tribunal could provide. However, if agreement can be reached it saves on court time and legal costs for all concerned.

As a process, mediation has been available for a range of legal disputes for some time. There are free local mediation services in many areas of the country. In the employment context, employers and employees can seek mediation from a commercial mediation organisation such as the Centre for Effective Dispute Resolution (CEDR). Some large employers have actively harnessed mediation services to their human resources functions.

More recently, in the Employment Tribunals Service, a pilot mediation project was set up in Newcastle, Birmingham and London Central Regions and ran between August 2006 and March 2007. It was targeted at more complex claims of disability, sex and race discrimination claims. Parties were invited to take part free of charge and could withdraw from the process at any stage. Tribunal chairmen who acted as mediators took no part in the formal aspects of the cases they had mediated in.

A review of the pilot was undertaken by the University of Westminster in late 2007 and although the results were not available at the date of writing it appears likely that it will signal continued use of mediation in the employment tribunals.

ACAS has also been developing its mediation service over a number of years, having piloted it from 2003 with positive results. It is possible that ACAS will be given a stronger role as a statutory mediation body in future. The Tribunals, Courts and Enforcement Act 2007, s.7B provides for mediation to be a part of the statutory process of conducting tribunal claims. New regulations may provide for practice directions in which mediation will be provided by tribunals after consultation with ACAS. All this will be in the future, depending on how both this piece of legislation and the Employment Bill 2007 finally take shape.

Mediation is therefore still a developing service in many areas of employment disputes but it does appear to be one which is growing in status and it will be well worth considering it as a possible option to resolve a workplace dispute, especially where the employment relationship is still continuing. It should however be noted that the services of external employment law mediators are subject to a fee, and it is not every employer that will be able to or prepared to defray the cost of using such services.

3.5   THE COMPROMISE AGREEMENT

A compromise agreement is a creature of statute. Under ERA 1996, s.203(1), there is a provision which states that any attempt to contract out of proceedings in the employment tribunal will be invalid unless it complies with the provisions set out in that section. All the main statutes giving rise to proceedings in the employment tribunal have similar provisions and state that contracting out is only permitted if it complies with the requirements in that statutory provision relating to a valid process of contracting out.

Thus a compromise agreement is a valid, contractual way of settling the employment tribunal dispute.

The compromise agreement is drawn up and agreed between the parties directly. Where both parties feel confident that they can communicate well through their representatives and hopefully reach agreement easily and speedily, a compromise agreement will avoid involving a third party (as in the ACAS settlement) which could make the process slower.

Tactics in negotiating a settlement between the parties

Before looking at the form and effect of a compromise agreement, it will be worth noting that in order to get to the point of entering into a compromise agreement, the two parties in conflict will have entered into direct negotiation with each other in order to settle their differences and record the terms of settlement. This process of negotiating the terms and reaching a final outcome that both parties can accept requires a number of skills and tactics.

The first principle of settling a case is to ensure from day one that settlement is seen as a positive option. Many cases are settled by parties' representatives at a relatively late stage, and some clients may feel that they have been pressurised into settling because their adviser has some ulterior motive. They may believe that you do not wish to go to court or that you wish to use the time saved for other work. Where you are acting on a conditional fee agreement, your client may be particularly wary of offers to settle. However, any meaningful settlement is likely to be worth striving for, no matter how late in the day, to avoid the risk, costs and stress of litigation. It is important that the parties see settling as a statutory, viable, route to resolving the dispute.

Claimants should from the outset be calculating as accurately as possible what their losses are and what the tribunal is likely to award them if they win. The claimant will have drawn up a schedule of loss. This is not only relevant for the purposes of calculating compensation but also keeps both parties focussed on the claimant's actual losses and helps to see them in the context of the cost and time involved in continuing with a claim. For the same reasons, respondents will wish to know what the claimant's continuing losses are as the case is progressing. This approach will help the parties to keep an open mind on the option of a settlement.

To help their clients put the idea of a settlement into perspective, advisers for each party need to advise on the costs of preparation, noting that legal costs (where the client is paying) rise steeply in the final stages of preparation and at the Hearing itself.

Where the adviser embarks on negotiations designed to lead to a settlement there are certain principles which it will be useful to be aware of:

1. Settlement negotiations between the parties are 'off the record' or 'without prejudice'. The employment tribunal is not entitled to know any details of the discussions or indeed that any attempt has been made to settle the claim.
2. The claimant is unlikely to recover 100 per cent of what the claim would actually be worth if it were to be completely successful. The claimant and the respondent need to understand that the level of settlement will reflect the fact that both parties are avoiding the risk of litigation. Thus the rule of thumb figure is usually around two-thirds of the maximum which the claimant might be awarded by the tribunal if the claimant was to win on all counts.
3. Negotiations are sometimes conducted in an artificial framework. Initial figures put forward in negotiation may not reflect the figure each party will either offer or accept to settle a claim. Claimant advisers may ask for a higher figure than the one they have advised their clients they are likely to achieve on a settlement. Respondent advisers may come in with a first offer below that, perhaps as low as a third, or even lower. In spite of these tactics it will be important for each party to agree with their adviser or representative at the the outset of any negotiations the actual amount they are willing to settle for.
4. There will be typical stages at which a settlement might be achieved. A respondent may offer to settle as soon as the ET1 is received to avoid the costs and time of defending a claim. Parties may be encouraged to settle if

documents and witness statements have been fully disclosed by each party and strengths and weaknesses of each case are fully revealed. Finally there may be a last-minute settlement, either in the days running up to the Hearing (as the parties may decide they do not want the Hearing to go ahead) or at the tribunal immediately before or during the Hearing.

5. Settling a case is bound to involve giving ground. There is little to be gained by expecting your opponents to settle by convincing them that your case is bound to succed. For the purposes of negotiating you are likely to accept that both cases have strengths and that your aim is to accept that and move forward to a position where differences are put aside for the sake of a settlement which will save time, stress and expense in the tribunal.

What is covered by the compromise agreement

Assuming that negotiations have been successful the parties will be ready to start drafting a compromise agreement. It will contain the terms of settlement as well as certain information required by the legislation

The agreement serves to settle the subject of a claim in the employment tribunal. The wording of ERA 1996, s.203(2) (mirrored in the other relevant statutory provisions) also makes it clear that the agreement can cover proceedings not yet issued as it refers to 'instituting or continuing' with proceedings.

The agreement cannot include all or any proceedings which the claimant may institute in the future (see *Lunt* v. *Merseyside TEC Ltd* [1999] ICR 17). However, it can cover any complaints which the employee might have which could lead to proceedings, as well as the 'particular proceedings' which the parties want to compromise (see *Hinton* v. *University of East London* [2005] IRLR 552).

In the *Hinton* decision it was found that the wording of the compromise agreement excluding the claimant's right to pursue an unfair dismissal was not sufficient to exclude his right to pursue his right to claim automatic unfair dismissal as a whistleblower. As a result, employers are now much more careful about how they draft agreements and will list in detail all those claims they believe that the parties are agreeing to exclude or claims that the employee may make based on the issues which they have raised with their employer.

The employee who is ignorant of those potential claims may be able to pursue them even where he or she agreed to wording apparently excluding such claims. In *Hilton Hotels* v. *McNaughten* (unreported, EAT/0059/04) the employee had agreed to exclude her rights to pursue a claim under the Equal Pay Act, but later read in a newspaper article that as a part timer she could pursue a pension claim. She had not appreciated the meaning of that exclusion at the time when she signed the agreement. Where employees have access to an adviser who can explain the effect of what they are signing they are unlikely to be able to rely on their ignorance. Employee advisers should ensure that their clients fully understand the meaning of the claims they are agreeing not to pursue, relating them to the facts as they are known at the time.

Drawing up the agreement

The various statutes under which tribunal proceedings can be brought set out the requirements which must be complied with in order for the compromise agreement to be valid.

Because the effect of a compromise agreement is to allow the claimant or potential claimant to contract out of the tribunal proceedings, there are safeguards for the claimant, who must have been advised and assisted by a named adviser. The EAT has stated that the agreement is likely to be invalid if the adviser is not named, no matter if it is clear who the adviser is (see for example *Sankyo Pharma UK Ltd* v. *Bartlett* (unreported, EAT 687/1999)).

The classes of persons who will count as an adviser (known as an 'independent adviser') for the purposes of drawing up a valid compromise agreement are as follows:

1. A solicitor either in private practice or employed to give advice, with a practising certificate, or a barrister or a person who has rights of audience or is a litigator within the meaning of s.204 of the Courts and Services Act 1990. This can now include a member of the Institute of Legal Executives with rights of audience in the courts: see the Compromise Agreements (Descriptions of Persons) Order 2004, SI 2004/754.
2. An officer or official of a trade union certified by the union as being competent to give advice.
3. An employee or volunteer of an advice centre who gives free advice (e.g. a Citizens Advice Bureau).

An employer or associated employer cannot act as an independent adviser.

In addition, there are further formalities to be complied with in the wording of the agreement. These are:

*   the agreement must be in writing;
*   it must state the name of the independent adviser (i.e. 'identify' them);
*   it must state that the effect of the agreement has been explained to the employee by the named adviser (i.e. the 'contracting out' nature of it); and
*   it must also confirm that the independent adviser has in force, at the time the agreement is drawn up, a policy of insurance concerning the advice given to the employee covering the risk of a claim.

Common additional clauses

In addition to the statutory clauses, the typical compromise agreement will often contain a number of additional clauses. Note that some of these can appear to be more favourable to the employer than to the employee.

Confidentiality

A confidentiality clause may sometimes be referred to as a 'gagging clause'. The parties will agree not to disclose to anyone other than their legal or financial advisers the existence or the terms of the agreement. This clause would usually be requested by the employer, but the employee may also wish to move forward with a clean slate. In addition, this clause may also include a requirement for the employee not to disclose anything about the employer's business interests or affairs, where there was no such post-termination clause in the original employment contract. In this context, parties should be aware that it would be unlawful to exclude the employee's rights as a 'whistleblower' under the Public Interest Disclosure Act 1998 and any actual or potential claims as a whistle-blower would need to be specifically excluded (see *Hinton* above).

Tax indemnity clause

There is strictly no provision for excluding income tax liability for termination payments as HM Revenue and Customs will usually regard these as pay. However under s.148 of the Income and Corporation Taxes Act 1988 no tax is payable under the PAYE scheme for a termination payment of up to £30,000. The employer does not pay tax and hands over the full payment to the employee.

On the other hand, if there is a notice pay clause in the employee's contract, then any payment to compensate for lack of notice pay in lieu is taxable as it is income and not a compensatory termination payment.

To avoid doubt, however, the employer will usually expect the employee to indemnify the employer in respect of any liability after the agreement is concluded or, in the alternative, to agree to pay any income tax which may thereafter accrue. This almost 'fictional' agreement is one which many employees find hard to grasp, but employers will wish to cover themselves in relation to their legal liability to pay tax under the PAYE scheme.

References

As with the ACAS agreement, it is not uncommon for the parties to agree that the employer will provide a reference for the employee as part of the compromise agreement. There is, of course, no legal obligation to provide a reference and by the same token there is no requirement as to the content of any reference.

Employers should be aware, however, that they may be liable for negligence for an inaccurate reference which causes damage to the economic interests of the employee (see *Spring* v. *Guardian Assurance plc* [1994] IRLR 460). For this reason many employers may be reluctant to say very much about an employee, especially one who has already shown an inclination to be litigious.

When negotiating a reference, the parties should consider whether they will want the exact wording of the reference to be agreed and provided on headed paper for the employee to take away, or whether the parties can agree a 'shopping list' of the elements and comments in the reference to be provided when approached by a future or prospective employer.

The disadvantage of the first approach is that the employee will have only one document to show to prospective employers, and this document may well look like it has a history of negotiation behind it. In contrast 'the agreed items' approach gives the reference a freshness if requested.

However, the employee should be aware that if the ex-employer is approached for further information nothing could be said which could be seen as causing any possible damage to the employee's economic interests; but also the ex-employer cannot lie to a future or prospective employer. Strictly the respondent to the agreement should refuse to impart anything other than the agreed items. This may, of course, make a prospective employer suspicious.

Payment method and dates

The parties can agree any method or date of payment to suit themselves. However, some employers will expect the employee to agree to the proceedings being withdrawn prior to payment being received. The employee's adviser will, for obvious reasons, wish the withdrawal of proceedings to take place only after payment or other terms have been finalised. However, it would seem that a compromise agreement that has all the statutory elements in it will stand as a valid instrument to avoid proceedings in the tribunal, even if the terms are not complied with.

Enforcing a compromise agreement

Given that there are defined statutory elements in the compromise agreement, once these are complied with the agreement will be valid to exclude tribunal proceedings.

However, either party may not keep to their side of the bargain. Once the agreement is binding the employee will not be able to seek to reinstate the original claim, which was settled under the terms of the agreement. All that can be done is to seek to enforce the negotiated terms of the agreement. An employee could, however, still litigate against the employer for matters excluded in the agreement, and the case law tends to revolve around disputes over what matters were excluded (see *Lunt* (above) etc.).

The employer may fail to comply with its side of the agreement by, for example not paying money or not providing a reference. An employee may be alleged to have breached a term relating to the confidential nature of the agreement. If any terms of the agreement are not adhered to or are breached the appropriate action will be breach of contract. Employers should be careful how enforcement clauses are worded. In *CMC* v. *Zhang* [2006] EWCA Civ 408 the employer sought to recover the whole amount paid to the employee who it claimed had breached a term of the compromise agreement. The employer had failed to quantify its damages under the contract as a result of any breach. The Court of Appeal found that the wording requiring a repayment of all the money paid in the light of any breach was unenforceable as it operated as a penalty clause.

If the agreement has arisen on the termination of the employment contract it could be enforced (within the required three-month period) in the employment tribunal which can hear a contractual claim that 'arises or is outstanding on the termination of the employment' contract (see the Employment Tribunals (Extension of Jurisdiction) Order 1994, SI 1994/1623).

If the agreement has been reached before or after termination, breached terms will be enforced in the civil court, as for any other breach of contract claim. This would also be pursued as an alternative to commencing the breach of contract claim in the employment tribunal. Although fees will be payable in the civil courts, the time limit of six years for commencing breach of contract claims gives more latitude.

Using our fictional example of *Molly Martin* v. *Just in Time*, an example of a compromise agreement which might be drawn up in Molly's case is provided at **3.7**.

3.6 WITHDRAWING THE CLAIM

It is possible for the claimant to withdraw a claim once it has commenced in the employment tribunal. Claimants often decide that they can no longer cope with the stress associated with continuing with the case.

Rule 25(1) states that a party may withdraw a claim at any time. The request to withdraw must be made in writing (a letter is sufficient as long as it clearly states which case is being withdrawn).

The tribunal office will send a copy of this document (which becomes known as the notice of withdrawal) to the other party or parties. The date upon which the tribunal receives the notice of withdrawal is the date upon which the claim is withdrawn. Once the claim is withdrawn a respondent can apply to have the proceedings dismissed.

Where the proceedings have been dismissed the tribunal has no power to reinstate the proceedings. In *Khan* v. *Heywood and Middleton Primary Care Trust* [2006] ICR 543 the employee had written to the employment tribunal to withdraw his claim and then received advice from a solicitor, following which he asked the tribunal to set aside the notice of withdrawal. The EAT stated that the tribunal had no power to set aside a claim that had been withdrawn; the effect was the same as a claim that had been dismissed. A claimant with a dismissed claim will be prevented by the doctrine of estoppel from litigating twice in respect of the same matter. The wording of r.25 is slightly ambiguous as it states that the withdrawal of a claim brings the proceedings to an end against that respondent as well as providing for the respondent to apply for the proceedings to be dismissed once the claim is withdrawn (r.25(4)). The Rules, however, give no power for the tribunal to reinstate a withdrawn claim, so claimants should be advised that they cannot restart a claim which they have withdrawn as it will be treated as having been dismissed.

There is no rule which states that the withdrawing party must pay the other party's costs to date, as there is in the civil courts. However, the tribunal has the power to award costs or preparation time under r.40(2) where, amongst other things, a party has acted unreasonably in the conduct of proceedings. So where a claimant withdraws a claim at a late stage the respondent may have grounds for a costs application. Rule 25(3) also states that proceeding in relation to costs are not affected by a withdrawal.

Claimants should be aware that they do always have the right to withdraw but should be aware of their timing as respondents will have spent time and expense on preparing for the Hearing. In any event if the claimant does decide to withdraw at any stage it would be prudent to write to the respondent and explain the reasons for doing so, to avoid a costs application being made or being successful.

3.7 SETTLING AT THE TRIBUNAL

Where a claim is settled on the day of the Hearing or part-way through a Hearing, it will usually be recorded as a tribunal judgment. Given that a tribunal judgment may include an award of compensation (see r.28(1)), a judgment can be drawn up by the tribunal which reflects the agreed terms and will state either that the case is stayed until the terms have been complied with or that the claimant will withdraw or has withdrawn the claim.

A breach of the tribunal order will mean that the employee will have to enforce the judgment like any other tribunal judgment. Note, however, that sometimes the parties will agree on the wording of a tribunal order which keeps the settlement figure confidential and will only state that the proceedings are (for example) withdrawn on payment of an agreed sum. For more on tribunal judgments, see **Chapter 11**.

Case study: Molly Martin's compromise agreement

An agreement to refrain from instituting or continuing with proceedings before an employment tribunal.

This agreement is made between Molly Martin of 4 View Road, Anytown XYZ 12X (hereinafter known as 'the Employee') and Just in Time Catering Limited of Unit 405, Springfield Road Anytown XYZ OPJ (hereinafter referred to as 'the Employer').

It is agreed between the parties as follows:

1. The Employer will pay the Employee the sum of £5000 (five thousand pounds) within 14 days of both parties' representatives having signed this agreement.
2. The Employer will provide a reference in respect of the Employee to any future or prospective employer in the terms agreed as set out in Appendix 1 to this agreement.
3. The Employee will refrain from continuing with her complaint against the Employer which is the subject of the proceedings numbered 33333/2008 in the Employment Tribunal at Anytown. The employee has also agreed that she will refrain from instituting proceedings in respect of the claims listed in Appendix 2 hereto. Furthermore she will send a copy of the letter seeking a withdrawal of this particular complaint to the Employer within 7 days of receiving the sum referred to in paragraph 1 above.
4. The Employee agrees not to discuss the terms of this agreement with anyone other than her legal advisers.
5. The Employee acknowledges that before signing this agreement she received independent legal advice from Jenny Carter, an independent adviser employed as an employment adviser at The Last Stop Advice Bureau as to the terms and effect of this agreement and in particular the effect on her ability to pursue these claims before an Employment Tribunal.
6. The conditions regulating compromise agreements under s.203 of the Employment Rights Act and s.77(4A) of the Sex Discrimination Act are satisfied in relation to this agreement.

Signed (Employee)   Dated

Signed (Employer)   Dated

STATEMENT BY COMPLAINANT'S LEGAL ADVISER

I, Jenny Carter of the Last Stop Advice Bureau, Anytown confirm that I am a solicitor and an employee of the above advice bureau and that the advice given by the bureau is free and that the bureau carries an appropriate policy of insurance and that I have advised the Employee as to the terms and effect of this agreement and as to its effect in relation to her rights to continue with her claims of unfair dismissal and sex discrimination (as well as the claims listed in Appendix 2 hereto) in the employment tribunal.

Signed

Dated

CHAPTER 4

The claim and questionnaire

4.1 FIRST STEPS

Before submitting a claim to the employment tribunal there are a number of preliminary steps to be taken. This chapter will deal with those and sets out the steps to be taken in submitting a claim to the tribunal. Although the chapter is aimed at claimants and their advisers, respondents will need to understand the preliminary stages that the claimant is likely to have followed prior to and upon issue of their claim.

Before starting a tribunal claim, the claimant adviser should set out the facts of the employment relationship as well as the legal wrong which the employee is saying gives rise to his or her complaint. From this factual outline, the issues in dispute which the employment tribunal will be asked to reach a decision on can begin to be identified and extracted.

The adviser should also advise the potential claimant how strong the proposed claim (or claims) appears to be before any claim is commenced, and outline what compensation the claimant is likely to receive from the employment tribunal if the claim is successful. The adviser should also discuss how the claim will be funded and give an explanation of costs in the employment tribunal.

It will be necessary to explain to a client who has no experience of employment tribunal proceedings that once a claim is commenced in the tribunal there are key stages which will occur as the case progresses towards a final Hearing. Timings will vary according to the complexity of the issues, the facts of the case, and whether there will need to be a pre-hearing review. Lengthier and more complex cases are likely to be listed for a number of days and this will usually mean a longer wait for a date available in the tribunal and convenient for all concerned. Nevertheless the key stages can be outlined to clients to prepare them for the tribunal process (see **Figure 4.1**).

When acting as a claimant adviser, it may be useful to prepare a standard letter for the client contemplating a tribunal claim which outlines the procedure of following a claim step by step. In addition the letter can outline what steps the adviser will take on the client's behalf. In interviews between the client and the adviser to discuss preparation for a Hearing these procedures and steps can be further discussed and explained, referring back to the outline letter. Respondent clients will also no doubt seek to understand the process of a tribunal claim and may find **Figure 4.1** and an outline letter helpful.

Checklist of first steps

For the claimant the following checklist may be useful to ensure that all the relevant preliminary points have been covered during the initial contact with the client:

1. What are the facts of the case.
2. What are the legal issues.
3. What are the time limits for presenting the claim(s).
4. Has the employee has complied with any required statutory procedures and/or is the claim in time.
5. Is the employee is in any way excluded from claiming due to employment status, type of job, location, or some other factor.
6. The merits of the case at this stage – can a percentage be put on them.
7. What is the claim worth and how will compensation will be assessed.
8. What outcome is the client seeking – compensation in the tribunal, to have his or her job back, or to try to achieve a settlement.
9. How an adviser will conduct the claim on the client's behalf.
10. Who will represent the client at tribunal.

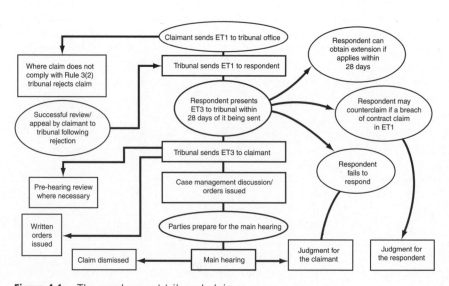

Figure 4.1   The employment tribunal claim

4.2 THE FACTS ABOUT THE EMPLOYMENT RELATIONSHIP

There are a series of specific questions to which short and accurate replies will be needed in order to establish the contractual and statutory status of the employment relationship. The answers will tell you whether any documents can assist in deciding the employee's contractual rights, what the employee's length of service is or was (for the purpose of calculating qualifying period and/or compensation). Most of this factual information will also need to be included in the claim form (ET1) (see later).

Factual questions checklist

---

1. Date started job.
2. Whether still employed.
3. Whether written terms and conditions were provided.
4. Job title and/or job description.
5. Name and address and telephone number of the employer. If this is a head office, also the details of the employee's workplace.
6. If not still employed, last date of work. (NB: The adviser will then need to establish precisely when the Effective Date of Termination (EDT) was and/or the date of the act being complained of and also carefully calculate the time limits within which the claim can be commenced.)
7. How many hours worked per week.
8. Pay (client to produce any pay slips if possible).
9. Contractual or statutory holiday entitlement or pay in lieu outstanding (details).
10. If dismissed, whether the employee worked out notice or received notice pay, or whether the employee was summarily dismissed with or without notice pay.

The facts of the case

At the outset, it will be necessary to identify the facts as closely as possible, then decide on what claims might arise out of these facts. It will help to try to establish whether the employer will be likely to dispute the facts (or has already done so). These facts, once established, may throw up a range of interwoven issues. For example, exploring an unfair dismissal claim may mean that other claims may be added in, such as notice pay or holiday pay. Possible acts of discrimination should also be identified.

This factual outline will form the basis of the claimant's statement, and a first working draft should be drawn up after the first interview.

Case study: establishing the facts

Returning to the case example outlined in **Chapter 1**, in Molly's case, examples of facts which need to be established would be:

1. Where and how often she worked for Just in Time.
2. What were her pay arrangements.
3. What aspects of her job were under the control of Just in Time.
4. The exact details of the conversations with her manager in November.
5. What Molly said in her letter to her manager in her letter of 26 November.
6. The details of the changes to her shifts after she complained to her manager.
7. The exact details of her conversation with her manager in December just before she left for the last time.
8. Whether there had been any earlier references to her pregnancy.

4.3 THE LEGAL ISSUES

Once the facts have been established, the legal issues need to be identified and a view taken on how strong these are. This can be done in the following way:

1. Identify the nature of the claim or claims in law (e.g. unfair dismissal, wrongful dismissal, sex discrimination).
2. Decide how each claim can be proved and what witnesses and documentation will assist.
3. Assess what evidence is currently available to the claimant.
4. Decide if the claimant has any claims in the alternative (e.g. unfair dismissal for capability and/or automatic unfair dismissal as a pregnant employee) and, if so, which of the possible claims appears to be the stronger.
5. Establish whether the claimant has any knowledge as to how the employer will deal with its evidence (e.g. witnesses).

At this point it should be possible to assess the merits of the claim, preferably on a rough percentage basis (e.g. 60/40 in favour). This assessment of the relative strength of a claimant's claim will need to be reviewed and probably revised once the employer's response to the claim is received by the claimant.

4.4 COMPENSATION AND COSTS

At the outset, the potential claimant should be given an idea of what the claim is likely to be worth. This may only be a rough estimate at this stage, as the claimant's financial circumstances may have altered by the time the Hearing takes place. How the tribunals assess compensation is looked at in **Chapter 12**.

Note that claimants in employment tribunal claims will in nearly all circumstances have a duty to 'mitigate their loss'. This means ensuring that they do what they can to minimise their present and continuing loss, by, for example obtaining alternative employment.

If the claimant is unemployed, it is important that from the outset a record of attempts to find work and any fluctuation in income is kept. Some tribunal offices require the claimant to file a schedule of loss shortly after the claim has been registered; others will order it to be prepared as part of case management. The schedule will show the total financial losses incurred at that time (for example: wages, loss of pension, expenses incurred looking for work) and will need to be updated nearer to the date of the main Hearing.

The example below is only for guidance. It is taken from Molly's case study and combines a job search record with her ongoing schedule of loss. It refers to her ongoing loss in relation to the money she took home on average each week, including her bonuses and commission. This can be regularly updated or added to, and can be sent to the tribunal or the opposing party either as ordered or as part of the preparation for the Hearing.

Case study: Molly Martin's initial schedule of loss

Weekly wages at Just in Time average £300 a week

Date	Income/ source of income	No of weeks after dismissal	Job applications made	Results of job applications	Loss
20 Dec	Nil/None	1	2 applications made via local paper for Christmas waitressing jobs	Told no vacancies left	£300 – 1 week's net pay
11 Jan	Nil/None	3	1 application for receptionist job at local taxi firm	Told 'no relevant experience'	£900 – 3 weeks' pay
11 March	Nil/None	7	No jobs applied for (unwell)	N/A	£2,100 – 7 weeks' pay*

* Note that Molly needs also to calculate any notice pay she is owed and any outstanding holiday pay she is owed. She will also be claiming compensation for her discriminatory dismissal as a pregnant employee – see **Chapter 12** for more on remedy.

Costs

The adviser will also discuss with the client the way in which the case will be funded. Whatever method is used (private paying, conditional fee agreement, or free advice under a Legal Services Commission contract), an employee could potentially face the risk of being liable to pay costs at the end of the proceedings.

Employment tribunals are given the power to award costs against a party. The tribunals can decide on costs awards up to £10,000 and can refer for assessment in the civil courts a costs award which exceeds that amount. With one exception (where an adjournment has been necessitated by an employer's failure to provide evidence of a suitable job for an employee seeking to be reinstated or re-engaged) the award of costs in the employment tribunal is discretionary. This means that they are not automatically awarded at the end of every Hearing to successful parties. Tribunals have the power to award costs against a party whom they find to have acted vexatiously, abusively, disruptively, or otherwise unreasonably, in bringing the proceedings, or where the bringing or conduct of the proceedings by a party has been misconceived.

In addition the tribunal has the power to award costs against a party's representative. Costs are dealt with in full in **Chapter 13** but the question of costs orders in the employment tribunals should be discussed with the client at the outset. Many employees are unrepresented in the conduct of their tribunal claims and may be more at risk of having costs orders made against them.

Case study: Molly's possible claims

Looking at Molly's case, there is the possibility that she can pursue a claim for either unfair dismissal and/or for automatically unfair dismissal (for a reason connected with her pregnancy). There are also possible claims for sex discrimination, in relation to remarks made to her about her appearance as a pregnant woman, her dismissal as a pregnant woman and the detrimental change to her shifts after she complained about her treatment. She is also likely to have claims for notice pay and/or a breach of contract and a deduction of wages. Molly's claim form is set out later in this chapter.

At the outset, careful thought should be given to which of the claims is most likely to succeed. There will be a risk of costs being awarded against her if unmeritorious claims are added in 'for good measure'.

4.5   GRIEVANCE STATEMENT AND LETTERS BEFORE ACTION

The claimant adviser may be asked to write her client's Step 1 grievance letter for her. As we have seen in **Chapter 2**, a legal adviser's letter can constitute a grievance in order to comply with the pre-action steps. The letter may also seek to clarify the client's claim and seek a remedy.

Case study: Molly's grievance

In the case of Molly, she has already written to her employer, setting out her grievance. It will be recalled that Molly only needs to raise a grievance about what she regards a discriminatory treatment and not about any subsequent dismissal even if she believes that dismissal also to be an act of discrimination. This is what Molly wrote to her employer on 26 November:

To:
Just in Time Catering Ltd
Unit 405
Springfield Road
26 November

Dear Sirs,

I am writing to complain about the way my manager has been treating me at work.

Ever since I told the Events Manager in November that I was pregnant he has made life very difficult for me. He has said that he cannot guarantee that I will be allowed to take maternity leave. He has also made remarks to me which are discriminatory and sexist

He has said that pregnant women have caused him problems taking time off for medical appointments and having morning sickness. He has also commented that he doesn't want me looking fat and unladylike in my uniform, referring to the fact that I am pregnant.

I believe this to be discrimination against me as a woman and a mother-to-be and I have found it very upsetting and distressing.

I would like you to deal with this complaint and tell me what you intend to do to stop this type of thing happening again.

Yours sincerely
Molly Martin
4 View Road

Letter before action

If the employee's claim is one where the employee is obliged to follow the statutory grievance procedure and wait 28 days before starting a claim, that time interval could be used to write a letter before action.

There is no obligation in the Rules to write such a letter, only a requirement, as we have seen in **Chapter 2**, to follow certain preliminary steps before commencing the tribunal claim. If the time frame allows, there are reasons why a further preliminary letter, or letter before action, could be sent to the employer:

1. *To confirm that the statutory grievance procedure has been complied with.* Since both parties have an obligation to comply with the statutory procedures, a letter which sets out the way in which the employee believes the matter to have progressed to date will be helpful if there is any disagreement about what has happened to date.

2. *To attempt to avoid litigation and save costs.* Even if the statutory procedures have been followed, a letter before action which summarises the claim which the employee is contemplating and which seeks a remedy without resorting to tribunal proceedings may have the effect of saving costs and assist in defending a costs application once the case has been heard.

3. *To seek written reasons for a dismissal.* Where the employee is uncertain as to the reason for a dismissal, a letter can be sent to the employer seeking written reasons. Note that if the employee was employed for a year or more, by virtue of ERA 1996, s.92(1) an employer is required to provide written reasons for dismissal. A woman who is dismissed whilst she is pregnant is also entitled to written reasons no matter how long she has worked for her employer (see ERA 1996, s.92(4)). If the employer fails to provide a written reason, the tribunal can make a finding as to what the reason was and award compensation of two weeks' pay (see ERA 1996, s.93).

4. *To deal with the statutory defence in discrimination claims.* In discrimination claims the employer may rely on the statutory defence of 'reasonably practicable'. See, for example, SDA 1975, s.41(3). This says: 'In proceedings brought under this Act against any person in respect of an act alleged by an employer of his it shall be a defence for that person to prove that he took such steps as were reasonably practicable to prevent the employee from doing that act, or from doing in the course of employment acts of that description.' Similar provisions exist in the other five discrimination enactments. Therefore the employer should be given an opportunity to say if potential discrimination has been dealt with or remedied. There is a fairly high standard of what the employer would be required to do to show that they have done all that they could to eliminate the discrimination complained of (see e.g. *Caniffe* v. *East Riding of Yorkshire Council* [2000] IRLR 555).

Case study: Molly's letter before action

To
Just in Time Catering
Unit 405 Springfield Road

Dear Sirs,

Re: Ms Molly Martin

I should be grateful if you would note that we have been consulted by Ms Martin concerning her employment with you.

We have advised our client that she was dismissed by you on 6 December when you indicated that she should leave her employment when she was told that she was already beginning to show and she should think about leaving straight away. We have advised her that these are unambiguous words of dismissal.

We have advised her that she was your employee throughout the time she worked for you as you exercised full control over her employment, including how and where and when she worked for you.

In addition Ms Martin wrote a Step 1 grievance statement to you on 26 November to complain about discriminatory treatment of her relating to her pregnancy and gender. Following that letter being sent she suffered detrimental changes to her shifts which made it very hard for her to make arrangements for childcare.

We have therefore advised her that she can bring a claim for unfair and wrongful dismissal, unpaid wages and outstanding holiday pay, and that furthermore she was treated less favourably as a woman, including treatment amounting to harassment and victimisation, and was dismissed for a reason connected with her pregnancy and that her dismissal was an act of sex discrimination.

We should be grateful if you would reply to this letter indicating what remedy you are prepared to offer our client for her losses and injury to feelings, failing which she will have no option but to pursue her claims in the Employment Tribunal. She is no longer employed.

Yours faithfully,
Jane Carter
The Last Stop Advice Bureau

4.6 ENSURING CLAIMS ARE PRESENTED IN TIME

As we saw in the previous chapter it is important for advisers to know when to send in a claim form, particularly where the statutory procedures apply, and to have a system for checking that responsibility is taken by advisers and the organisations they work for to ensure claims arrive in time.

Many claimant advisers will aim to ensure that claims go in to the tribunal at the earliest opportunity (as long as their clients are willing to start claims off) to avoid any possible finding that claims are late and that the tribunal therefore has no jurisdiction to hear them.

There are various issues to bear in mind when calculating the right time to claim, and these are set out in **Figures 4.2** and **4.3**.

Case study: time frames for starting Molly's tribunal claims

Molly has claims both for unfair dismissal and for discrimination. Her time limits will look like this:

Unfair dismissal, wrongful dismissal and discriminatory dismissal claims

(i)   There is no evidence that her employer has started any DDP and so she must make sure her claim for unfair dismissal goes in within three months of the date of her dismissal as she cannot have a reasonable belief that any dismissal procedure is still being followed.
(ii)   She is also claiming notice pay and for wrongful dismissal has no requirement to use a statutory procedure.
(iii)   Furthermore she is asserting that her dismissal was an act of pregnancy-related discrimination and sex discrimination, but because the claim is about the act of dismissal itself she has no requirement to use a statutory GP. She must therefore ensure that all her dismissal claims are presented to the tribunal on or before 5 March, three months following the date of her dismissal.

Other discrimination claims

Molly is asserting that derogatory remarks were made to her on 5 November and that these continued until she was dismissed on 6 December.

She put in a complaint about these on 26 November (her Step 1 Statement). She therefore has six months from 5 November (5 May) to put in her claims for discrimination.

Given however that she also wishes to claim unfair dismissal, she and her adviser have agreed that she will put all her claims into one ET1 which will be sent to arrive at the employment tribunal office no later than 5 March, her deadline date for the dismissal claims.

Note, however, that you may see clients who have already started some claims (e.g. for unfair dismissal) within time and who have other claims which will require the use of a grievance procedure and a careful calculation will be required as to when those claims can be commenced and whether they too can be presented in time.

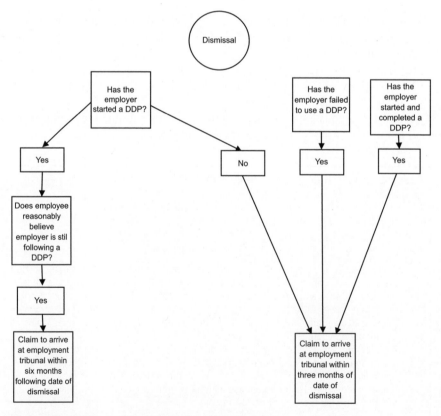

Figure 4.2 DDPs and time limits for tribunal claims

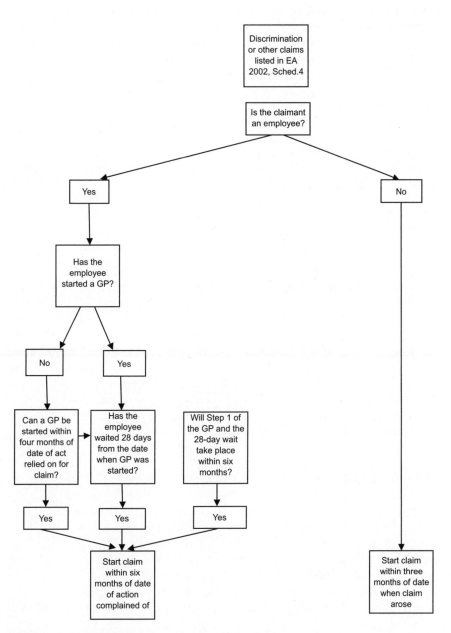

Figure 4.3   GPs and time limits for tribunal claims

Where a claimant starts two claims one after the other, arising out of the same employment relationship, the claimant can ask the tribunal to consolidate or join those claims together so that they will be heard at the same time in a Hearing. As we shall see in **Chapter 7** the tribunal has quite wide powers of case management and will be able to manage multi-claims in a time effective way prior to the Hearing.

4.7 WHERE TO SEND THE CLAIM FORM

Before drawing up the claim form (see below) you will need to know where to send it.

Rule 1(1) of the 2004 Rules states that:

> a claim shall be brought before an employment tribunal by the claimant presenting to an employment tribunal office the details of the claim in writing.

The form should be sent to the tribunal nearest to the place where the employee actually worked (not the tribunal nearest to the employer's head office).

It is possible to locate the relevant office by visiting the Employment Tribunals Services website (**www.employmenttribunals.gov.uk**). This allows you to search on the postcode of the claimant's workplace to find the nearest tribunal office. In addition, the booklet 'How to Apply to an Employment Tribunal' may be downloaded from the website. This provides a list of all the tribunal offices and cross-refers each office to the postcodes it serves. Even if the claim is sent to the wrong tribunal office, it will be still be registered on the day it was received and it will be forwarded to the correct office by the tribunal staff.

If the claim is sent online it will be forwarded to the appropriate employment tribunal office.

4.8 THE FOLLOW-UP LETTER TO THE CLIENT

At the first meeting with the adviser, the employee client should have been advised on the merits, likely compensation, procedures, costs and the funding of the case.

The adviser may also have offered to draft the ET1 form and to send it to the correct tribunal office on behalf of the claimant.

The adviser should then prepare a follow-up letter for the client which confirms the preliminary advice. Other letters should also be sent to the employee client, as follows:

1. The 'Rule 15' or the 'client care' letter (from the Solicitors Regulation Authority Rules of Conduct 2007). These letters can be standardised in solicitors' firms and advice agencies.

2. The initial advice letter covering facts, issues, advice, merits, key dates and steps the adviser will take. This letter will also explain how the case will be funded.
3. A letter about how the case will be conducted and what happens about representation and possible settlement. This letter will also often be standardised.
4. A copy of the claim form ET1 drafted on the client's behalf (if this step has been taken).
5. If appropriate, a copy of the letter before action that the adviser has written to the employer.

4.9 THE CLAIM FORM

The Secretary of State was given power by EA 2002 to bring in a prescribed form in employment tribunal proceedings, and the ET1 has been mandatory since October 2005 with some slight changes having been made since then. The form is available from tribunal offices, ACAS, job centres, Citizens Advice Bureaux and many advice centres. It is also available and can be downloaded from the employment tribunals website. The current form is some 13 pages long but that may change if and when the Gibbons recommendations (see **Chapter 1**) are implemented. It also contains an Equal Opportunities Monitoring Form which does not have to be completed. The blank form is accompanied by a Tribunal Service booklet 'How to Apply to an Employment Tribunal' which contains clear and helpful guidance.

The ET1 contains requests for some information which must be supplied under r.1(4). That information should be clearly marked on the form. Extra care must be taken to respond to these requests, as the consequences of not giving the required information can be quite draconian (see **Chapters 2** and **7**). The claim form also deals with those aspects of EA 2002 which introduced statutory procedures and, in particular, the requirement that an employee should, in a number of instances, try to resolve problems through an internal grievance procedure. See **Chapter 2** for details of the statutory procedures.

Guidance notes accompany the claim form but it is possible that some potential claimants, particularly those without advice or assistance, may find this section confusing. Separate guidance was also issued by the Department for Business, Enterprise and Regulatory Reform (BERR, formerly the DTI) in 2004 (**www.berr.gov.uk**) but this guidance was written for lawyers, small businesses and employees, and may not be as helpful as when the procedures were newer. As we have seen the commonest situations where the statutory grievance procedure is relevant when issuing a claim are constructive unfair dismissal, unpaid wages and discrimination cases – although for 'actual' unfair dismissal, it will not apply.

Drafting claim form ET1

Much of the advice here would apply to the drafting of any legal or formal documents. The first point is to be clear on the claim or claims made and the factual basis of the claim(s). The claim form will be read first by a member of the administrative staff and if registered, copies will be sent to the respondent and, after the date for receipt of the ET3 (Response), it will be read by an employment judge.

This document will also probably be the first thing that is read by the tribunal when the matter comes to the Hearing. Try to make a good impression by using accessible language, and do not include bad points or irrelevant facts. Avoid legalistic language, or even worse, Latin phrases, although there is no harm in specifying the legislative basis of the claim by references to section numbers of Acts of Parliament or regulation number. If you do so, also explain, in plain language, the meaning of that section or regulation.

So, for instance, you may wish to say that the claim is for discrimination on the grounds of race and religion. It may be sufficient to state just that and give details of each act complained of. There is no harm in mentioning the Race Relations Act 1976 and the Employment Equality (Religion or Belief) Regulations 2003, SI 2003/1660. In some circumstances your claim may be in the alternative. For example, it may state that it was a dismissal on the grounds of raising a health and safety concern and therefore automatically unfair (under s.100 of the ERA 1996) or 'ordinarily' unfair under s.98 of the ERA 1996. In these circumstances it may be wise to refer to the statutory provisions. It will be even more important to do so if you are claiming under a little-used provision.

The form should, of course, be easily legible and if possible the information should be typewritten. Now that the ET1 can be filled in online, this is becoming a very common way for it to be done. An example of a blank form may be found at **Appendix 6**. The form is also available on the employment tribunals website. The advice below is based on the form being used at the time of publication, but it is possible that the forms may change so do check carefully.

(1) Your details – name, address, etc.

The mandatory information in this section is the claimant's first name and surname (which should be completed in capital letters) and address. Whilst this information is mandatory, the EAT have indicated that a fairly flexible approach should be adopted. In *Hamling* v. *Coxlease School Ltd* [2007] IRLR 8 it was decided that the fact that the claimant's address was missing did not mean that the claim should have been rejected, particularly as details of her solicitors with their address were on the form. However, it is wise to be careful and complete sections which are mandatory to avoid the possibility of rejection. Make sure that you complete this fully and legibly and include the postcode. Other important information is date of birth, which is used for calculating compensation. It is also obviously particularly important for age discrimination cases.

(2) Respondent's details

Here the mandatory information is the name and address of the respondent. Again check the information and write legibly. Mistakes in these apparently simple parts of the forms can delay matters considerably and even lead to the time limits being missed. The rule is that the tribunal will send a copy of the claim form to the address for the respondent on the form. Make sure it is correct and, if the respondent is a limited company, that it is the registered office.

There is also a space here for other respondents (usually individuals apart from the employer). This should only be completed if you genuinely mean to add respondents and they could be legally liable, most commonly in discrimination cases only. Do not be tempted to include everyone who had involvement in, for example, the grievance process, as there is a risk that individually named respondents might apply for costs if they have spent time and incurred costs in defending a claim where there was no chance of them being found liable.

(3) Action before taking a claim

There are a range of options for people completing the form. Great care must be taken at this point as this is where the rejection procedure (see **Chapters 2 and 7**) becomes relevant.

The claimant has to state whether he or she was an employee of the respondent. Again, although it is a mandatory requirement, the EAT has given some guidance. In *Richardson* v. *U Mole Ltd* [2005] ICR 1664 the claimant's claim was on the previous form before the new ET1 became mandatory and he, therefore, did not state whether he was an employee. The EAT stated that that question could be answered by other information provided by the claimant and his claim should not have been rejected.

The question of whether a person is or was an employee is, in any event, a complex legal question and one which many claimants, employers and representatives might find difficulties in answering. It may well have implications for how the case progresses. If in doubt, the claimant would usually be well advised to say 'Yes' as those who are not 'employees' have fewer rights. In particular, they do not have the right to claim unfair dismissal.

If you need to check this point there are a number of sources of information. There is a statutory definition contained within ERA 1996, s.230 and case law regularly further defines and re-defines the position.

However, the situation has been further complicated by the introduction of the statutory procedures, as these apply only to employees and not to workers. So, in some circumstances, as will be obvious from the rest of this chapter, claimants who are employees may not be allowed to proceed unless the statutory grievance procedure has been commenced. As this does not apply to 'workers', there may be some circumstances in which you wish to establish that the claimant is a worker not an employee. The claimant is also asked to state whether they are a 'worker' on the form. Consider the claims carefully and answer with care!

The claimant then must state whether the claim is about dismissal. Whilst the majority of claimants may have no difficulty with this question, it is complicated by the fact that if the claim is for constructive dismissal (which is a dismissal in law under ERA 1996, s.95), the claimant is expected to have followed the statutory grievance procedure and waited 28 days. Where employees have resigned, the booklet instructs them to tick the box which states that the claim is about a dismissal and the following box, 'Yes' to the question as to whether the claim is about anything else in addition to the dismissal. A claimant claiming constructive unfair dismissal must then go on to complete the sections that deal with the grievance process.

This then leads into the questions about the requirement to follow an internal procedure before bringing a claim. As the notes on the Tribunal Service website state:

> If you are or were an employee of the respondent and your claim or part of it does not relate to you being dismissed, you must also tell us
>
> - whether you have raised your complaint in writing with the respondent, and
> - whether you have waited 28 days before presenting your claim

Reference is then made to the BERR guidance which gives clear information on when someone does not have to go through the procedures. These are:

- after the end of employment and it is not reasonably practicable to put it in writing;
- if the claimant has reasonable grounds for believing that writing to the employer would result in significant threat to the claimant or someone else's person or property;
- the claimant has suffered harassment and has reasonable grounds for believing that further harassment might result from putting it in writing;
- where there has been a collective complaint;
- where the employer is a sole trader with a long-term illness.

Other valid reasons would include the fact that the claimant is not an employee, that the only claim is breach of contract, or there is a national security question.

The case of *Basingstoke Press Ltd* v. *Clarke* [2007] IRLR 588 emphasises that there must be a clear 28 days from the date the complaint was sent to the employer and the claim being presented.

This part of the claim form will need careful completion in any claims that are for anything other than 'straightforward' unfair dismissal.

(4) Employment details

This section will provide important information both to the tribunal office and to the respondent but it is not mandatory at this stage. However, to assist in the efficient management of the case, it is best to provide as much information as possible here (see **Chapter 7**).

(5) Unfair dismissal and constructive dismissal

A large box is provided for the details of an unfair dismissal claim. If it is insufficient, extra pages can be added. (Be sure to mark any additional pages clearly in case they become detached from the form.)

The extent of the information entered on the form will depend on a number of factors, including the complexity of the case and your own particular style. What is of fundamental importance is that the basic details are covered. This is not the witness statement for the claimant, which will come at a later stage. However, it should refer to all claims made even where those arise out of the same set of facts. So, in one of our examples above, the allegation that an unfair dismissal has come about because the employee has made a complaint about health and safety should state why it is believed that it is so. It should also state, in the alternative, that the dismissal may be an 'ordinary' unfair dismissal because of a failed procedure or because it was unreasonable to dismiss in the circumstances. It may be useful to put matters in list form, particularly where there are a number of claims. Paragraph numbering may aid reading and analysing the claim. Do not include 'background' information unless it is highly relevant. Use short sentences and plain language.

Be careful to consider which remedy is being sought and note that the options now make it clear that an order for reinstatement or re-engagement will also include an element of financial compensation.

(6) Discrimination

The first part of this section contains a number of boxes to tick – i.e. sex, race, disability, religion or belief, sexual orientation or age. Do *not* be tempted to tick those that do not apply. In discrimination claims the initial burden of proof rests with the claimant so, consider what the facts are and how you believe they amount to discriminatory treatment.

The detailed information follows in that section. Again, make it clear here what are the acts that are complained of and on which grounds it is alleged that they were discriminatory. If it is a direct discrimination claim, say so. If a number of the protected grounds are thought to be relevant, make that clear.

Specify the less favourable treatment, why the claimant falls within a protected group, and whether there is an actual comparator who can be named or identified or whether the claimant relies on a hypothetical comparator. If the claim is for disability discrimination, it is useful to state what the health condition is and how it amounts to a disability and to state clearly whether the claim is for direct discrimination, disability related discrimination and/or a failure to make reasonable adjustments.

If the claim is for indirect discrimination, this should be stated. You will need to state which 'provision, criterion or practice' was applied, which protected group is disproportionately affected, and why and how the claimant is adversely affected. It may well be that further particulars will be sought unless the facts are relatively straightforward and the claim is clear. Assistance with a discrimination claim may be obtained by looking at the Equality and Human Rights Commission (EHRC) website (**www.equalityhumanrights.com**). The EHRC is relatively newly formed (October 2007) following the amalgamation of the EOC, CRE and DRC. Assistance may also be obtained from a Citizens Advice Bureau or a Law Centre (see **Appendix 7** for useful websites).

If a claim for harassment or victimisation under the discrimination legislation is alleged, this should be made clear as this can form a separate claim. Give details of the harassment or state the nature of the protected act for victimisation.

It is vital that you give dates or approximate dates for when the alleged discrimination took place as the respondents and the tribunal need to be clear about the allegations and whether they raise any issues of jurisdiction.

(7) Redundancy payments

State here why you believe you are entitled to a redundancy payment and the amount that you believe is due. See the Ready Reckoner at **Appendix 4** to calculate the amount due.

(8) Other payments that you are owed

This section asks for a breakdown of the sums claimed. Be as precise as possible, because this information will be used when deciding whether to allocate the claim to the short track (if it is your only claim) and which fixed period of conciliation will apply (see **Chapter 7**). Make sure that any calculations are correct. If this is the only claim, a precise calculation at this point could lead to a default judgment on liability *and remedy* if the respondent fails to put in a response in time.

(9) Other complaints

You can only include matters which fall within the jurisdiction of the employment tribunals. Do not be tempted to scour through the list of possible claims to see if there is anything to add. A claim should be made only if it is valid and has a reasonable prospect of success, or you run the risk of the claim being struck out and/or a costs order being awarded against you (see **Chapter 13**). Again, if your claim is unusual, it should be clearly stated, and you should provide a reference to the statutory provision.

(10) Other information

Claimants are requested not to send a covering letter with the form, and you should avoid doing so unless absolutely necessary. If extra sheets have been attached these should have the names of the claimant and the respondent on each page in case they are separated from the rest of the claim form.

(11) Disability

This part is *not* concerned with whether there is a disability discrimination claim but is for the tribunal to consider whether there are any adjustments that need to be made during the progress of the case or at the Hearing. Be clear about any special needs that you have and whether you expect the tribunal to arrange them.

(12) Your representative

The name of a representative should be included only if there is an agreement between the claimant and the representative. If the claimant has had advice only or hopes to be represented at a later stage, the name of the relevant person or organisation can be added later.

Always remember to sign and date the form where indicated. Representatives may sign on behalf of claimants but they should check the contents for accuracy first.

Case study: Molly Martin's claim form (ET1)

1.1   Ms

1.2   Molly

1.3   MARTIN

1.4   23/06/72 Female

1.5   4 View Road, XXXX

1.6   020 7266 1400

1.7   Post

2.1   *Just in Time Catering Limited*

2.2   *Unit 405, Springfield Road, XXXXX*

3.1   Are you, or were you, an employee of the respondent?   *Yes*

3.2   Are you, or were you, a worker providing services to the respondent?   *No*

3.3   Is your claim, or part of it, about a dismissal by the respondent?   *Yes*

3.4   Is your claim about anything else, in addition to the dismissal?   *Yes*

3.5   Have you put your complaint in writing to the respondent?   *Yes – 26/11/07*

3.6   Did you allow at least 28 days between the date you put your complaint to the respondent and the date you sent us this claim?   *Yes*

4.1   Please give the following dates
When your employment started   *2002*
When your employment ended   *06 December 2007*
Is your employment continuing   *No*

4.2   Please say what job you do or did

I worked as a waitress for over 5 years. I had to go to lots of different venues catering for private functions.

4.3   How many hours do or did you work each week?   *About 30*

4.4   How much are or were you paid?
Pay before tax   *£350 per week*
Normal take home pay (including overtime, commission, bonuses and so on)   *£300*

4.5   If your employment has ended did you work a period of notice?   *No*

5.1   Unfair dismissal or constructive dismissal

When I told my boss, the Events Manager, that I was pregnant in early November, he asked me how long I would continue working for them. I said that I wished to take maternity leave just before the baby was due in June and then maybe a few weeks before returning to work but that I might need more notice for events as I would have to arrange childcare. He then said that this would be difficult because of the nature of the business. He said that he had had some bad experiences with pregnant staff before as they had to take lots of time off for medical appointments and had morning sickness. He said to me "We'll see how it goes".

The Events Manager also made comments about how pregnant staff look in the uniform. I was really upset and wrote to Just in Time on 26 November complaining about this treatment because I don't think he should say things like that just because I was pregnant. After that, during early December, there were a number of last minute changes to my shifts which were difficult for me as I have two other children. A week after I sent the letter, on 6 December, the Events Manager asked me when my maternity leave was starting as "it was already beginning to show". He said I should think about leaving straight away. I thought he was sacking me and have heard nothing from the company since.

I think that was very unfair as I should have been able to stay at work and not be dismissed just because I was pregnant. I have not been able to get another job because of my pregnancy and I have been quite ill.

5.2	Were you in your employer's pension scheme?	*No*

5.3 If you received any other benefits from your employer, please give details.

Travel to work, food at the venue

5.4	Since leaving your employment have you got another job?	*No*
5.5 and 5.6		*N/A*

5.7 Please say what you want if your case is successful
A To get your old job back and compensation (reinstatement)
B To get another job and compensation (re-engagement)
C Compensation only   *X*

6.1	Discrimination	*Sex*

6.2 *The first conversation mentioned in 5.1 took place with the Events Manager, Mr Jones on or around 5 November. Someone has told me that it is sex discrimination to sack a woman who is pregnant and I think it is as he would not have sacked a man for being away for a while. I also think he made a sexist remark about my appearance and mentioned problems he had with other women who had been pregnant. I think the changes to my shifts were because I'd sent a letter complaining about him as he knew it would be hard for me because of my childcare commitments.*

7.1	Redundancy	*N/A*

8.1 Please tick the box or boxes to indicate that money is owed to you for

	Holiday pay	*Yes*
	Notice pay	*Yes*
	Other unpaid amounts	*Yes, unpaid wages*
8.2	How much are you claiming?	*£3,000*
	Is this Before Tax	*No*
	After Tax	*Yes*

8.3 Please explain why you believe you are entitled to this payment and set out the calculation you have used to work out this amount

Holiday pay 4 weeks @ £300	*= £1,200*
Notice 5 weeks @ £300	*= £1,500*
Last week's wages	*= £300*
Total	*= £3,000*

9.1	Other complaints	*N/A*
10.1	Other information	*N/A*
11.1	Disability	*N/A*

12.1	Representative	*Jane Carter, Last Stop Advice Bureau*
13	Multiple cases	N/A
Signed		Date
Molly Martin		*3 March*

4.10 QUESTIONNAIRES UNDER DISCRIMINATION LEGISLATION

If there is a potential claim for sex, race or disability discrimination, the claimant can serve a questionnaire on the respondent. This statutory procedure specifically provides for the claimant or a potential claimant to ask questions to assess whether discrimination is likely to have occurred. The procedure can be used before the claim has been made or within a period of time after the claim has been made. It is not required as part of a discrimination claim in the employment tribunal but is a useful way of eliciting information about alleged discriminatory treatment and equal opportunities practices in the employee's workplace and will form part of the claimant's documents. An example of the questionnaire procedure is contained within SDA 1975, s.74, with the Race Relations Act 1976 and the Disability Discrimination Act 1995 having similar provisions. The EHRC website has some good basic advice and suggestions, particularly on the race discrimination questionnaire (**www.equalityhumanrights.com**).

A statutory questionnaire can be sent to an employer even if no tribunal claim is pending or is likely to be made, to try to resolve a complaint about alleged discriminatory treatment at work. If the claim has not been made, there are no time limits which apply to the questionnaire itself, but it will be important to comply with the time limit to apply to an employment tribunal (generally three months – see **Chapter 2**).

If a claim has been started, any questionnaire should be sent to the employer within 21 days of the claim form being submitted to the tribunal office. It is possible to get an extension of time for this but you must ask the employment tribunal for this extension if more than 21 days have elapsed. As usual, a good explanation for the delay and other factors such as the length of delay, when the matter is likely to be listed for hearing and the views of the respondent will be taken into account.

The questionnaire will often contain a statement which is identical, or very similar, to the statement of the allegations made in a claim form. If a claim form has already been completed, it is advisable to check that you cover the same points. It is usually helpful to use the same format, as this form will be familiar to the respondent and is on the tribunal file. Answers to the questionnaire can be used as evidence in the employment tribunal proceedings.

It provides an opportunity for collecting information that in other employment-related claims may not become available until very close to the Hearing or at the Hearing itself. Employment tribunals can take a respondent's failure to give responses to a questionnaire as itself evidence of discrimination.

The EHRC provides standard forms of questionnaires and useful guidance on how to complete forms.

Case study: questionnaire prepared by Molly Martin

In Molly Martin's case, it would be unlikely that she would serve a questionnaire before putting in her claim form because she believes she has been dismissed. The time limit for unfair dismissal claims will apply and, as she has not heard from Just in Time for three months, there is little time for a questionnaire to be sent before a claim is submitted. However, she could request some useful information to prepare for her case. The SDA questionnaire includes a standard part 2 of the form which asks the claimant to set out the discrimination alleged.

The form then continues at part 3:

I consider that this treatment may have been unlawful because [*with a space for completion*].

At part 4:

Do you agree that the statement in 2 is an accurate description of what happened? If not, in what respect do you disagree or what is your version of what happened? [*with a space for completion*].

At part 5:

Do you accept that your treatment of me was unlawful discrimination by you against me? If not:

(a) **Why not?**
(b) **For what reason did I receive the treatment accorded to me?**
(c) **How far did my sex or marital status affect your treatment of me?**

Part 6 provides the opportunity to ask further questions. Although there might be many more pieces of information that could also be sought and the EHRC website makes suggestions, it is possible that Molly's extra questions may be along these lines:

1. How many employees/workers do you have?
2. Please give a breakdown of your employees/workers by sex.
3. Please supply a copy of your equal opportunities policy.
4. How many employees/workers have taken a period of maternity leave in the past two years?
5. How many employees/workers are currently on maternity leave?
6. How many employees/workers have school age children?
7. How many requests have been made for flexible working in the past two years?
8. How many employees/workers are currently absent for other reasons?
9. How many of the above employees/workers are men and how many women?
10. How many employees/workers are currently pregnant and at what stage is their pregnancy?
11. Please state what training your managers have received with respect to family friendly statutory provision and/or maternity rights.
12. Please confirm that I have received no informal or formal warning.

In conclusion

The serving of a questionnaire will be particularly useful in the more complex claims of indirect discrimination and equal pay. In the case of indirect discrimination, the forms available from EHRC suggest questions that might be asked. In equal pay claims, there is a different form and given the complexity of that area of law and the fact that it also has separate rules of procedure, great care should be taken. For these complex claims it is advisable to seek specialist help.

CHAPTER 5

The response

5.1 RECEIVING A CLAIM

This chapter is aimed at respondents and their advisers, where the respondent has been sent a claim from the employment tribunal by a claimant. It outlines the first steps to take upon receiving the claim, and details how and when to respond.

Some respondents may ask an adviser to become involved as soon as the claim has started. Many employers now have in-house staff or external employment consultants who will take responsibility for advising on and preparing a response to an employment tribunal claim. An officer or manager within the employing organisation who is aware of the situation and who has the authority to give instructions in relation to the company's position should be quickly identified. Later, once the claim is ready for a hearing, it may be referred to a solicitor and/or barrister. Early preparation and a clear plan of action is important.

In examining the claim form and considering the claim or claims made against the respondent, the following areas should be examined prior to drafting or sending in a response:

1. The statutory procedures and how far these have been followed by either party.
2. Any other preliminary issues (such as whether the claim was in time) which are thrown up by the claim as set out in the ET1.
3. The strengths and weaknesses of the claimant's case.
4. Details of the respondent's case and its current strengths and weaknesses.
5. Any possible counterclaims (where breach of contract claimed).
6. The relevant time limit for responding to the claim.
7. Costs and settlement.

5.2 STATUTORY PROCEDURES FOR THE EMPLOYER

Examining the ET1 for a breach of EA 2002, s.32

In **Chapter 2**, we noted the requirement for the employee to follow a grievance procedure (GP) for certain types of claim. The ET1 requires a claimant who has not followed the procedure to explain why this has not been done. This will allow an employee to rely on the permitted exceptions to using the procedures, as discussed in **Chapter 2**, in order to be allowed to proceed. The respondent employer needs to decide if it agrees that the employee is entitled to rely on any of these exceptions or if it wishes to challenge the claim as being in breach of EA 2002, s.32(2)–(4).

Respondents should also be checking to see if the claimant employee has waited 28 days after commencing a GP with the employer before putting in the claim. Under EA 2002, s.32(6)(b) a tribunal can take into account a respondent's representations that an employee has not used the GP or waited 28 days after commencing a GP when deciding if it has jurisdiction to hear a claim. Employers should be examining their own records as well as the claim form to check all these matters and to decide whether they accept that an employee claimant has followed the necessary pre-action steps. The employer may need to raise these matters in its response form.

The appropriate juncture for deciding on jurisdiction was looked at in the case of *DMC Business Machines* v. *Plummer* (unreported, EAT 0381/06). The EAT indicated that unless the tribunal decides it has no jurisdiction when the claim is first sent to it and rejects the claim under s.32(2) or unless the respondent has raised this issue in its response form (the ET3), the question of jurisdiction is no longer relevant and the claim should proceed. The only option thereafter would appear to be that the respondent would need to seek leave to amend its ET3 to raise this issue. So respondents must ensure they raise this matter if needs be in their response form.

Ensuring that the employer has used a DDP prior to dismissing

The employer who receives a claim for unfair dismissal must check to see if it is one where they will need to have used the statutory disciplinary and dismissal procedures (DDP). These apply to dismissals for reasons of misconduct, capability, some other substantial reason and redundancies where the employer is contemplating dismissing fewer than 20 employees at that time by reason of redundancy. They also apply to dismissals where a fixed term expires. See below for the main categories of dismissals where a DDP will not need to be used.

If the employer fails to initiate the statutory DDP at the time when it is contemplating a disciplinary sanction, but then goes on to use one where it is contemplating a dismissal arising out of the same set of facts, it will not be penalised for a failure to use the required statutory procedure (see *A to B Travel Ltd* v. *Kennedy* (unreported, EAT 0341/2006)).

The requirement to use the procedure is paramount since employees with at least a year's service will succeed in an automatic unfair dismissal claim arising out of an employer's failure to use a DDP. Employers who default are also likely to face a penalty uplift in any compensation awarded to the employee. There is a power under EA 2002, s.31 to increase compensation by between 10 and 50 per cent for non compliance with the statutory disputes procedures. These remedies will be discussed in more detail in **Chapter 12**.

The compensation uplift will apply in all cases. The way in which remedy operates under ERA 1996, s.98A in relation to the employer's failure to use the DDP or other procedures is set out in **Chapter 12**.

Under reg.4 of the Dispute Resolution Regulations, the requirement to use a DDP does not apply to all dismissals. Dismissals to which the requirement does *not* apply include:

- dismissals for contravention of a statutory duty or obligation as referred to in ERA 1996, s.98(2)(d);
- where there is a dismissal to be immediately followed by a re-engagement (perhaps because the employer needs to reorganise the business in some way and uses this method to bring existing contracts to an end and re-engage on new terms);
- redundancy dismissals where the provisions of s.188 of the Trade Union and Labour Reform Consolidation Act 1992 applies (the statutory duty to consult for large scale redundancies);
- dismissals where the employer's business suddenly ceased to function in unforeseen circumstances;
- retirement dismissals introduced under the Employment Equality (Age Discrimination) Regulations 2006, SI 2006/1031, where there is a separate procedure under ERA 1996, s.98ZF.

In any event it will be good practice for the employer to use the DDP or a contractual equivalent for all dismissals, even where the employer does not believe the employee could have a claim, in order to avoid penalties arising under claims not only of unfair dismissal but wrongful dismissal or automatically unfair dismissal, where there are no qualifying service requirements. Employers and their advisers are reminded to follow the guidance contained within the ACAS Code of Practice on Grievance and Disciplinary Procedures which includes advice on the use of the statutory disputes procedures (**www.acas.org.uk/media/pdf/l/p/CP01_1.pdf**). This Code is likely to be much more firmly embedded into the unfair dismissal regime in employment tribunals under the Employment Bill in relation to fair procedures, and any employer who does not have recourse to it should now begin to do so.

The statutory disciplinary and dismissal procedure

There are two types of disciplinary and dismissal procedure: the standard procedure and the modified procedure. The steps themselves are set out in EA 2002, Sched.2 in paras.1–5.

The standard procedure will be used where the employer contemplates a disciplinary action or is contemplating a dismissal as defined above.

The modified procedure will be used where there has been a summary dismissal for gross misconduct and no statutory DDP has been used prior to dismissal and it is regarded as 'reasonable to do so'. The employment tribunal may have to judge whether it was reasonable when deciding if the statutory procedure has been followed, but it is likely to be appropriate in situations where gross misconduct has required swift action to be taken. The modified procedure effectively gives the employee a right of appeal against the dismissal.

The process

The statutory disciplinary and dismissal procedures have similar steps to the statutory grievance procedure outlined in **Chapter 2**.

STANDARD PROCEDURE

The standard procedure is a three-step one:

Step 1 – The employer must send a statement to the employee detailing the employee's conduct or other circumstances which have led the employer to initiate the procedures. The statement must also invite the employee to a meeting.

Step 2 – The meeting takes place. Afterwards, the employer must inform the employee of the decision and the reasons for it. It is not necessary to do so in writing but this would be good practice. The employee must also be informed of the right to appeal.

In a similar way to which the standard grievance procedure operates, prior to the Step 2 meeting the employer must inform the employee what the basis was for including the grounds set out in the Step 1 statement. The employer must also allow the employee a reasonable time to consider his or her response to the information. Employers should note that employees (and workers) will be entitled to be accompanied to disciplinary meetings by either a trade union representative or a workplace colleague under s.10 of the Employment Relations Act 1999 and they will need time to arrange this and to discuss the employer's concerns with that person.

Case law has examined what information employees should be given in a Step 1 statement and by the time they attend their Step 2 meeting. In *Alexander* v. *Brigden* [2006] IRLR 422 the EAT stated that the information to be given in the Step 1 statement could be in broad terms; the employee should be told that he or she is at risk of dismissal and why. The reason for possible dismissal should be given (for example redundancy, misconduct). By the time employees attend the Step 2 meeting they should have more information. For example if the reason is misconduct they will need sufficient detail to be able to provide their side of the story. If the reason is redundancy they should know the basis upon which they have been selected, the selection criteria used and their own assessment in that process.

An employer must ensure that both Step 1 statements and Step 2 information are provided. As with the grievance procedures, there is a relatively low threshold as to the type of information which should be provided in the Step 1 statement – see *Draper* v. *Mears* [2006] IRLR 269 where it was found that the employee knew that the accusation was that he had been drunk and insubordinate, in spite of the contents of the Step 1 statement referring rather generally to conduct which put the health and safety of himself and others at risk. Inadequate information in the Step 1 statement cannot be remedied by compliant Step 2 information, but the detail required in Step 2 may depend on what the employee could have been expected to infer from the information provided. In *Ingram* v. *Bristol Street Parts* (unreported, EAT 0601/06), the accusation involved a technical accounting fraud which was not spelt out in full detail but which the employee would have understood the import of in order to prepare herself for the Step 2 meeting. Furthermore in *YMCA* v. *Stewart* [2007] IRLR 185 it was held that the procedure would still be complied with where following the Step 2 meeting more information was provided to the employer of a similar nature, which the employer also relied upon in order to dismiss. The same case also said that it would not be in breach to indicate during the Step 2 meeting or towards the end of it that the employer had reached a decision to dismiss.

Step 3 – The employer's decision will be communicated to the employee after the Step 2 meeting has taken place. The employee then has the opportunity to appeal against the decision and at Step 3 the appeal hearing takes place. The hearing may be held before or after the disciplinary sanction or dismissal takes effect. After the appeal the employee must be informed of the decision. Employers should not be too rigid about the time frame for lodging grounds for appeal once the decision is communicated to the employee. Many employers have contractual procedures with strict time frames for appealing and must bear in mind that EA 2002, Sched.2, para.12 only requires steps to be taken within a reasonable time – see *Wilson* v. *Mars UK t/a Masterfoods* [2007] ICR 370 where an employer refused to entertain an appeal sent after its contractual period of five days had elapsed and it was found to have been in breach of the requirement to use the statutory procedures.

MODIFIED PROCEDURE

The modified procedure is a two-step one:

Step 1 – The employer must send to the employee a statement of the alleged misconduct, the reason why the employer thought it was appropriate to dismiss as a result and the employee's right to appeal against dismissal.

Step 2 – The appeal hearing. After the appeal hearing, the employer must inform the employee of the final decision.

At the date of writing there is no case law clarifying the circumstances in which the modified disciplinary procedure would be appropriate. Given that the process denies the employee an opportunity to take part in the process prior to the decision being reached, employers would be wise to use the standard procedure wherever possible to avoid allegations of an unfair process.

Note, however, that there is no requirement for the employer to use the modified procedure if the employee puts in the tribunal claim before the employer has complied with Step 1 (i.e. has sent the employee written reasons for dismissal): see reg.3(2) of the Dispute Resolution Regulations.

After two attempts to hold a meeting which has been postponed because the employee's representative was not available to attend, the employer will no longer be required to hold the meeting (and will not be penalised for failing to properly use the statutory procedures). See reg.13 of the Dispute Resolution Regulations.

Time extensions for the employee's unfair dismissal claim

Regulation 15 of the Dispute Resolution Regulations provides that where a DDP is underway but not complete, the employee's three-month time limit for putting in an employment tribunal claim will be extended by a further three months where the employee has reasonable grounds for believing that a statutory or contractual procedure is being followed. So employers will find that employees will be relying on this extension where they reasonably believe that a statutory dismissal procedure is still being followed.

Employers may seek to challenge the employee's reasonable belief that the procedures are being followed. Note that particularly in relation to appeals, there is only a requirement under the statutory procedures to follow each step within a reasonable period of time. In **Chapter 2** we looked at circumstances where employees put in appeals after some considerable time (see *Codemasters Software Company* v. *Wong* referred to there) and where the tribunal will examine as a question of fact whether the employee reasonably believed that a procedure was being followed.

In the employment tribunal decision of *Tenby* v. *Smee Advertising Ltd* 2202595/05 (see IDS Brief 803) an employee who was made redundant later obtained information which led her to believe that her redundancy dismissal was unfair. She then wrote to the employer seeking clarification. Her claim was sent to the tribunal five months after she was dismissed and two months after she sent in the letter. It was held that her letter constituted an appeal under the standard procedure and that she did have a reasonable belief that the statutory procedures were still being followed.

In contrast in *Piscatelli* v. *Zilli Fish* (unreported, EAT 0638/05) a solicitor wrote to the employer on behalf of an employee client seeking reinstatement. No right to appeal was sought and the employer did not offer an appeal. Therefore the employee could not reasonably believe a procedure was being followed. Similarly in *Van Dieren* v. *G and C Edwards* (unreported, EAT 0166/06) the employee appealed against dismissal having failed to attend his disciplinary hearing. There was no response from the employer to his appeal. Therefore he could not have a reasonable belief that the procedure was being followed and would have to have sent the claim form in within the normal three-month time limit.

Deemed compliance with the DDP

There are circumstances in which both parties will be deemed to have complied with the DDP. One will be where the employer has its own 'appropriate' contractual procedures in place and this procedure has been used in the dismissal proceedings. The alternative procedure must have been agreed between an employer or employer's association and a trade union and must give the employee an effective right of appeal against the dismissal.

If the employee has claimed an automatically unfair dismissal and has applied for interim relief but has not yet appealed this will be regarded as complying with the DDP. Interim relief will be granted in claims for unfair dismissal arising out of business transfers, trade union membership and activities, the Working Time Regulations 1998, and the Public Interest Disclosure Act 1998 (whistleblowers). Since the interim relief application has to be made seven days after the dismissal, the employee is effectively being given a right of appeal.

It should be borne in mind also that the exceptions for the need to comply referred to in **Chapter 2** (fear of threats or harassment or not practicable to commence or complete the procedure within a reasonable period) apply also to the employer in the context both of the GP and the DDP.

5.3   LOOKING AT THE CLAIMANT'S CASE

Preliminary legal issues – looking at the ET1

The ET1 should be carefully examined to look for any preliminary points which might mean that the claimant's claim as it stands is misconceived or appears to have flaws which may prevent it going forward.

Claim out of time

An example of this would be a claim that has been started out of its statutory time frame. It will be necessary to understand how the normal statutory time limit is calculated, including what extensions may apply as a result of statutory procedures being used.

In discrimination claims, for example, matters raised which on first sight appear to be out of time may still be allowed by the tribunal. Discrimination time limits can sometimes be difficult to calculate, or allegations which are out of time may be allowed in as background evidence of other issues. The 'just and equitable' time extension may also be applied (see **Chapter 2** generally for calculation of time limits).

Other preliminary issues

There may be other preliminary issues which the respondent might believe would make the employee's claim fatally flawed or which might need to be overcome before the claim can proceed. Examples of these preliminary issues are:

1. Was the claimant an employee or self-employed? This will be relevant to unfair dismissal claims as only an employee can claim unfair dismissal. Bear in mind that workers and contractors can also pursue some claims.
2. Was the claimant in an excluded class to claim unfair dismissal (e.g. police officers)?
3. Has the claimant sufficient service as required under ERA 1996, s.108 to pursue an unfair dismissal claim?

If issues such as these are raised by the respondent or are drawn out by the tribunal on looking at a claim form, they are likely to be dealt with as preliminary issue at a pre-hearing review or a case management discussion (see **Chapters 7** and **8**).

Main legal issues

The next step for the respondent adviser will be to identify the legal issues which have been raised by the claimant on the claim form, so that a proper response can be made to those issues and the relevant documents and evidence can be identified.

Case study: legal issues for Molly Martin's claim

Looking at Molly's ET1, the following legal issues present themselves to be decided on by the employment tribunal.

1. Molly is stating that she was an employee and not self-employed or a 'casual worker'. This may be regarded as a preliminary issue to be tried.
2. Molly is asserting that she was dismissed by Just in Time.

---

3. Molly is asserting that her dismissal was unfair and she has the requisite service to pursue an unfair dismissal claim.
4. Molly is also asserting that she was automatically dismissed for a reason connected with her pregnancy.
5. Molly claims that as a worker and/or employee she was subjected to harassment, victimisation, and discrimination under SDA 1975 when she told Just in Time she was pregnant and comments were made about her appearance, and shift changes were made after she complained.
6. Molly also has a number of money claims, for unpaid wages, holiday pay and notice pay, in accordance with her statutory and/or contractual rights to these payments.

Factual issues

A check should be made to see if the respondent agrees with the factual information provided by the claimant.

1. Has the claimant correctly set out details of employment, place of work, the employer's correct title, dates of service and information regarding wages?
2. Can the respondent agree with the facts, such as any details provided by the claimant of the history of the employment relationship or the date and manner of dismissal?
3. Furthermore, has the claimant set out the claim in sufficient detail for the respondent to meet it?
4. Are there any statements made in the claim form which the respondent disputes? Take a note of the respondent's version of events.

Check also whether the claimant has put in a claim for breach of contract existing at or arising out of the termination of their employment contract. If the claimant has, and it is appropriate, the respondent may counterclaim for any breaches of contract that the respondent may assert have occurred (see below).

5.4 THE RESPONDENT'S CASE

Having identified the facts and legal issues raised by the claimant, it will be necessary to decide what the respondent's case will be.

Background facts about the respondent

The adviser to the respondent should make sure they are familiar with the respondent's organisation, how it is run, the management structure and the process used to dismiss (or whatever issue the claim is about). The adviser will also need to know who was involved in the claimant's employment.

The respondent should provide a list of relevant documentation and details of managers and other employees who have or had dealings with the claimant over the issues raised. Examples of relevant documentation will be:

- the claimant's personnel file;
- memos and emails concerning the matters claimed;
- any letters or grievance complaints received by the claimant; and
- the respondent's disciplinary and grievance procedures.

It will also be important to clarify line management responsibilities and (where relevant) who handled disciplinary or grievance procedures.

The respondent's legal issues

Having looked at the claim and highlighted the legal issues which it has identified (see the example of Molly above) it will now be necessary to decide on how the respondent will deal with each of these issues.

The respondent may, for example, have documentation which will support the legal argument that the claimant was not an employee. There may be sufficient documentary evidence that a dismissal was fair within the definition of a fair dismissal set out in ERA 1996, s.98. These will be used to support the legal argument.

Is there a counterclaim?

If the claimant has claimed a breach of contract and this has been claimed upon termination of the employment contract, the respondent may have the option, where relevant, of pursuing a counterclaim for breach of contract. Typical claims may arise, for example, out of the employee's misuse of the work telephone or email leading to higher utilities bills for the employer, or taking paid annual holidays in excess of the contractual or statutory entitlement.

Counterclaims must be lodged in the employment tribunal within six weeks of receiving the claimant's ET1. No award for breach of contract can be more than £25,000 in the employment tribunal. The Court of Appeal decision of *Fraser* v. *HLMAD Ltd* [2006] EWCA Civ 738 stated that claims worth over £25,000 should commence in the High Court, rather than limiting the part of the claim worth up to £25,000 to the tribunal's jurisdiction and reserving the rest for a High Court claim. Once a tribunal has adjudicated on a breach of contract claim there would be no jurisdiction for another court to hear what was effectively the same claim again.

5.5 PROCEDURES FOR RESPONDING TO THE CLAIM

Is the respondent in time to respond?

The claim form

If the respondent decides to send a response to the ET1 claim form it must arrive at the relevant employment tribunal office within 28 days of the date when the ET1 was sent to the respondent (see r.4).

The respondent can apply for an extension of that time limit under r.11 and the application for the extension (which can be by way of a letter) has to be sent within the 28-day period (see r.4(4)). The application will need to explain why the respondent cannot comply with the required time limit of 28 days for filing a response and the judge will only extend time if the judge considers it 'just and equitable' to do so. A good reason for requesting the extension should therefore be provided, such as sickness or unforeseen absence of key personnel who have the necessary information to prepare the response.

The statutory questionnaires

If in a discrimination claim the claimant has sent the respondent a statutory questionnaire, the time limits for replying must be observed.

A discrimination questionnaire sent to a respondent by a claimant after proceedings have been issued must be received by the respondent within 21 days of the ET1 being presented at the tribunal office.

The respondent then has eight weeks in which to respond. If the respondent does not do so within that time, the employment tribunal can draw an adverse inference in respect of the discrimination alleged based on equivocal or evasive replies or a failure to respond. See for example SDA 1975, s.74(2)(b).

No response entered

Under r.8 the tribunal can enter a default judgment where no response is entered or accepted (for non-acceptance see below). This means that there will be no hearing and a tribunal judge can decide in the claimant's favour on liability only or on liability and remedy.

Respondent advisers may be approached for assistance by a respondent whose time limit for putting in a claim has run out or who has been informed that a default judgment has been entered. The respondent can become involved in the tribunal proceedings at this stage as the Rules allow for either party to apply for a decision (which includes the default judgment) to be reviewed under r.33.

The application for a review must be made in writing and presented to the tribunal office within 14 days of the date when the default judgment was sent. It should state reasons why the judgment should be varied or revoked. In addition, the proposed response form and an application to extend time to present a response should be attached. The respondent may rely on any or all of the grounds for review set out in r.34, namely:

- the decision was wrongly made as a result of an administrative error;
- a party did not receive notice of the proceedings leading a decision;
- the decision was made in the absence of a party;
- the interests of justice require such a review.

The review of the decision to enter a default judgment is a public hearing held by a judge sitting alone. This means that both parties can attend and can be heard. The judge will then decide whether to confirm, vary or revoke the decision to enter a default judgment and will inform all the relevant parties in writing.

The tribunal judge is given discretion by r.33 to revoke or vary a default judgment on application if the respondent has a reasonable prospect of successfully responding to the claim. The judge may take a view of the merits in deciding on this issue, and so this should form a significant part of the respondent's representations on the review application. The judge must have regard to whether a good reason exists for failure to present a response within the time limit.

Note also that if a claim is settled at the point where the judge is deciding on and issuing a default judgment, the default judgment will have no effect. See **Chapter 7** for more on these procedures and **Chapter 14** on reviews.

Non-acceptance of a response by the tribunal

In some circumstances, the tribunal can refuse to accept a response. These are where:

1. The response lacks information which r.4(3) requires should be provided.
2. It has been presented outside the 28-day time limit (and no application has been made to extend time).
3. It is not on the prescribed form.

The administration section of the tribunal office will take a preliminary view and then refer the matter to a judge to make the final decision on whether the response should be accepted.

If the judge decides not to accept a response the respondent can apply for a review of that decision under r.34. However the grounds upon which that decision can be overturned (reviewed) are very narrow. Only two of the grounds under r.34 can be relied on for a review of a decision to reject a response. These are the first (that the decision was wrongly made as a result of an administrative error) and the final one (that it is in the interests of justice that the matter should be reviewed).

The application for the review must be made in writing within 14 days of the date on which the decision was sent to the parties by the tribunal office. The review will be carried out by the same judge who made the original decision and it may be confirmed, varied or revoked (see **Chapters 7** and **14**).

Amending a response already sent in

If the respondent has already sent in a response and it needs to be amended, perhaps as a result of receiving advice for the first time, the respondent should bear in mind the employment tribunals' case management powers under r.10. Under r.10(2)(q) leave can be granted by the tribunal to amend a response. The application should be made as early as possible. It must be requested in writing at least 10 days before a Hearing (if any) and will be regarded as an application in the proceedings (see r.11(1)). The claimant should be informed by the respondent of this request and will be given the opportunity to comment on it.

A response may need to be amended to comply with the requirements to contain all relevant information (see below) or to add factual circumstances not originally known or thought relevant (for instance, in the case study of Molly Martin, details about how she was paid, which might affect her employment status).

5.6 GUIDELINES ON THE CONTENT OF THE RESPONSE

Assuming that these preliminary issues have been satisfactorily dealt with, it is now time to examine what should go into the response form (ET3).

Rule 4 requires the response to contain all the relevant information. This is set out in guidelines which will be attached to the ET1 when it is sent to the employer.

How much detail is required? The following guidelines may assist:

- *Unfair dismissal claims.* These should contain full details of the reason for the dismissal, the way in which the decision to dismiss was arrived at, and the procedures followed. Names of staff should be supplied where they have played a part in the dismissal, especially where they are likely to be witnesses. There is no virtue in seeking to withhold details as the burden of showing a potentially fair reason for dismissal lies on the employer.
- *Automatically unfair dismissal claims.* The respondent who wishes to defend these claims will need to show that the real reason for the dismissal was not the statutory reason raised by the claimant, although it will be for the claimant to establish the reason for dismissal in such claims.

- *Discrimination claims.* The respondent must demonstrate clearly the way in which the respondent intends to deal with the claim. Is the respondent relying on the statutory defence that the respondent did all that was reasonably practicable to deal with the alleged discriminatory behaviour? Expert assistance may be required to draft a response due to the way in which the burdens of proof in discrimination claims operates.
- *Other claims.* Tribunal claims now cover a broad range of complex issues. Where these arise (for instance, equal pay claims, European law and/or Human Rights Act claims) specialist drafting may be needed.

For an example of how the response form would look in the case of *Molly Martin* v. *Just in Time*, see **5.8** below.

5.7 CHECKS BEFORE DRAFTING THE RESPONSE

As well as general advice about the law, and the merits of the claim, the respondent needs to plan how to deal with each stage of the preparation for the Hearing. Furthermore, the finances of running the case should be examined at this early stage.

Checklist: practical planning

- Who will continue to give instructions on behalf of the employer?
- Is there a diary note of when replies to the statutory questionnaires and/or the response form must be sent to the tribunal office and is it clear who will take responsibility for this (check statutory deadlines)?
- What documents are relevant to the case?
- Are the documents readily available, in order and/or is preparation in hand to ensure that they are?
- Which witnesses are relevant? Contact details need to be taken and any non-availability noted at a very early stage – in any event, before any case management discussion.
- Are any expert witnesses necessary? If a Disability Discrimination Act case, consider if these should be joint.
- Who will represent the respondent at any tribunal hearings? If counsel, have counsel been recommended and accepted by the respondent?

Financial planning

As part of the preliminary preparation with the respondent, the financial planning of the case should be considered. How the case will be funded will be balanced against any possible risk of costs and the context of a possible settlement or any alternative route for disposing of the complaint.

Costs

Since the introduction of r.14 of the 2001 Rules and rr.38–48 of the 2004 Rules, costs orders are becoming more frequent in employment tribunal proceedings. The costs regime is dealt with in **Chapter 13**. There should at all stages be a consideration as to: (a) whether there is any risk of a costs order being made against the respondent; or (b) whether the respondent should apply for a costs order against the claimant at any stage.

Settlement

Settlement should always be considered even at an early stage, and this is discussed in detail in **Chapter 3**. Often the claimant will have left the employment and it may not be known what his or her employment situation is. Information should be sought from claimants about their financial circumstances. Tribunals usually require the claimant to provide a schedule of loss as part of case management. The respondent should be made aware of the claimant's duty to mitigate loss by seeking other employment.

Once the respondent has been advised on the strength of the claim and the likely legal costs have been assessed, the respondent should be asked to weigh this up against the cost of settling at an early stage, or indeed at any stage.

Now that the preliminary preparation has been done the respondent is ready to prepare the response to the claim.

5.8 THE RESPONSE FORM

As with the claim form, the response form became mandatory from October 2005. Also, as with the claim form, there will be some information that must be provided. There are strict time limits, as we have seen, but to repeat, the response must be received by the tribunal office within 28 days from the date when the copy claim form is sent. Strict rules apply to late responses as the 2004 Rules give the tribunal a power to order judgment in default.

It is important to complete the response form (ET3) carefully. Use plain language, remembering that it has to be read and understood by the claimant, representatives, administrative staff and the tribunal consisting of a legally qualified employment judge and, usually, two lay members. As with the ET1, the form should make a good impression and be clear to all those who need to understand your case. It may be necessary to refer to the legal position and you may wish to refer to relevant legislation, but if you do, be sure to explain the effect of the relevant statutory provision. For instance, if the claimant does not have one year's service and they are claiming unfair dismissal, you might want to mention ERA 1996, s.108 (the qualifying period for claiming unfair dismissal) but not if the claim is very clearly for one of the 'automatically unfair' dismissals such as pregnancy, health and safety, and so on.

If it is a claim to which the statutory grievance procedure applies, that is constructive dismissal or discrimination not connected to dismissal, or unpaid wages, you may want to state that EA 2002, s.32 has not been complied with, as discussed above, if there has been no complaint in writing or the employee has not waited 28 days after putting it in writing. This is particularly important because of the provisions of s.32(6)(b) which prevents the tribunal from hearing the claim if the procedures apply and:

> the tribunal is satisfied of the breach as a result of his employer raising the issue of compliance with those provisions in accordance with regulations under section 7 of the Employment Tribunals Act 1996 (c17) (employment tribunal regulations).

Be cautious, however, about relying too heavily on the proposition that steps taken by the employee do not constitute a grievance, as case law has indicated that there should be a wide interpretation to what constitutes a grievance (see *Shergold* v. *Fieldway Medical Centre* [2006] IRLR 76). Consider whether, if there is something in writing from the employee, or someone acting on the employee's behalf, it is likely to be sufficient.

The other problem that might arise is where the claim is made up of a number of claims and some have been accepted and some rejected. In these circumstances, the respondent should have been informed by the tribunal and should only answer those parts accepted. However, if it is clear to you, as respondent, that the other claims are likely to be accepted at a later stage, you may choose to complete one ET3 and simply send a copy when the other claims are accepted. For the smaller claims, such as unpaid wages, it may be as easy to deal with the issues at an early stage.

Drafting the response form

For the most part the ET3 is self-explanatory and there are guidance notes which accompany it. Explanatory booklets can also be obtained from the employment tribunal website (**www.employmenttribunals.gov.uk**).

(1) Your details

Either complete legibly or type these details. Enter the respondent's full name including any abbreviations which indicate the nature of the legal entity, such as Limited (or Ltd), plc or 'trading as'. Use only well-known abbreviations and include the postcode. If the details differ from those on the ET1, inform the tribunal office.

(2) Action before a claim

As can be seen, this part of the response form mirrors section 3 of the claim form (see **Chapter 2**) in that it is an attempt to elicit information with respect to the new statutory procedures and ascertain the claimant's right to bring a claim. Again, it is quite complex and there are guidance notes to assist. Unlike the information given by the claimant on this area, it is not mandatory for the respondent to answer, although the respondent certainly will want to do so if there are inaccuracies in the claim form.

(3) Employment details

This section asks the respondent to confirm or dispute the information given by the claimant. It is therefore important to read what has been said on the ET1 carefully. The details cover dates of employment and job title or description. If you do not have accurate records of the dates of employment, make every effort to obtain that information. It may be important for the claimant's right to claim: for instance, if the claimant does not have one year's service and is claiming unfair dismissal. If there has been a transfer of employment, it would probably be useful to make that clear on the form.

(4) Unfair or constructive dismissal

Questions are asked here about pensions and other benefits.

(5) Response

It is vital that the respondent deals with each and every aspect of the claimant's claim. It is usually useful to use the same structure as the claimant has used, perhaps mirroring the paragraph numbering used in the claim form, for instance. This may not be possible if the claim form has been completed in an unhelpful fashion. Do not make bad points and raise irrelevant issues here. Any points on the claimant's right to claim should be raised, for instance, that the claimant does not have sufficient service to claim unfair dismissal. If you dispute the facts, be clear what your version is. If you accept the facts but dispute the claimant's analysis of them, make that clear. It may be that you accept the claimant's version of some facts but that other important facts have been omitted, such as the number of warnings given.

So, for example, where the claimant has stated (as in **Chapter 2**) that the dismissal is either automatically unfair on the grounds of pregnancy or, in the alternative, that it is 'ordinarily' unfair, deal with those points separately. You might, for instance, accept that the woman's pregnancy was raised by her but wish to state that the dismissal was unconnected to that issue. You may accept that the procedure used was defective in some way but you may wish to state that it did not affect the overall fairness of the dismissal or that it made no difference to the outcome – see **Chapter 12** for how the tribunal will approach the question of fair procedures in assessing remedy for unfair dismissal.

Because EA 2002 has introduced ERA 1996, s.98A which deals with procedurally unfair dismissals, it will be important to read carefully the claimant's complaint and assess your response in line with those procedural requirements. You should be clear about your position with respect to any relevant procedures. If you have followed any statutory disciplinary procedure, say so or give an explanation why you did not do so. If you have followed your own procedures which are actually an improvement on the statutory procedures, that should also be made clear. You should if at all possible refer to the fact that you are aware of and have taken account of the ACAS Code of Practice on Disciplinary and Grievance Procedures. This is also your opportunity to state, where relevant, that you believe the claimant should have used a grievance procedure and has failed to do so.

(6) Other information

Here you may wish to raise something that the claimant has not mentioned but is relevant. For instance, if the claim seems to have been made out of time, that aspect should be raised when you respond. Avoid unnecessary point scoring. The tribunal does not need to know how well you treat all your employees and how many days the claimant has been allowed to be absent from work if it is not part of the case.

(7) Your representative

Only put in the name of a person or organisation that has agreed to be named as representative.

(8) Signature and date

The completed form should be signed and dated.

Case study: Just in Time Catering Ltd's response form

1.1	Name	*Just in Time Catering Limited*
	Contact	*Alan Jones*
1.2	Address	*Unit 405, Springfield Road*
1.3	Phone number	*7666 4333*
1.4	How would you prefer us to communicate with you?	*Post*
2.1	Is, or was, the claimant an employee?	*No*
2.2	Is, or was, the claimant a worker providing services for you?	*Yes*

2.3	If the claim, or part of it, is about dismissal, do you agree that the claimant was dismissed?	*No*
2.4	If the claim is about something other than dismissal does it relate to an action you took on the grounds of the claimant's conduct or capability?	*No*
2.5	Has the substance of this claim been raised by the claimant in writing under a grievance procedure?	*Yes*
2.6	If 'Yes' please explain what stage you have reached in the procedure	*N/A*
3.1	Are the dates of employment given by the claimant correct?	*No*
3.2	If 'No' please give dates and say why you disagree with the dates given by the claimant	
	When their employment started	*10/09/02*
	When their employment ended or will end	*N/A*
	Is their employment continuing	*Yes*

I disagree with the dates because, although Molly Martin is not an employee, she is a casual waitress – she did start working for us on the date above and can continue to work for us if she contacts us for work. She has not been dismissed.

3.3	Is the claimant's description of their job or job title correct?	*No*
3.4	If 'No' please give the details you believe to be correct below	

Molly is a casual waitress.

3.5	Is the information given by the claimant correct about being paid for, or working, a period of notice?	*No*
3.6	If 'No' please give details you believe to be correct below. If you gave them no notice or didn't pay them instead of letting them work their notice, please explain what happened and why.	

Molly was not dismissed and no notice was given. She was not entitled to notice anyway as she was a casual worker.

3.7	Are the claimant's hours of work correct?	*Yes*
3.8	If 'No' please enter details	*N/A*

3.9	Are the earnings details given by the claimant correct?	*No*

3.10   If 'No' please give the details you believe to be correct below

Her pay varied depending on the hours she did.

4.1	Are the details about pension and other benefits given by the claimant correct?	*Yes*

4.2	If 'No', please give details you believe to be correct below	*N/A*

5.1	Do you resist the claim?	*Yes*

5.2   If 'Yes', please set out in full the grounds on which you resist the claim.

Molly was a casual waitress for us for a number of years. She was contacted when work was available but she was quite regular as she was reliable and always agreed to do the work. She was a good waitress and we have no complaints about her.

In November she spoke to Mr Jones, the Events Manager, and mentioned to him that she was pregnant. Mr Jones asked her for more information about this as some of our other waitresses have given up the work when they become pregnant as it involves a lot of time standing and carrying things. Mr Jones also mentioned Molly's appearance as there would be a problem with the uniform when Molly's pregnancy was more advanced. He was only suggesting that Molly might take maternity leave early but she seemed to get upset and walked away. Mr Jones was aware that Molly had written a letter about him but it was being dealt with by Head Office. It was necessary to change some of Molly's shifts because other staff had rung in sick. Mr Jones had another short conversation with Molly on 6 December but he did not sack her. We have not heard from Molly since and assumed she had decided to give the work up.

She was definitely not dismissed. She was not an employee. She hasn't followed any grievance procedure so we haven't been able to deal with her concerns. We did not discriminate against her because of her sex and we have a large number of females working for us.

As to her claims for holiday pay and unpaid wages we are checking the position and if we owe her anything we will pay her.

6.1   Other information

7.1   Representative

Name	*Mr Brian Brown*
Name of the organisation	*Employment and Discrimination Law Direct*
Address	*14 Bolton Road XXXX*
Phone number	*333 4444*
Reference	*BB*

How would they prefer us to communicate with them?	*Post*
Signed	Date
Alan Jones	*7 April*

5.9 DISCRIMINATION QUESTIONNAIRES

If a discrimination questionnaire is received it is, of course, important to respond. This is because the discrimination statutes dealing with sex, race and disability specifically state that failure to respond within a reasonable period without reasonable excuse or giving an evasive or equivocal reply may lead to the employment tribunal drawing any inference that is just and equitable, including an inference that there has been discrimination (SDA 1975, s.74, RRA 1976, s.65 and DDA 1995, s.56). It may be necessary to gather a considerable amount of information and this may take some time, so it is often advisable to write to the claimant (and the tribunal, if proceedings have started) to indicate how long it may take to reply.

The questionnaire procedure does have, as we have indicated, statutory authority. However, you may not be able to (or you may not need to) answer all the questions put. Only if you have the information or it is relatively easily obtainable do you need to reply. Do not be 'evasive or equivocal' (see above) but it would be acceptable to reply that you do not have information if that is genuinely the case. If you have not kept records of promotion interviews and you cannot find out by asking questions, particularly if your record-keeping is poor and the person or people with knowledge have left the organisation, it may be acceptable to explain that that is the position. Much will depend on the size and type of organisation of the employer as to what would be considered acceptable in these circumstances. You also only need to give information which is relevant to the allegation of discrimination. So, for example, if the employee or claimant alleges that they have been discriminated against on the grounds of their sex, you do not need to answer questions on the breakdown of your workforce by ethnic origin.

Case study: response to Molly Martin's questionnaire

In our case study, Just in Time may well respond in this way to the extra questions at point 6 in the questionnaire served by Molly Martin in **Chapter 4**.

Just in Time's response to Q6 of Molly Martin's SD74

1.   25
2.   10 men and 15 women
3.   enclosed
4.   one employee and one casual waitress have taken maternity leave
5.   none
6.   we do not have details of this
7.   none
8.   2 employees
9.   one women and one man
10. we have no knowledge of this
11. all our managers are well aware of their duties
12. confirmed

CHAPTER 6

Progressing the case

6.1 INTRODUCTION

Depending somewhat on the size and location of the tribunal office and the number of days for which the Hearing is to be listed, the parties may have to wait up to six months for the main Hearing. This time frame will also be affected by the statutory conciliation periods of seven or 13 weeks for non-discrimination claims (see **Chapters 2** and **7**).

Claims with an element of discrimination are likely to be listed for more than a day and the waiting time will be longer. However, do not be caught out by an early hearing date. Where, for example, the claim is in respect of a statutory right or is only for notice pay, the hearing date may be listed fairly soon after the shorter conciliation period of seven weeks. See **Chapter 7** for how the tribunals now have 'short track' allocation for some types of cases.

Case management is now fundamental to the preparation of a claim to be heard in the employment tribunal. It is important that the parties take responsibility for managing the progress of the case at an early stage. The tribunal will expect a case to be clearly set out, properly prepared and fully ready for a Hearing. There is no point in letting the preparation stages drift 'in case the claim settles'. Whilst it may settle, the twin activities of trying to achieve a settlement and ensuring that the case is properly prepared will need to be addressed at all times. In addition you will feel more in control of the case if you are actively managing its progress rather than waiting for a case management order to come crashing down on you unawares.

In addition it should be noted that the parties' representatives have a duty to assist the tribunal in its 'overriding objective' to deal with cases justly and expeditiously (see reg.3) and for this reason they should both be working towards the presentation of a fully prepared case and be prepared to cooperate with each other as well as the tribunal, in progressing the claim to the main Hearing. The tribunal will take an active part in that process through its case management powers. These will be discussed in **Chapter 7**.

From the early stages, there are a number of useful steps that should be considered by both parties to 'move the case along'. You may need the assistance of the tribunal in obtaining information or relevant documentation from your opponent as you prepare the case even prior to or following on from the case management discussion.

6.2 MAKING REQUESTS AND APPLYING FOR ORDERS

Some six weeks or so after the claim has been presented to the tribunal, the claimant will receive the respondent's ET3 (response form) from the tribunal. This means that each party will now have the details of the other's case.

At this stage it is often helpful for parties to exchange correspondence seeking more clarification from each other if necessary. Examples might be:

- asking for documents referred to in claim or response form which the other party says they have not seen;
- asking for background documents such as employee handbooks or equal opportunities policies;
- asking for clarification of when meetings took place or telephone conversations occurred;
- asking for further details of how money claims are made up.

If you have asked for information which you think is important, such as an employee's personnel file, and your opponent has not responded, you may refer your request to the tribunal. There is no set format for framing requests in the tribunals, but a letter seeking information from your opponent should refer to r.10 of the 2004 Rules which gives the tribunal a general power to manage proceedings (see **Chapter 7**). This means that if a request has not been met voluntarily an application can then be made under r.11 for an order to be made concerning the subject matter of the request letter. You may therefore ask the tribunal to order your opponent to provide further details of the matters they refer to in their ET1 or ET3 as requested (sometimes referred to as a request for further and better particulars) or to provide the requested documentation.

Rule 11 states:

(1) At any stage of the proceedings a party may apply for an order to be issued, varied or revoked or for a case management discussion or pre-hearing review to be held.

(2) An application for an order must be made not less than 10 days before the date of the hearing at which it is to be considered (if any) unless it is not reasonably practicable to do so, or the chairman or tribunal considers it in the interests of justice that shorter notice be allowed. The application must (unless a chairman orders otherwise) be in writing to the Employment Tribunal Office and include the case number for the proceedings and the reasons for the request. If the application is for a case management discussion or a pre-hearing review to be held, it must identify any orders sought.

(3) An application for an order must include an explanation of how the order would assist the tribunal or chairman in dealing with the proceedings efficiently and fairly.

(4) When a party is legally represented in relation to the application (except where the application is for a witness order described in rule 10(2)(c) only), that party or his representative must, at the same time as the application is sent to the Employment Tribunal Office, provide all other parties with the following information in writing –

   (a) details of the application and the reasons why it is sought;
   (b) notification that any objection to the application must be sent to the Employment Tribunal Office within 7 days of receiving the application, or before the date of the hearing (whichever date is the earlier);
   (c) that any objection to the application must be copied to both the Employment Tribunal Office and all other parties;

   and the party or his representative must confirm in writing to the Employment Tribunal Office that this rule has been complied with.

(5) Where a party is not legally represented in relation to the application, the Secretary shall inform all other parties of the matters listed in paragraphs (4)(a) to (c).

(6) A chairman may refuse a party's application and if he does so the Secretary shall inform the parties in writing of such refusal unless the application is refused at a hearing.

You will write a letter to the tribunal asking for an order and copying them into the request you have already made to your opponent. Note in particular r.11(3) which requires you to state how you believe the order would assist the tribunal in dealing with the proceedings efficiently and fairly. The r.11 application must also comply with r.11(4) where the person making the application is a legal representative. You must give the details of your application to your opponent in writing, invite them to object within seven days of receiving your application or before the hearing in question, whichever comes first, and remind them that their objection needs to be copied to you and the tribunal.

Tribunals will usually make orders requiring a party to comply with them within a particular time – see r.10(3). Non-compliance with an order can mean that a party will have to pay the other party's costs at the main Hearing or that the claim will be struck out (using powers under r.13). Note that, however, as indicated in **Chapter 7**, orders for strike out will be very rare. Nevertheless a tribunal order is a strong incentive to comply with the request.

Case study: examples of requests for further details of the claim and response

Requests made to Molly by Just in Time

Just in Time want Molly to be clear as to how and when she worked for them as they dispute that she is an employee. They also want her to clarify the comments she alleged were made which she claims to be discriminatory. They require her to specify her shift changes which she alleges were done to victimise her under the SDA 1975. Just in Time therefore writes to Molly with the following requests for 'further and better particulars' of these matters which she has raised in her claim form:

1. Please provide full details of the exact working arrangements between yourself and Just in Time including the exact procedure followed prior to your working each event and how often you worked for Just in Time. Please provide full details of the occasions you were unable to work for Just in Time and the reasons offered by you.
2. Please give details of the exact comments allegedly made to you by the events manager concerning how pregnant staff looked in their uniform.
3. Please give details of the alleged last-minute changes to your shifts stating when these occurred and how often.

Requests made by Molly to Just in Time

In order to clarify the same issues Molly is likely to put the following requests to Just in Time:

1. Please provide full details of the way in which you arranged my work for you at each event.
2. Please give the exact details of the conversation I had with the events manager about how I looked in my uniform, stating when this conversation took place and whether there is a written record of it.
3. Please state which employees had rung in sick and when their shifts were due to take place for the period I worked for you after I told you I was pregnant.

6.3 DRAWING UP THE ISSUES

Both the parties involved in a tribunal claim should be working towards a point where they are clear about the matters in dispute. In **Chapter 8** we shall see that the issues in Molly's case are clarified at the conclusion of the pre-hearing review. However, the tribunal will expect you to have agreed with each other what the issues are and ideally to attend a case management discussion with an agreed list of what issues you want the tribunal to try. This means preparation of the issues at an early stage.

For example, if you cannot agree that words said to someone amounted to harassment as defined in SDA 1975 then the tribunal will be asked to decide on this issue for you. You may be able to agree that the words were used but not that they amounted to harassment, so the question of whether harassment occurred as defined in that statute is the issue to be tried.

It is for this reason that you will be seeking as much information from your opponent as they can provide about what their case is, and will be providing them with information about your case, as you will need to reach a point where you are both clear on the issues you are in dispute over. Asking for more information is not to be used as a tactic to put undue pressure on your opponent, nor should it be done simply to run up costs by insisting that your opponent provides extra information whether or not it may be relevant (which lawyers often refer to as 'fishing expeditions'). Case law guidelines (see *Byrne* v. *The Financial Times Ltd* [1991] IRLR 417) have made this clear. The main purpose of seeking and providing extra information is to clarify a party's case as already set out in the claim form or the response form, and to ensure that the parties know in advance the nature and details of the case. In *Byrne* it was said that 'pleadings battles should not be encouraged'. This is particularly so now in the more open approach to conducting civil litigation in the courts and tribunals.

Case study: issues in *Molly Martin* v. *Just in Time*

In **Chapter 4** we saw that Molly was claiming that she had been unfairly dismissed and discriminated against on the grounds of her sex. She is also claiming pregnancy discrimination, harassment and victimisation and money claims of notice pay and holiday pay. Her employer's response (see **Chapter 5**) was that she was not an employee, and therefore has no right to claim unfair dismissal, and that she was not treated unfairly because she was pregnant. They also deny that anything said to Molly might amount to harassment in law or that they victimised her or discriminated against her as a woman. They have stated that they are looking into her claims for notice pay and holiday pay.

The issues which are therefore beginning to emerge will look something like this:

- Was Molly an employee?
- Was Molly dismissed?
- If Molly was dismissed:

  - Was her dismissal unfair?
  - Was the main reason or one of the principal reasons for her dismissal her employment status or was it the fact that she was pregnant ?
  - Was her dismissal an act of direct sex discrimination?

- Was Molly treated to discriminatory harassment on the grounds of her sex?
- Was Molly victimised on the grounds of her sex because she had carried out a protected act, namely she had complained to her employer about discriminatory treatment?
- Is Molly entitled to unpaid wages, notice pay and/or holiday pay, and if so how much?

The tribunal will need to decide on all these issues and then if the judgment is in Molly's favour, assess her compensation. Most of these involve a mixture of fact and law, but the preliminary issue as to whether Molly is an employee is a question of law and must be decided if her unfair dismissal claim is to proceed.

We will see in **Chapter 8** how this may be dealt with as a preliminary issue by the tribunal at a pre-hearing review. It is also possible that this issue could be deferred to the main Hearing along with all the other issues.

If the parties can agree on the issues in advance of a case management discussion or a pre-hearing review they will be able to discuss them at those hearings with the judge who will clarify them, having satisfied him or herself that they are the proper issues to be tried in the case, and will then set them out for the parties in a letter recording the outcome of those hearings as well as any orders made arising out of them.

If you are representing the claimant it would be useful to write to the respondent some time in advance of a case management discussion setting out what you believe are the issues to be tried and asking them if they agree.

You can then both come to the case management discussion with a clear idea of what the issues are and what it is you want the tribunal to decide for you at the main Hearing.

6.4 DISCLOSURE OF DOCUMENTS

Introduction

Tribunals will usually require the parties to exchange a list of their documents within a reasonable period of time and in advance of the Hearing. They may send out a standard letter as part of the process of case management under r.10 once both the claim form and the response have been received (see **Chapter 8**). Where there has been a case management discussion they will require the parties to ensure they have disclosed to each other all relevant documents by a certain date prior to the main Hearing, usually 14 or 28 days (see **Chapter 8**).

It is often said that documents can make or break a party's case and this must be borne in mind when preparing for a tribunal Hearing. The sooner you have got the relevant documents assembled and organised (see more on this in **Chapter 9**) and have obtained copies of the other party's documents, the better. Documents will often be crucial in demonstrating the truth of a statement made in a tribunal claim or response form. For example if the respondent states that there was a full investigation into allegations of misconduct, or that holidays were taken and paid, the claimant should ensure he or she obtains the documentation that the respondent has to support these statements and puts them to the test.

Both parties should therefore begin to look at their own and their opponent's documents as soon as possible and not necessarily leave it until the final date for discovery set out in a tribunal order. The process of disclosure will assist in clarifying the issues as well as whether a party is likely to be able to persuade the tribunal to find in their favour at the main Hearing.

As indicated above, if you believe it is important at an early stage to see copies of certain documents you know that your opponent has in their possession, you can make a specific request for that documentation under r.11, referring in your letter to the tribunal's powers to order discovery under r.10.

At this stage the process will be called voluntary disclosure. In spite of its voluntary nature, it will be necessary to ensure that it is nevertheless full and helpful. It cannot be unfair or selective (*Birds Eye Walls Ltd* v. *Harrison* [1985] IRLR 47), leaving out, for example, internal memos about a claimant from the claimant's personnel file which may not help the respondent's case.

Certain types of claims may lead to extensive documentation being disclosed by the respondent. In discrimination claims, for example, it will usually be thought reasonable for the respondent to disclose documents about the claimant's past in the organisation or about other staff, to see if a discriminatory pattern of treatment can be shown to exist (see *West Midlands Passenger Transport Executive* v. *Singh* [1988] IRLR 186). In redundancy unfair dismissal claims there may need to be extensive discovery of paperwork surrounding a selection process operated by the respondent.

The key documents

All claims will have in common certain key documents. These are likely to include:

1. the claimant's statements of terms and conditions of service and any other allied contractual documents (e.g. disciplinary and grievance procedures);
2. equal opportunities policy (discrimination claims);
3. the claimant's disciplinary and grievance records (including the copies of the statutory steps documentation);
4. the claimant's personnel records; and
5. any internal memos or correspondence surrounding the subject of the claimant's claim(s).

All of these documents will of course be in the respondent's possession.

Case study: documents in Molly Martin's case

In Molly's case the following documents may have particular significance:

1. her contract and pay records (to assist in ascertaining her employment status and payment of holiday pay);
2. any complaints about her performance on her personnel file (to assist in establishing if the dismissal was fair);
3. any history of employees taking maternity leave or being granted flexible working arrangements after returning from maternity leave (to assist in her discrimination claim);
4. any written memos recording meetings and discussion between Molly and the Events Manager in the latter part of her employment (possibly relevant to all her claims).

Below is a composite example of a letter written seeking further information and documents written to Just in Time by Molly's adviser.

Case study: sample letter seeking further information and discovery

To:
Just in Time Catering Ltd
Unit 405
Springfield Road
Anytown
XYZ 0PJ

105

Dear Sirs,

Re: Ms M. Martin v. Just in Time – Tribunal Case No: 333333: XXXX South West employment tribunals

(1) Requests for further and better particulars of the respondent's response

We refer to paragraph 5.2 in your response form and should be grateful if you would fully particularise the conversations referred to there between the claimant and your Events Manager both in November when she told him she was pregnant and on 6th December. Please state if any written records of these conversations were made by yourselves.

(2) Request for disclosure:

(i) Please provide a copy of any written records referred to in the preceding request.
(ii) Please provide copies of Ms Martin's personnel and pay records during the time she worked for you.
(iii) Please provide a copy of your disciplinary and grievance procedures.

Please note that if you do not comply with these requests within the next 14 days then an application will be made to the employment tribunal under Rule 11 of the Employment Tribunals (Constitution and Rules of Procedure) Regulations 2004 that you should be ordered to provide this information by the tribunal.

We look forward to your reply.

Yours faithfully,

Jane Carter

The Last Stop Advice Bureau

As we have seen, the applying party who seeks an order in respect of requests made needs to write to the tribunal office (a letter will suffice). The letter must state the case number (as should all correspondence with the tribunal). It must state the reason for the request. Finally, it should state how in the view of the party applying an order would assist the tribunal or chairman in dealing with the proceedings efficiently or fairly. Although the Rules do not specify this, it will also be helpful to enclose a copy of the original request.

When making the request to the tribunal, you must, if you are a legal representative, copy the opposing party into your correspondence with the tribunal, as you have an obligation to inform them of the application and the reason why you seek the order. You must also inform them that they have seven days to object to your application and must do so in writing to the tribunal. The opposing party must send a copy of any objection to you. Rule 11(4) is set out above.

When making the original requests, therefore, what you ask for and how the request is framed will be done while bearing in mind how the Rules will require you to approach the tribunal for an order if necessary.

Note that in relation to disclosure any order made by the tribunal will only be to the extent that it will be necessary in order to dispose fairly of the case or to save expense. So in seeking discovery and then applying for an order, bear in mind that the tribunal will not always ask the other party to provide everything you have asked for as it will apply the above test in making the order.

However, orders in respect of all the above matters should be applied for if you believe that they will assist in clarifying the issues and will help the tribunal in exercising its obligations under reg.3.

6.5 COMPLYING WITH THE TRIBUNAL TIMETABLE FOR ORDERS

The orders timetable

As indicated above and as will be discussed in more detail in **Chapter 7**, the tribunal office will sometimes send out standard case management letters with a timetable built into them which lead up to the final step being taken a certain number of days prior to the main Hearing (even though that date may not have yet been allocated by the tribunal). The order may also have dates for compliance.

A tribunal judge may also hold a case management discussion (see **Chapter 8**), after which the judge will write to the parties to record the orders made and setting out the timetable. In each case, it will be necessary for the parties to diarise the dates for complying with the orders and to communicate with each other to ensure that they are both 'on track' with the required preparation for the main Hearing.

Where there has been a case management discussion, the judge will have asked each party at that hearing if there are any relevant outstanding requests for further and better particulars, discovery or for clarification of a party's case.

If, for example, your opponent has asked you for discovery and you have failed to provide it, then at the case management discussion, the judge will either suggest a timetable for you to comply on a voluntary basis or may order you to comply with an outstanding request by way of an order under r.10.

Delays in meeting requests or complying with orders

Whether or not there has been a case management discussion, it is good practice to write to your opponent setting out any reason why there may be delays or difficulties meeting requests or complying with any order. For example, there may be an unavoidable delay in obtaining documents, or there may be difficulty in obtaining a medical report by the required date.

This is not only a matter of acting openly and fairly, but also may prevent or forestall an application being made by your opponent for a costs order or a strike out order.

6.6   TRIBUNAL CORRESPONDENCE

All letters from the parties to the tribunal office are placed before a judge, usually after the judge has finished sitting for the day, as part of the duty to administer the business of the tribunal. A reply will be sent indicating the judge's view of the contents of the letter.

It used to be the case that parties could apply for orders without any recourse to the other party and the tribunals were often required to take a preliminary view of the matter or delay replying until they had sent a copy of that letter to the opposing party.

Rule 11(4), as we have seen, requires a legal representative to inform his opponent of any applications he is making to the tribunal. The aim is that the parties should be assisting the tribunal in its overriding objective and will only need to involve the tribunal where the parties believe there are good grounds for an application to be made for an order.

Sometimes you will have to wait to know the outcome of a request for an order you have made. You can ring the tribunal office and ask a clerk for the progress of your application. They will be able to tell you when the application is likely to be looked at by a judge or whether it has and how long you will have to wait for a response to your application. They will not give you the decision on the phone; you will need to wait to be informed of the decision by letter. The decision will be sent out to both parties at the same time even where it was an application made by only one party. If you do not have very much time before a Hearing you will need to be aware of how this process of dealing with applications takes place. Always ring the tribunal office in mid-afternoon, as if the matter was not referred to a judge at the end of the previous day's business you may be able to persuade the clerk to place it before a judge later in the afternoon when the judge has finished sitting for that day.

6.7   PARTY SEEKING A POSTPONEMENT

As will be seen in **Chapter 8** parties may seek postponements of Hearings where there are extenuating circumstances, for example when it becomes clear that a crucial witness cannot attend. We saw that the tribunal would only be able to grant a postponement in exceptional circumstances.

If a date is sent out by the tribunal for the Hearing and you or your key witnesses cannot attend you should immediately inform the other party that you cannot proceed on the date fixed for the Hearing and ask if there would be any objection to asking the tribunal for a new date.

If the other party does agree, then both parties can write applying for the adjournment under the application process in r.11. This may make the likelihood of an adjournment being granted slightly higher.

If your opponent objects to an adjournment then immediately write to the tribunal to make the application. Send with the letter of application any documentary evidence to support the reason for the application. The tribunal will have to bear in mind the overriding objective and to balance that against the interests of the party concerned to obtain a fair hearing.

6.8 OTHER PREPARATORY STAGES

As well as corresponding with each other, the parties should carry out the following steps at an early stage.

1. Ascertain who will be their witnesses and discover their availability to attend a hearing in the next few months. Prepare outline witness statements. Where witnesses are not willing or able to attend without an order, make a note to apply for a witness order (see **9.3**).
2. Begin a document file separate from the main office file on the client.
3. Begin drafting the main client's statement (e.g. claimant, dismissing manager) and add to it as further information becomes available.
4. Ensure that the claimant keeps a running record of any losses (e.g. job hunt record, benefits, etc.) so that the schedule of loss can be kept up to date.
5. Finally, ensure that you keep in mind what you need to prove to the tribunal and how you will do it at the Hearing. Remember that all this preparation is geared towards this aim and it is important to keep focussed and not get too overwhelmed in documentation!

Chapter 9 will deal with the preparation for the main Hearing. Prior to that there may be interim hearings, which will be looked at in **Chapters 7** and **8**.

CHAPTER 7

Case management – matters dealt with without a hearing

7.1 THE PRINCIPLES

The increased use of what has become known as 'case management' as cases proceed through the system has been encouraged by a number of factors. These include its apparently successful use in the civil courts following the Woolf reforms, the report of the Employment Tribunal System Taskforce, and the need for greater efficiency. Another factor is the increase in more complex employment tribunal cases, particularly those alleging discrimination and those claiming under a number of jurisdictions, sometimes known as 'multi-claims'. The 2004 Rules reflect this aspect giving greater powers to judges to give directions and deal with a significant number of factors during the progress of the case. Not to be forgotten, there remains the central importance of the overriding objective at reg.3 of the Regulations. In essence, judges will be concerned to ensure that the case progresses at a reasonable speed, that all necessary documents and witnesses will be available to the tribunal that hears the case, and that realistic time scales are agreed or imposed for the parties to prepare properly and for the hearing of the matter. The judge will expect the parties and their representatives to co-operate (and reg.3 specifically states that the parties shall assist the tribunal with furthering the objective). The judge will discourage, possibly with the threat of sanctions, including costs awards and strike out, those who attempt to delay or obstruct the process.

Communications from the tribunal are usually accompanied by a letter and may include orders or a request for information. It is vital that you attempt to comply with orders and any time limits or date for compliance or you risk being 'struck out' under rr.13 and 18. There are a number of steps in the process and these will be considered in roughly chronological order although they may arise at any time up to (and in some cases beyond) the merits Hearing.

7.2 ACCEPTANCE OF CLAIM AND RESPONSE FORMS

Claim form

As soon as the form is received, the tribunal office will date stamp both the form and the envelope (if it is sent by post or hand delivered). Mail delivered on Saturday will be date-stamped on Monday but with Saturday's date. Sunday postings (through the letter box, etc.) will be date-stamped on Monday. These dates are kept on the file for reference purposes, especially if there is an issue over whether the claim was made in time. The next procedure is to check that the claim can be accepted but, as long as it is accepted, the claim is registered and given a case number which is retained throughout the progress of the case and should be quoted in all correspondence. In practice, most cases are registered quite quickly, usually within a few days. Claims can now be presented online and may be received the same day but it is important to check as there is no guarantee of same-day delivery. (See *Akhavan-Moosavi* v. *Association of Local Government* (unreported, UKEAT 501/04) and *Initial Electronic Security Systems Ltd* v. *Avdic* [2005] ICR 1598 which suggested that a claim sent by fax or email more than 60 minutes before the time limit expires might be considered to be in time, but also see *Miller* v. *Community Links Trust Ltd* (unreported, UKEAT 0486/07) where an online claim received 8 seconds past midnight was out of time.) An automatic receipt is generated when a claim is submitted online.

The tribunal office will then 'code' the claim. This is done by assigning initials which will identify, for office use only, the nature of the claim. So, for instance 'UDL' for unfair dismissal, 'SXD' for sex discrimination, 'RRD' for race discrimination, 'WA' for unpaid wages and so on. There is no legal significance in these codings, which are used for statistical purpose but do not bind the parties in any way whatsoever.

This is the point at which a decision is made whether or not to accept a claim. As spelt out in **Chapter 4**, the claim should be made on the claim form ET1. There is some information which is compulsory and without which the claim cannot be accepted (but see *Grimmer* v. *KLM Cityhopper UK* [2005] IRLR 596 about how that rule can be interpreted). The information required is set out in r.1(4) and is essentially the name and address of the claimant, the name and address of the respondent, details of the claim, whether the claimant is or was an employee of the respondent and whether the claimant was dismissed by the respondent. There is then some extra information which is required for the tribunal office to ascertain whether the requirement to follow the statutory procedure has been followed, and thus the claimant has to state whether the claimant has raised the matter in writing with the respondent within the previous 28 days (EA 2002, s.32) and, if not, why not. This information is not required if the claimant was not an employee, or if the claimant was dismissed and the only claim is for 'actual' unfair dismissal. This means it is not required for unfair dismissal although it is for constructive dismissal. It is required for all other claims for discrimination (unless the only allegation is that the dismissal itself was discriminatory), unpaid wages, public interest disclosure claims and less common claims relating to part time workers, fixed term workers, failure to provide pay statements etc.

The first task for the tribunal is for the secretary (that is, a member of the administrative staff) to consider whether the claim should be accepted under r.3. If it is accepted the normal procedure of registering the claim and giving it a case number, sending a copy to the respondent, informing the parties of the role of ACAS and the fixed period of conciliation will be followed (see below at **7.3**).

There are two possible reasons why the claim would not be accepted. The first is where the secretary decides that the claim cannot be accepted because it is not on the prescribed form, and it will then be returned to the claimant explaining why it has not been accepted (r.3(1)).

The second situation is rather more complex, and these possibilities are listed in r.3(2). They arise from situations where there is a perceived failure to provide some of required information or the tribunal does not have jurisdiction or there has been a breach of the requirement to follow the grievance procedure under EA 2002, s.32.

Where the secretary decides that the claim should not be accepted, the matter must be referred to a judge under r.3(3) with a 'statement of reasons'. At that point the judge may decide to accept the claim but can only do so if the statutory grievance procedure has been complied with where it applies. This is a mandatory requirement under EA 2002, s.32(6):

> An employment tribunal shall be prevented from considering a complaint presented in breach of subsections (2) and (4) but only if –
>
> (a)   the breach is apparent to the tribunal from the information supplied to it by the employee in connection with the bringing of the proceedings . . .

It may be that, when a judge reads the claim form, it is clear that the only discrimination claim is one which relates to the dismissal and there is therefore no need to follow the statutory grievance procedure (under reg.6(5) of the Dispute Resolution Regulations and see *Lawrence* v. *HM Prison Service* [2007] IRLR 468). If a decision is made by the judge not to accept the claim, that decision is to be recorded with reasons and the claimant is to be informed of the rejection and given information on reviews and appeals (see **Chapter 14**).

One of the recurring problems that has emerged is the complexity that has arisen over part rejected claims. Very often, part of the claim is accepted, most commonly the unfair dismissal claim but another claim, for example, the relatively minor aspect of unpaid wages, is rejected. This complexity is increased where, for instance, a claim is made for holiday pay which might be for statutory holiday under the Working Time Regulations for which a grievance is required or under the employment contract for which a grievance is not needed. Where a claim is part rejected, the claimant will be sent a letter which specifies which part is accepted and which rejected. When, and if, it is re-submitted, it will be given a new case number and file and another ET3 should, strictly speaking, be presented. Although the respondent should have been told which claims have been accepted and which rejected this may not always be as clear as it might be, particularly for unrepresented respondents. The result can be a number of fairly messy files with questions about jurisdiction and the necessity for considerable case management, often at a Hearing. The latest Tribunals Service statistics on claims between April 2006 and March 2007 that were rejected and not re-submitted show over 10,700 rejected with a little over 3,800 subsequently re-submitted and accepted. This means over 6,000 never come back or are not accepted when they do. You should be careful, therefore, to try to ensure that your claim is not one which is rejected at this stage by checking the form thoroughly and giving all necessary information.

Response form

The time limit for responding to a claim is perhaps the most common stumbling block for respondents. Under r.4 a respondent must present the response within 28 days of a copy of the claim form being sent by the tribunal office. As with the claim form the response *must* be on the prescribed form. It will be rejected if it is not, regardless of whether it has all the relevant information. As with the claim form, there is required information but this is less onerous than that required of the claimant and amounts to name, address, whether the respondent wishes to resist the claim and the grounds on which the respondent does so. The question of what is sufficient for the grounds of resistance is explored further in **Chapter 5**. As stated above, it may be that part of the claim form has been rejected and the response need only deal with accepted claims.

As far as the 28-day time limit is concerned, the 2004 Rules are stricter than previous rules. A respondent may apply for an extension of time under r.11 (which covers all applications to the tribunal, specifying that they must be made in writing) but it must be made within 28 days and must explain why the respondent cannot comply with that 28-day time limit. Rule 4(4) states explicitly that time may only be extended if it is just and equitable to do so. Extensions *cannot* be given after the time limit has expired – even if there has been an extension within that further period. So, for example, if the ET3 was due by 31 October and an extension has been granted to 14 November, a further extension requested on 7 November cannot be granted. The consequence of not responding, not doing so in time, not using the prescribed form, or not supplying the required information is that there will be a refusal to accept the response, which means one of the two results set out below.

Default judgments

First, and most likely, is that there will be a default judgment, the power to issue such judgments having been introduced in 2004. This is set out in r.8. The default judgment may determine liability only or, if there is sufficient information on the claim form, liability and remedy. Under r.8(2)(c) a default judgment can also be made if the respondent has stated that it does not resist the claim as well as when the response is late or has not been accepted because it is not on the prescribed form or does not contain the required information. Rule 8 states that the judge 'may' issue a default judgment 'if he considers it appropriate to do so'. This clearly allows for some discretion although, in practice, it might be necessary for the judge to justify any decision given the right to apply for review. In *Moroak t/a Blake Envelopes* v. *Cromie* [2005] ICR 1226 the EAT President said 'it would appear to be an entirely discretionary matter on the part of the tribunal as to whether, in a particular case, it does or does not, issue a default judgment'. In practice, this judgment is not made by a tribunal but by a judge on the papers. The circumstances where a default judgment is more likely to be made are where the claims are clear, where there is sufficient factual information to substantiate the claims, where there is only one respondent and no issues of jurisdiction arise. Where there are multiple respondents, where the claimant may not be an employee, have insufficient service or be out of time, or where there are discrimination claims where the initial burden of proof rests on the claimant, it is less likely to occur.

There is a clear right to ask for a review of a default judgment which is set out in r.33 but there is no power to stay or set aside a default judgment pending the review. Rule 33(4) clearly envisages a Hearing ('A review of a default judgment shall be conducted by a judge in public') but, given considerable guidance from the EAT on the limited circumstances that such a review would not succeed, some employment judges now write to claimants seeking to invite consent to the revocation of the default judgment as it is arguable that it is an unnecessary burden to have such a Hearing. If the matter does go to a Hearing, we set out guidance in later chapters.

Rule 9

The second possible result of a failure to respond in time, not on the form or without the required information arises under Rule 9.

9 Taking no further part in proceedings

A respondent who has not presented a response or whose response has not been accepted shall not be entitled to take any part in the proceedings except to –

(a) make an application under rule 33 (review of default judgments);
(b) make an application under rule 35 (preliminary consideration of application for review) in respect of rule 34(3)(a), (b) or (e);
(c) be called as a witness by another person;
(d) be sent a copy of a document or corrected entry in accordance with rule 8(4), 29(2) or 37;

and in these rules the word 'party' or 'respondent' includes a respondent only in relation to his entitlement to take such part in the proceedings, and in relation to any such part which he takes.

One of the important things to note is that the application of r.9 does not formally require a decision by a judge or tribunal. It happens, as it were, automatically, because of a failure by the respondents. In practice, if a default judgment is not made, the respondent will be sent a letter that informs them of the application of r.9 and that they can take no further part in the proceedings. Although this would seem, on a strict reading of the Rules, to allow for no review, as there has been no decision or judgment, the respondent does have such a right under r.34(1) with the grounds limited to those in r.9 or under r.34(3), either (a) (decision made as result of administrative error), (b) (a party did not receive notice of the proceedings) or (e) (the interests of justice require a review). Again, guidance from the EAT (see for example, *NSM Music Ltd* v. *Leefe* (unreported, UKEAT/0663/05)) suggests strongly that a review should be granted if the respondent has a reason for the failure and a has reasonable defence. Again, if the matter does proceed to a Hearing, further advice can be found in later chapters.

Case study: Just in Time's late response and default judgment

Molly Martin's claim form (see **Chapter 4**) is dated 3 March and is received by the tribunal office on Tuesday 4 March. It is accepted and sent to Just in Time on 6 March. Twenty-eight days from 6 March brings us to 3 April.

Just in Time's response form (see **Chapter 5**) is dated 7 April and received by the tribunal office on 9 April, i.e. six days late.

A default judgment had already been made on 8 April for 'liability only' with respect to unpaid wages, unfair dismissal and sex discrimination and a remedy hearing to follow. Just in Time receive written notification on 10 April of the default judgment and, on the same day, apply in writing for a review under r.33.

The application states that the claim form was not received by the respondent (presumably because of a postal strike) until after the Easter holiday period on 31 March, the respondent had to get legal advice, and the response form was completed on the day that the respondent met the legal adviser. The respondent apologises and requests an extension of time, and includes a further copy of the ET3.

A public hearing of the application is listed for 19 May and Molly Martin and Just in Time are invited. Molly Martin does not attend and the judge decides to revoke the default judgment with respect to the unfair dismissal and sex discrimination claim as there is a reasonable prospect of successfully defending the claim, and the judge is satisfied that there was a good reason for the delay. (Note that the judge may have written to Molly's representative asking whether they consent to the revocation of the default judgment. As it is highly likely that it will be revoked, it is worth giving serious consideration to giving consent and saving costs and time.)

The respondent has satisfied the claim for unpaid wages and holiday pay, so that part of the claim is also revoked. A pre-hearing review to deal with the question of whether the claimant is an employee is listed for 3 July.

7.3   FIXED PERIODS OF CONCILIATION AND TRACK ALLOCATION

Fixed periods of conciliation

This was another concept introduced by the EA 2002 and incorporated into the 2004 Rules, and likely to be removed when the Dispute Resolution Regulations are abandoned. The idea and the policy background was to encourage settlements without hearings, perhaps to concentrate the minds of parties, representatives and ACAS conciliation officers but it appears to have been unpopular and largely unsuccessful. Fixed periods will be repealed when the Employment Bill becomes law.

Rules 22–4 deal with the procedures. Note that although cases will not have a merits Hearing during these fixed periods, they may be listed for Hearing. Case management discussions and any pre-hearing reviews will be listed and heard to ensure that there are no unnecessary delays in the matter being listed and that they are dealt with if there is no settlement. The fixed period runs from the date that the copy claim form is sent to the respondent, yet another reason for all parties to get to grips with the case at an early stage.

There is also provision for early termination of the fixed period set out in r.23 where there has been a default judgment, withdrawal, a notification to ACAS that one or both parties do not wish to attempt conciliation, where there has been a settlement or where there is no response, no default judgment and 14 days have elapsed. A stay of proceedings, for example, where there are other ongoing court proceedings, will also suspend the conciliation period. Note that there are no fixed periods of conciliation for discrimination claims.

Checklist: fixed periods of conciliation

- 'Short' – seven weeks – wages, guaranteed payment, suspension, redundancy.
- 'Standard' – 13 weeks – unfair dismissal and other claims where judge decides it is appropriate.
- Extension of two weeks – where all parties agree (see r.22(7)).
- No fixed period – discrimination.

'Short track', standard and complex cases

One of the practices that has been adopted within the last few years in most tribunal regions dovetails nicely into these fixed periods. Track procedures now apply in all regions, and it is possible to allocate different sorts of cases on different 'tracks'. In particular, some less complex money claims may be allocated to the 'short track'. These are listed quickly to be heard as soon as possible after the end of the fixed 'short' conciliation period. If your case is allocated to a short track you will find that more concise and less onerous case management orders are given. A letter is sent to the parties with a copy of the claim form to the respondents, even before the response has been received, which gives a date and time allocation for the Hearing, usually one hour. That letter will typically include a number of case management orders, and suggestions for representatives to consider if they are involved in such a case are given below.

Checklist: short track procedure

What the notice will say and how parties or representatives might respond.

	Notice	Guidance
(a)	Time and date of Hearing and time allotted for completion	Usually one hour, but if this is insufficient tell the tribunal immediately with reasons
(b)	That it will be before a judge sitting alone	If you want a full tribunal, tell the tribunal immediately and give reasons
(c)	Instruction to parties to arrange for their own witnesses	Any witnesses must be relevant to the issues
(d)	That parties can conduct the case or get representatives	The tribunal should be informed of the representatives' details
(e)	That parties can attend in person or send written representations	Decide which is best in the circumstances, but if there is a dispute it is usually better to attend
(f)	That the claimant must provide details of how much is claimed and the calculation and send to the tribunal and respondent	This should be done in as much detail as possible
(g)	That the claimant should bring three copies of various documents	These will include pay slips, contract of employment and other supporting documents
(h)	That the respondents can present a response but, if they do not, they cannot defend	Do this if you dispute the claim
(i)	Parties reminded of the services of ACAS	This should be considered, especially if the claim is for a relatively small amount of money
(j)	What is enclosed (such as maps and explanatory booklets)	

A proportion of cases are considered appropriate for a range of customised case management orders and they appear to fit into the 'standard' period. These will include unfair dismissal or slightly more complicated money claims. The more complex discrimination or multi-claim cases require particular care, and do not have any fixed period of conciliation and are not allocated in a particular track. However, such cases may well be allocated to a named judge to deal with the case management aspects and are likely to be the subject of a case management discussion.

7.4 CASE MANAGEMENT ORDERS

Depending on the sort of case that is being dealt with, there will almost always be case management orders from the tribunal. The file will have been considered by a judge who will make an initial assessment on matters such as track allocation, what further information is required and what needs to happen to bring the case to a Hearing as soon as possible. The purpose of making case management orders is to encourage the parties to give as much information as possible to each other and the tribunal so that the case can progress to a final Hearing. In the future, it may be found that more cases settle as each party will become aware of the other party's case and the evidence available at an earlier stage.

In the majority of claims, the case will fall into the 'standard' conciliation period. A number of regions issue similar orders in this type of case, and this is expected to continue and increase. Although the orders are not 'standard' as they will vary depending on the information previously supplied by the parties, there are a number of orders which are commonly used. These will outline what the parties are expected to do to prepare for the Hearing, and the orders are expected to be complied with. They will usually cover disclosure of documents, witness statements and a schedule of loss for the claimant. If you receive such orders, read them and prepare accordingly. They will include time limits for compliance, usually giving an actual date for compliance or expressed in weeks or days in relation to a hearing. If the relevant date is not stated, you should immediately calculate the date yourself and diarise with enough time for slippage. If you consider that there is a good reason to depart from the orders, if possible agree that departure with the opposing party and ask for the tribunal to consent to a variation. As long as it does not interfere with the hearing, cause potential injustice or inconvenience to a party or the tribunal, a judge may agree.

In other more complex cases, there is no fixed period of conciliation. There may well be orders made at this stage, for instance, for the production of medical reports in disability discrimination cases. However, these are likely to be interim orders which may well be followed by further orders, a case management discussion or a pre-hearing review.

Example of common case management orders

Note that in this example the tribunal has inserted the actual date for compliance. Whilst this is recommended practice it may be that case management orders state periods of time to comply instead, such as within 21 days or no later than four weeks from the date of the order. In that case, it is obviously of great importance that representatives and parties calculate the date for compliance and diarise it immediately. A notice of hearing is often sent at the same time as the sort of case management orders set out below.

---

7 January

An employment judge has considered the case papers and has given the following orders which apply to both parties.

1   Any person who is to give evidence to the tribunal (including the claimant and the respondent) shall prepare a written statement containing all of the evidence he or she intends to give. These statements should be typed or legibly written and should be exchanged between the parties by 4 February. Six copies should be brought to the Hearing.
2   The claimant shall prepare a schedule setting out all the losses which are claimed in this case and serve a copy on the tribunal office and the respondent by 28 January. An example form for these purposes is enclosed.
3   Both parties shall disclose to the other party all documents in their possession, power or control that are relevant to any issue in this case by 28 January. This can be done by sending a list of documents or sending photocopies. Where the claim is for unfair dismissal or discrimination the claimant should ensure that he or she has disclosed all documents which relate to the alleged losses suffered including any documents dealing with his or her attempts to find alternative work.
4   Both parties shall by 11 February prepare a joint bundle of documents containing all the documents that they wish to rely upon. Each page of the bundle shall be consecutively numbered and there should be an index. Six copies should be brought to the Hearing. Unless there is a direction to the contrary these documents should not be sent to the tribunal in advance of the Hearing.

7.5 SPECIAL ORDERS

In some cases there will be a need to apply for or for the tribunal to make particular orders or give particular directions because of the type of case. We deal with the most common such cases here. Most of these applications can be dealt with on the papers, that is, by one party writing in, the other party having been given the opportunity to comment and the judge deciding on the information available to them. They may also be dealt with at a Hearing, case management discussion, pre-hearing review, review or merits Hearing, particularly if a Hearing is imminent or if there is a serious dispute between the parties. **Chapter 8** deals with orders that might be made at a Hearing with parties or representatives present.

Rule 11 covers the process that should be used to make applications. Rule 11(2) requires the application to be made in writing 10 days before a Hearing (if there is to be one). Rule 11(4) states that if the party making the application is legally represented, they must also notify the opposing party of the application (with the exception of witness order applications) and inform the opposing party that they have seven days to send any objections to the tribunal *and* confirm to the tribunal that this has been done. Note that, if you are a legal representative and you fail to comply with r.11(4) your application may be refused without consideration. Be aware also that r.11(3) requires the party making the application to explain how the order requested will 'assist the tribunal or judge in dealing with the proceedings efficiently and fairly'. Bear this in mind when considering any of the orders below.

Restricted reporting orders

These arise in two circumstances under r.50(1) of the 2004 Rules and are limited to these:

(a) where there is an allegation of 'sexual misconduct' (not limited to sex discrimination claims); and
(b) where evidence of a personal nature is likely to be heard in a Disability Discrimination Act case.

The tribunal must still exercise discretion and although there is rarely a problem in practice, representatives must give reasons within the scope of r.50 and r.11(3). Whilst the agreement of the other party should be sought (as in all these applications where possible), the tribunal will need to be satisfied that the order should be made (see *X* v. *Z Ltd* [1998] ICR 43). The judge may make a temporary restricted reporting order which will lapse in 14 days unless application is made to convert it to a full restricted reporting order.

In cases of sexual misconduct, the definition appears at s.31(8) of ETA 1996:

> the commission of a sexual offence, sexual harassment or other adverse conduct (of whatever nature) related to sex, and conduct is related to sex whether the relationship with sex lies in the character of the conduct or in its having reference to the sex or sexual orientation of the person at whom the conduct is directed

When considering whether to make a full restricted reporting order the tribunal must give both parties the right to be heard, which seems to suggest that the matter cannot be dealt with by written representations. In practice, the application will often be made at a case management discussion or at the commencement of the main Hearing. A notice is then placed on the tribunal hearing room to the effect that there should be no identification of the witnesses or the parties.

Note that the order can only delay publication of the names until after the decision has been promulgated (i.e. sent to the parties).

120

Sexual offences and the register

However, note that in the case of sexual offences, r.49 prohibits the publication in the tribunal register or any tribunal document of names or means of identifying those people against whom a sexual offence has allegedly been committed. This means that in such a case any names and means of identification will be omitted from the judgment.

Amendments to claims or responses

Amendments generally fall into two different categories, from the simple and uncontentious yet important (such as correcting the name of the respondent), to the complex and highly contentious (such as amending the grounds in the claim form). There is reference to the power for a judge to consider amendments to a claim or a response in r.10(2)(q) and as a matter of practice and case law, amendments can be allowed, depending on the type and timing of the request.

If the respondent's name is to be amended, consent of both parties should be sought. Generally, there is no particular difficulty with this but it must be clear to the tribunal or the judge that the claim is not against a new respondent. It is also possible to join further respondents under r.10 although this will be considered cautiously if the Hearing is imminent, particularly as further respondents would need to be served with the claim form and given an opportunity to respond. Where the respondent appears to be insolvent the Secretary of State for Business, Enterprise and Regulatory Reform (formerly the Secretary of State for Trade and Industry) may be added as a respondent and will be treated as a party.

Where the question is whether other important details in the claim form or response can be amended, until the 2004 Rules, it was assumed that the general power under r.15 of the 2001 Rules covered the situation. It remains a very difficult area and representatives should tread carefully when dealing with it, whether on behalf of the claimant or the respondent. The relevant guidance in case law can be found in *Cocking* v. *Sandhurst (Stationers) Ltd* [1974] ICR 650 and slightly more recently in *Selkent Bus Co Ltd* v. *Moore* [1996] IRLR 661. The tribunal or judge must consider the length and reason for the delay, what prejudice there might be to either party and the merits of the amendment sought. See also *Brock* v. *Minerva Dental Ltd* [2007] ICR 917 for a useful discussion of the guidance contained in *Cocking* and *Selkent*. The authorities suggest three different kinds of amendment as follows:

(a) altering the basis of a claim but with no new distinct head of claim;
(b) a 'relabelling', where there is a new cause of action based on facts already set out; and
(c) an additional or substitution for the original claim which brings in an entirely new claim.

Often it will be difficult to decide which of these it is and it is therefore useful to approach any application for amendment, whether making it or opposing it by a careful examination of the claim and response forms.

This is likely to be dealt with, if it is contentious, either at a case management discussion or, where the issue will affect a party's 'civil rights', at a pre-hearing review. If amendments to the claim form are allowed, consequential amendments will also be allowed to the response or, and this is less likely, to the claim form. It may be the case that the amendment is allowed but may give reasons for an application for costs to be made, possibly at a later stage.

Checklist: amending the claim or response

- Nature of amendment – simple error or substantial alteration altering basis of claim or response?
- Consider whether it is based on the same facts – is it relabelling?
- 'New' claim/response – in or out of time?
- Seek views of the opposing party as soon as possible – can you get consent?
- Time and manner of application – have you complied with r.11(4)?
- Consider case-law as suggested above.
- Consider what prejudice there might be to the other party.

Striking out

There are a number of rules which deal with the power of the judge or tribunal to strike out.

Rules 13 (non-compliance with orders and practice directions), 18 (at pre-hearing review) and 20 (non-payment of deposit) of the 2004 Rules deal with when part or all of the claim form or response may be struck out. This is a measure which effectively brings to an end all or part of a party's case, and can therefore be appealed if there is an arguable point of law.

A relatively old case giving guidance under the 'old' Rules may still be useful here: *Birkett* v. *James* [1977] 2 All ER 801. Where default is 'intentional and contumelious', and delay 'inordinate and inexcusable' it will prejudice the proper disposal of the case. The tribunal must send notice to the party concerned to give that party an opportunity to 'show cause' as to why the claim should not be struck out. In any event, there will be the opportunity to advance oral arguments at a Hearing. There is further explanation of this at **8.3**. With respect to the provision to strike out for failure to comply with orders and practice directions (r.13), guidance on dealing with the previous but identical rule can be found in *Weir Valves & Controls (UK) Ltd* v. *Armitage* [2004] ICR 371, EAT. That case makes it clear that a judge or tribunal should consider whether striking out or a lesser sanction will be the appropriate response. The EAT mentioned specifically the overriding objective, the magnitude of the default and whether a fair trial was still possible. An objective judgment of the possibility should be made. More recently the Court of Appeal in *Blockbuster Entertainment Ltd* v. *James* [2006] IRLR 630 stated that it is only in very unusual circumstances that a matter which has reached the Hearing should be struck out even where there has been unreasonable conduct. Interestingly, tribunals were said to be 'open to the difficult litigant as well as the compliant'. The proximity of the Hearing is therefore an important factor to consider when applying for a strike out.

Given the finality of a strike-out order, caution will be exercised by the judge. Parties should be aware of the consequences and ensure that, when asked to give reasons as to why strike out should not occur, they give cogent and clear explanation within the time indicated by the tribunal office. However, even if strike out is not ordered or if a strike out is overturned on review or appeal, another possible sanction is the making of a costs order. Now that there is the provision for a 'wasted costs' order under r.48 (see **Chapter 13**) it will be very important to avoid strike out.

Some strike out considerations will be on the basis of the written information (or lack of it) in the file, others will be at a pre-hearing review (see **8.3**). The most likely paper strike outs will occur in the most obviously hopeless cases and where a party, usually the claimant, has not been in communication with the tribunal. The power to issue 'unless orders', the sanction for not complying usually being a strike out, has led to judges exercising their discretion without the need to hear from the parties. So, for example and relatively commonly, where someone has made an unfair dismissal claim and has less than one year's service a letter or an unless order will invite the claimant to 'show cause' why the unfair dismissal claim should not be struck out because of lack of jurisdiction. Where the claimant does not reply by the required date or the reason given still does not give any indication of why the claim could be considered (for instance, the unfair dismissal relates to a health and safety matter under ERA 1996, s.100), the unfair dismissal claim is highly likely to be struck out. Other claims may remain and will proceed. For more complex issues, a pre-hearing review will be arranged so that both parties can make representations.

Requests for postponement and adjournment

The usual notice of hearing states that 'unless there are exceptional circumstances' no postponement will be allowed unless there is an application within 14 days. If there is good reason and application is made within the 14 days of the date of the notice of hearing, a postponement will be very likely to be granted. Where the application comes outside the 14-day limit, it will be much harder to convince a judge to grant the postponement, remembering that the circumstances have to be 'exceptional'. Note that the unavailability of a particular representative is unlikely to secure a postponement, unless it can be

123

shown that there is a particular reason for that representative to be present and a good reason for the application to fall outside the 14-day deadline. However, a judge or tribunal do have the power to postpone or adjourn under r.10(2)(m).

It is particularly difficult to secure a postponement where the date has been agreed by the parties or fixed at a pre-hearing review, case management discussion or other interim hearing. Where, on the face of it, the judge takes the view that there may be exceptional circumstances (for example, the unavailability of a vital witness through ill health) the views of the other party will be sought, if at all possible. If there is time, it may be that a hearing will be fixed to deal with the application, or the party making the application may be refused the request but told that it will be possible to re-apply at the commencement of the full Hearing.

Another circumstance where an adjournment may be required is during the Hearing, perhaps to deal with remedy after a judgment on liability in the claimant's favour. However, care should be taken. Both parties should be ready to deal with remedy, and good reasons will be expected if you request time to prepare for something that you should have anticipated beforehand. Adjournments and postponements might well be granted with the condition that the party seeking the delay (or the representative under the new 'wasted costs' rule in the 2004 Rules) must pay costs (see **Chapter 14**). The more issues that can be agreed with the other party before the Hearing and put before the tribunal as a joint application, the better.

The question of whether to allow a postponement can be difficult and involves weighing the prejudice to each party either in forcing the case ahead or in delaying matters. Factors to be taken into account will include the likely delay which may be some months, the reason for the request, the centrality of the unavailable witness for example and whether there is any way a fair Hearing can proceed. (See *Sinclair Roche and Temperley* v. *Heard and Fellows* (unreported, UKEAT 0168/05 and 0169/05) where a joint application to postpone was made.)

Witness orders

Applications for witness orders can be made as outlined in **Chapter 9**. They are made where a witness has relevant evidence and is unwilling to attend. The party applying for such an order should be aware that the judge will consider the necessity of bringing a witness who is unwilling and representatives should apply for such an order only when they are sure that the witness is important to their case. If you believe that an important witness is needed and cannot or will not come without an order, make sure you apply in good time. Allow as much as a month if you can as files are not always referred to a judge for some time and the judge will want to be satisfied that any witnesses will have sufficient time to arrange their affairs to be able to attend.

Checklist: best practice for case management applications

- Can you agree with the other party?
- If not, apply to the tribunal for the order requested.
- Make sure there is sufficient time for the file to be referred to a judge and for the order to be given (leave at least four weeks, if there is time).
- If no agreement, consider your arguments for the order.
- Be clear and consistent in your requests.
- Always comply in time.

CHAPTER 8

Interim hearings

8.1 INTRODUCTION

This chapter deals with the hearings that take place whilst a case progresses through the system. Sometimes they are referred to as 'interlocutory' or 'interim' hearings. They may (but only in the case of pre-hearing reviews (PHRs)) dispose of the case entirely or they may deal with a specific issue or issues that need resolving before the matter proceeds to a 'full' or 'merits' Hearing. Not all cases will have interim hearings which, in the main, are either PHRs or case management discussions (CMDs). In some cases they are 'reviews' (generally of a default judgment), which are dealt with in **Chapter 14**. If the hearing is not listed as a CMD but it does not dispose of the case, it is very likely that there will be a CMD following immediately to plan for the full or merits Hearing. If the case is listed for an interim hearing the judge will attempt to deal with as many outstanding matters as possible so that there is no need for more than one interim hearing. This means that representatives should always be ready to deal with these matters as well as the matter listed. For instance, if the issue for a PHR is whether the tribunal has jurisdiction and the judge decides that it does, there will then be clarification of the claims and issues, consideration of orders and listing the matter for hearing.

8.2 PRE-HEARING REVIEWS

Matters that used to be dealt with at preliminary hearings before October 2004 are now dealt with at a pre-hearing review (PHR): see rr.18–20. Most PHRs are heard by a judge sitting alone *in public*, which means that usually the only time that there will be a full tribunal is at a merits Hearing.

Pre-hearing reviews (rr.18–19)

Rule 18 outlines the circumstances where a judge may carry out 'a preliminary consideration of the proceedings'. There is provision in r.18(3) for there to be a full tribunal where there has been a request by a party not less than

10 days before the Hearing and where the judge is of the view that issues of fact may have to be determined and it would be desirable for there to be a full tribunal and has ordered one. Rule 18(2) provides that the judge may:

(a) determine any interim or preliminary matter;
(b) issue any order (r.10);
(c) order that deposit be made (r.20);
(d) consider any oral or written representations or evidence;
(e) deal with an application for interim relief (Trade Union and Labour Relations (Consolidation) Act 1992, s.161 and ERA 1996, s.168).

The judge's powers are wide at this stage as r.18(5) states that the judge may give judgment and that it may result in strike out, dismissal or determination of the matter. Furthermore, under r.18(7) the judge has power to strike out for reasons listed there. These include:

(a) that the claim or response is scandalous, vexatious or has no reasonable prospect of success;
(b) the manner of conducting the proceedings by a party or representative has been scandalous, unreasonable or vexatious;
(c) that the claim has not been actively pursued;
(d) there has been non-compliance with an order or practice direction;
(e) where it is no longer possible for there to be a fair hearing.

Rule 18(7) also gives the judge power to consider a party's entitlement to take part in the proceedings and make a restricted reporting order. There is a requirement under r.19 for notice to be sent to the parties when strike out, a restricted reporting order or entitlement to bring or contest proceedings is to be considered although that does not apply if the party has been given the opportunity to make oral representations. Be aware that these orders may be made in the absence of the parties.

A PHR may be listed to determine such questions as whether the claimant was an employee, a worker or in employment as defined in discrimination legislation, whether the claimant was disabled within the definition contained within the Disability Discrimination Act 1995, and whether the claim has been presented outside an applicable time limit. It may be that the wording in r.18(2) that the judge *may* (our emphasis) carry out a preliminary consideration of the proceedings has led to some inconsistencies with respect to whether these issues are dealt with at a PHR or the full or merits Hearing. If a PHR is listed, representatives will want to consider whether they prefer a full tribunal to hear the particular issue and make an application under r.18(3)(a). If you do wish to make an application for a full tribunal, do so in good time, certainly no later than the 10 days required.

For example, consider these issues:

(a) whether the claim has been made within the relevant time limits (as in **Chapter 2**);

(b) whether the claimant is an 'employee' as defined in the relevant legislation;

(c) whether the claimant is qualified to bring a claim because of length of service;

(d) whether the claimant has complied with EA 2002, s.32 (the statutory grievance procedure).

Matters may be dealt with at a PHR particularly if they are likely to dispose of the case entirely. The notice of the PHR will state what the preliminary considerations are to be and you should prepare on that basis. Witness statements and documents should deal with those questions that the PHR is to deal with.

It is likely that orders have been made for documents exchange, preparation of a bundle and witness statements. If there are no such orders, it is still very important to prepare very carefully for a PHR, given the judge's considerable powers at this stage. It is quite common for PHRs to involve legal issues and you may decide, even if it has not been ordered, to prepare an outline argument and copies of cases. This is good practice and is especially valuable where that information is provided to the opposing party in good time. Witness evidence will be given, if appropriate and the format of the hearing will be very similar to that of the merits Hearing (see **Chapter 10**) but will depend on the issue(s) to be determined. Whichever party you are, this hearing is vital, not only because of the issue(s) but also because there is almost certainly going to be further clarification of the claims and issues of the claim(s) and it will be listed for the merits or full Hearing. This is one of your chances to get the best case going forward and making a good impression on the tribunal.

If the case has not been listed for a PHR and you believe it should be, make an application under r.11, setting out carefully why you think holding a PHR may dispose of all or a large part of the case and how it will be consistent with the overriding objective. Alternatively, it may have been listed for a PHR but not to determine points you think it could usefully deal with. Again, make an application in that case, saying why the PHR could also consider other points. Do be aware that listing for a PHR may delay the listing of the full or main Hearing although you could suggest that listing is done for both, which may happen at a CMD.

Case study: Molly Martin's pre-hearing review

Pre-hearing review and clarification of the issues

Our respondent, Just in Time, have already raised in the ET3 that Molly Martin was not an employee but was a 'casual' worker. Later they write to ask for a PHR to decide this question. Unusually, Molly's representative writes and asks that a full tribunal hear that issue and a judge makes an order to that effect.

A PHR is listed and the tribunal hears evidence on that point only. Having heard from the Events Manager, another witness for the respondent and Molly herself, the tribunal decides that Molly is an employee within the statutory definition. The matter is listed for a full Hearing on the merits, with orders being given in a short case management discussion which follows immediately. Note that there has been discussion and a large measure of agreement and the orders given reflect this.

The main text of the judgment from the PHR reads as follows:

Judgment

1. The claimant was an employee of the respondent and her claims for unfair dismissal and discrimination on the grounds of sex proceed to a full hearing listed for 18 and 19 September.
2. The claimant having received sums due to her for unpaid wages and holidays, her claim for unlawful deduction of wages is hereby dismissed on withdrawal.

Orders

1. The Hearing has been fixed for 2 days on 18 and 19 September, this time being considered to be sufficient to hear the evidence, submissions, time for the tribunal to deliberate and give its judgment and, if necessary, deal with the issue of remedy. The parties accept that this is a fixed date which will only be adjourned in exceptional circumstances. Both parties and their representatives are reminded of their duty to assist the tribunal in furthering the overriding objective.
2. The claimant is to send copies of all documents relevant to the issue of remedy including letters to and from prospective employers, and medical reports by 30 July.
3. The respondent has agreed to prepare a joint bundle agreed by the parties by 14 August and supply a copy to the claimant's representative and bring 5 copies to the tribunal hearing.
4. It has been agreed and is ordered that both parties exchange witness statements by 30 August.

Issues

It is agreed that the remaining issues requiring determination by the tribunal are as follows:

1. Unfair dismissal

(i) Was the claimant dismissed during the conversation on 6 December?
(ii) If the claimant was dismissed, was one of the reasons for that dismissal connected to her pregnancy?
(iii) If the claimant was dismissed and the reason was not connected to her pregnancy, was there a potentially fair reason under ERA 1996, s.98(1) or (2) and, if so, what was the reason?
(iv) If there was a potentially fair reason, was it fair or unfair under ERA 1996, ss.98A and 98(4)?

2. Sex discrimination

Are there facts from which the tribunal could conclude that the claimant was subjected to less favourable treatment when:

(a) Comments were allegedly made by Mr Jones about her appearance and/or that of other pregnant waiters on or around 5 November and 6 December?
(b) Changes were made to her shift patterns in early December?

(i)   If there are such facts, was the less favourable treatment on the grounds of her sex?

(ii) If there were changes to her shift patterns, were they made because she had written a letter of complaint?

(iii) If there was such treatment does it amount harassment as defined in section 4A of the Sex Discrimination Act 1975?

(iv) Or, has the respondent satisfied the tribunal that there was a non-discriminatory reason for the treatment?

3. Remedy

If the claimant is successful in her claims for sex discrimination and/or unfair dismissal, what is the appropriate remedy, including any loss of earning and damages for injury to feelings?

Requirement to pay a deposit to continue with procedings

The purpose of this concept, introduced in 1993, was to discourage the pursuit of weak cases. Originally, a full tribunal was needed and it had the power to order a deposit of up to £500 as a condition of allowing the matter to proceed (this amount was increased from £150 in 2001). This power to order a deposit was retained within r.20 of the 2004 Rules but now, as with other PHRs, the matter may be dealt with by a judge alone who will decide, and if:

> the contentions put forward by any party in relation to a matter required to be determined by a tribunal have little reasonable prospect of success, the judge may make an order against that party requiring the party to pay a deposit of an amount not exceeding £500 as a condition of being permitted to continue to take part in the proceedings relating to that matter.

The judge must take reasonable steps to ascertain the party's ability to pay. The party must pay within 21 days, or a further period of up to 14 days if representations are made, then the matter will be struck out. In practice, the question of whether a deposit should be ordered is often considered at the same time as r.18(7)(a), the question being whether the claim has no reasonable prospect or little reasonable prospect being very closely linked. The power to order a deposit is still relatively rarely used but is worth considering as judges may be loath to strike out but may feel that they wish to make it clear that they believe that the claim is weak.

8.3 CASE MANAGEMENT DISCUSSIONS

Case management discussions (CMDs) are specifically provided for within the 2004 Rules. Rule 17 gives broad discretion to the tribunal to arrange for hearings conducted by a judge alone in private. Such hearings are to deal with 'matters of procedure and management' and notice must be sent to the parties to allow them to make written or oral representations. It is clear that there can be no final decisions on 'a person's civil rights or obligations' taken at these discussions. Rule 17(2) specifically refers to r.10(2) to give examples of what can be dealt with (time limits, information, deciding on a fixed conciliation period, staying the proceedings, witnesses, joining of parties, etc.). See r.18(7) for examples of what cannot be dealt with at a CMD but must be decided, if necessary, at a pre-hearing review (see above). If the judge has not listed the matter for a CMD but you feel it would be helpful in preparing for the merits Hearing, it is advisable to suggest it. Make sure that you leave plenty of time for one to be arranged and consider whether some or all of the issues and orders could be arranged by writing rather than needing a hearing.

CMDs are very important hearings particularly in complex cases or where either party has one or more difficulties with presenting their case, perhaps because they are unrepresented or poorly represented, do not have English as their first language or have problems understanding the law or procedure. It is absolutely vital that the representative prepares with care for all CMDs as much can be achieved at this stage. The notice of hearing for a CMD usually indicates that the hearing will attempt to clarify the claims and/or issues and make any orders to prepare for the Hearing. Read the notice with care as it may contain some other suggestions for what will be considered and will state who should attend and whether any preparation by the parties is ordered. In some cases, usually where the parties are both legally represented, there may be an order for those representatives to prepare an agreed draft list of issues or agreed draft orders. Even if the notice does not order such preparation, it is still worth doing as it is work which will pay huge dividends later in the case. Although practice may vary from region to region, you can expect the judge at a CMD to get agreement on the claims and issues to be determined at the merits Hearing and make all necessary orders so that the case can be properly heard. From time to time, it is necessary to have more than one CMD where there have been particularly difficult issues to resolve or where there have been long delays. In those cases, the matters discussed at the CMD may be limited, for instance to listing the case.

Another consideration before the CMD is whether it might be held by telephone. There are some variations in regions and between judges here. The practice in many regions is only to hold CMDs by phone where both parties are represented and there is a large measure of agreement. In that case, you will often find that the judge agrees to a telephone CMD on the condition that an agreed list of issues and orders are provided, often at a specified time before the CMD. In one region almost all CMDs are by telephone. If you feel it should be by telephone if it has been listed as a hearing or that it should not be by telephone where it has been listed as such, make an application, complying with r.11(4) if you are a legal representative, giving good reasons for your request in plenty of time.

Much will depend on the type of case, whether a party is represented and the judge but, as a general rule, the CMD will follow this pattern and you should prepare accordingly. Remember, this hearing is relatively informal and the overriding objective is to assist the tribunal in ensuring a fair trial.

Claims and issues

The first point at the hearing may well be identifying what the claims are. Sometimes this is clear but often it is not. So, for instance, a claim for sex discrimination may well be a direct discrimination claim but may also include a claim for indirect discrimination, harassment and/or victimisation. Similarly, a claim for disability discrimination may be a claim for direct discrimination, disability related discrimination, harassment, failure to make reasonable adjustments and/or victimisation. Whether you are the claimant or the respondent or a representative for either, read the claim form and the response with extreme care before the CMD.

- What claims are clearly made?
- What are the defences?
- Are there any preliminary issues which might be better dealt with at a PHR?
- List what you consider to be the claims broken down into their constituent components.

So, for instance, if there is a disability discrimination claim, do the respondents accept that the claimant fits within the definition of a person with a disability within the Disability Discrimination Act 1995? If not, that will be the first issue for the tribunal. Always consider jurisdiction questions first: for example, is the claim in time, has a grievance been raised if it should have been, and has the claimant met any qualifying period of employment?

If there are no jurisdiction issues, go through each claim one by one, breaking it down into its constituent parts, considering what facts are relevant.

The judge will wish to go through the claims, clarifying those that are unclear and checking whether there are any jurisdictional issues that arise. Sometimes, an unrepresented claimant (and perhaps even a respondent) might attempt to raise new claims at this stage. If any such claim is in time, it is likely that this might be treated as an application to amend the claim and that it might be granted. However, it is more likely that any such claim will be out of time and the judge should consider any such application to amend in accordance with the guidance set out in **Chapter 7**. If there is a serious dispute, it may well need to be listed for a PHR.

Once it is clear what the claims are, the judge will move on to clarify the issues that will need determination at the merits Hearing. You might find that the judge plays a very active role here, particularly where a party is unrepresented and the claim or response is unclear. It may be that the judge suggests that a party reconsider pursuing a weak claim or response. In some cases, judges ask claimants to concentrate their minds on the strongest part of their claim, possibly by asking them to list their best points.

So, for instance, if it has become clear that the claims are as follows:

1. Unfair dismissal under ERA 1996, s.104 (asserting a statutory right).
2. Race discrimination (direct discrimination on dismissal).
3. Race discrimination (direct and harassment for comments made by work colleagues).
4. Unpaid wages (non-payment of outstanding holidays).
5. Breach of contract (no notice).

What issues does the tribunal need to determine from the above claims? The list below is suggested but will depend on the respondent's case and the attention to detail of the parties and the judge.

ISSUES

- Reason for dismissal – what does respondent say is the reason?
- Facts from which the tribunal could conclude discrimination – does the burden shift?
- Holidays – how many claimed, what taken and what outstanding?
- Notice – is it contractual or statutory?
- Remedy – what is claimed?

Listing and orders

Having clarified and agreed claims and issues, the CMD will move on to list the matter for the merits Hearing or take other steps if that is not possible. *Be ready for this part of the CMD.* You will need to have a note of any dates when parties, witnesses and representatives will be unavailable. The Hearing may not be listed for some time, sometimes between three and nine months ahead, depending on the tribunal region and the length of Hearing. You can ring the tribunal office to get an idea when they are listing but it would be advisable to have a rough idea of how long you think the Hearing might be. The more witnesses, the more documentation and the more complex cases take longer. Whilst considering the length of the Hearing, be realistic about what can be covered. Remember that, as well as hearing oral evidence and hearing submissions, the tribunal will need to read the documents (which can sometimes be lengthy), deliberate and give judgment as well as dealing with remedy if the claimant is successful. As a rough rule of thumb, the Hearing needs to be almost twice as long as the time it takes for oral evidence. So, where as the respondent you have four witnesses, the claimant has two and you expect that evidence to take between two and three days, you would be expecting a listing of five to six days.

When arranging the listing of a case, it is becoming more common to try to timetable the Hearing so as to ensure it finishes in the allocated time and to avoid part-heard cases. It might be wise for you to think about this and perhaps draft an outline timetable which you can try to agree with the other party. This might include reading time for the tribunal if there are a lot of documents, time for the oral evidence, submissions, tribunal deliberation time, the giving of oral judgment (usually with reasons) and remedy. This might look something like the timetable below, although it may be even more detailed.

FIVE-DAY HEARING – ALLOW FOUR TO FIVE HOURS PER DAY

- First day – reading day for tribunal.
- Second day – claimant's evidence.
- Third day – evidence from three respondent witnesses.
- Fourth day – representatives' oral submissions (supplementing written argument) and tribunal deliberations.
- Fifth day – oral judgment and remedy.

Some judges will be interested in giving precise timings for each aspect. For instance, '3 hours for evidence-in-chief, 3 hours for cross examination, submissions limited to 30 minutes each' and so on. This should be done by agreement and it should be remembered that it will not necessarily bind the tribunal that eventually hears the case.

Following on from the listing of the case for merits Hearing, the CMD will go on to make orders for disclosure of documents, consider expert and medical reports, a schedule of loss, witness statements, and so on. If you have any specific requests, for instance if you wish to receive a particular document, it is wise to have asked the other party to disclose it voluntarily so that the judge is aware of what problems there are, if any, with the request.

See the case study example above for the sorts of orders that might be made.

Checklist for interim hearings

---

1   What sort of hearing is it? If it is a PHR, what is the issue?
2   Read the notice with care. Do you want to request any changes to the date and what might be dealt with?
3   Can you agree any alteration to the proposed hearing with the other party?
4   If PHR and you believe another preliminary matter can be dealt with at same time, write to tribunal to request this.
5   Do whatever you are told to do, in plenty of time.
6   If there are no instructions, consider what preparations can be made. Read all relevant documents, particularly the claim form and response.
7   What can you agree with other party?

8   If there is enough agreement between the parties, consider whether there is still a need for a CMD at all, and consider a possible request for a phone CMD.

9   After the hearing, do whatever is ordered by the date stated.

10 Note any dates for orders, as some may arise before you receive the written order.

CHAPTER 9

Preparing for the main Hearing

9.1 TIMETABLES

In most cases the parties will need to prepare for the final Hearing in accordance with the timetable as outlined in previous chapters. In this chapter we suggest an approach to getting ready for the Hearing based on good case management principles. However, in following this proposed timetable it is important also to keep an eye on the timetable directed by the tribunal (if there is one) as that must take precedence.

This chapter attempts to mirror the order in which the tribunal will usually expect things to happen. If no order has been promulgated by the tribunal then it is suggested that the order should, logically, be as set out here.

9.2 DOCUMENTS AND BUNDLES

Assuming that the Hearing is now a few weeks away, both parties should by now have a file or folder containing a neatly paginated copy of their own client's documents. Such a folder should ideally be set up at an early stage and if necessary added to and refined as time goes on.

One party, usually the claimant, will be required to prepare the bundle. There are no rules which provide for this, but the claimant often prepares the trial bundle as it is the claimant who has commenced the claim. Some respondents' representatives will prepare the bundle on the basis that they then will have some say in the final layout and can be assured of sending a clearly presented bundle to their counsel. It will, of course, often depend on sources of funding for the case. If the respondent's case is funded under insurance, for example, the insurer may decline to cover the cost of this item.

In any event, it may be worth discussing this issue with the other party. Impecunious claimants can always ask, either in correspondence or at a case management discussion, whether the respondent would be willing to prepare the trial bundle.

Preparing the bundle

Whoever has taken responsibility for preparing the trial bundle should first list all the documents which they have in their possession, either from their client or through inspection of the other party's documents. They should then prepare a draft index for the other party (or representative) to approve. At this stage the list should be numbered but not paginated.

The order of preparation of the final trial bundle should be:

1. Combine the documents provided by both parties.
2. Place the documents in order (see later).
3. Prepare an unnumbered index.
4. Send the index to the other party (or representative) for approval.
5. Once agreement is reached on the content, re-index as necessary and prepare a paginated index.
6. Send out the paginated index and/or one copy of the trial bundle to the other party (or representative) to check.
7. Prepare seven copies of the paginated bundle. One is for the client, three are for the tribunal, one for the other party, one for counsel (where needed) and one for the file. In addition, as a matter of courtesy, a spare copy should be prepared for the witness table.

Note that, if at all possible, the bundle should be paginated before witness statements are finalised (see later) so that witnesses can refer to pages by number in their statements.

What to include

Be careful to include only documents that are relevant to the issues that you wish the tribunal to decide on for you. It can often be the case that the tribunal does not have the opportunity to read many of the documents included in the bundle. This can occur for a variety of reasons. Representatives may be unwilling to exclude any document on the basis that it may ultimately prove to be of relevance. This is not the best use of resources, and documents should only be placed in the bundle if they will be of assistance to the parties and the tribunal in trying the issues.

Alternatively, a representative may neglect to take their witness through the documents or will overlook important documents in taking the witness through their paces. The person conducting the advocacy at the Hearing should ensure that the witness statements refer at all times to any relevant documents and that these documents are referred to by page and number in the statement so that they are not overlooked (see **9.3** for guidance on preparing witness statements).

Failure to agree on the contents of the bundle

If agreement cannot be reached on what documents should go before the tribunal at the main Hearing, a common bundle should still be prepared. The tribunal will prefer a common bundle to two separate ones. If the parties cannot agree on what is relevant or if there are some documents which a party objects to going into the bundle (as they may think they are not relevant or are not genuine), the party preparing the bundle should indicate in the index which documents are not agreed. One approach might be to mark the documents which are not agreed with an asterisk on the index. This would preserve the chronological order of the documents. Another approach would be to place any documents not agreed at the end of the bundle in a separate section.

The order of documents for the Hearing

The trial bundle should contain its own internal logic. This will be partly driven by the nature of the case. However in most (and in the most common) employment tribunal claims, the following order of documents is to be recommended:

1.   *Section 1* – Pleadings (ET1 and ET3).
2.   *Section 2* – Requests and replies (both parties).
3.   *Section 3* – Employment tribunal orders, including directions (but not witness orders).
4.   *Section 4* – Personnel documents relevant to the individual, namely the employment contract, any procedural or policy documents, letter of job offer, job description and/or person specification, letter of dismissal, sample pay slips, P45 (all in chronological order).
5.   *Section 5* – Other documents relevant to the issue being decided. In unfair dismissal claims, this might include:

     (a)   conduct – the disciplinary proceedings: minutes, memos and notes;
     (b)   sickness incapacity – the sickness procedures: minutes, memos, medical reports;
     (c)   redundancy – the redundancy policies and procedures: copies of letters of consultation, interview notes.

     In discrimination claims, this might include:

     (a)   copies of statutory questionnaires and replies;
     (b)   equal opportunities policies;
     (c)   grievance procedures;
     (d)   minutes, memos of meetings;
     (e)   medical records (DDA claims).

6.   *Section 6* – Any correspondence between the parties or their representative once the proceedings were started which is relevant. An example

might be where one party has raised an objection to a certain course of action and indicated that a costs order will be sought. Another will be where correspondence deals with a preliminary issue raised by one party which they want to be dealt with at the outset of the main Hearing, such as the order in which witnesses should be called.

It will not be necessary to put into the bundle all correspondence as some of it is likely to be purely administrative and not relevant to the matters to be decided on by the tribunal at the hearing.

7. *Section 7* – The claimant's schedule of loss and any supporting documents (e.g. letters from employers regarding job applications or letters from the Benefits Agency regarding benefits claimed or paid).

Make sure that each section is clearly separated out and numbered, with a guide at the beginning of the file stating what is in each section.

9.3   WITNESS STATEMENTS

Witness statements should be placed separately. Where they have been exchanged in advance of the Hearing a numbered section containing them can be prepared, preferably in the order in which the party calling the witnesses will ask them to give evidence.

Preparing witness statements

All the key witness statements for each side should be 'in the making' from the outset. They will need to be regularly reviewed. For example, what the claimant tells the adviser at the first interview will often be added to or varied after sight of the respondent's ET3, and so a running note of the client's instructions should be held. This will be an 'organic statement' which gradually develops as the final Hearing approaches.

The main witnesses for the respondent (e.g. the dismissing officer in an unfair dismissal claim) should also have an early draft of their statements in the making.

Some claimants and/or key witnesses for the respondent will prepare their own statements. This will not only save time and costs but will mean that the statement is the witness's own and not that of the solicitor, or of another member of staff in the solicitor's office asked to draft a statement who may only have a limited grasp of the case. Nevertheless the adviser will need to ensure that certain essential ingredients are in the witness statement, even if a draft has already been prepared by the witness.

If you have applied for a witness order you may not be able to prepare a statement for those witnesses, as the order will require them to attend as required by the tribunal. Witness orders are discussed further below.

Good practice when preparing witness statements

1. Make the paragraphs short – remember that a nervous witness will have to read out the statement at the Hearing.
2. Ensure that the statement is, as far as possible, in the witness's own words. A tribunal may be disapproving of a situation where a witness appears to be struggling to read a statement containing complex words or legalistic phrases. Remember that witnesses will need to be cross-examined and must fully understand and be familiar with their evidence-in-chief as set out in their witness statement.
3. Ensure that the statement deals with the order in which events occurred and does not leap around in time.
4. Ensure that the statement refers to the relevant documents in the bundle and, as far as possible, in the order that they are placed in the bundle. The last stage in the preparation of the statement occurs once the bundle is paginated. At that point the adviser goes back to the statement and for each document inserts a reference to the correct page number in the final paginated bundle where that document can be found.
5. Do not allow the witness to give an opinion (for instance 'my view is that the dismissal was fair'). Witnesses (unless an expert witness) will be witnesses of fact and should confine themselves to what they saw, heard or know about the circumstances of the case.
6. Do not allow witnesses to state what the law is, or what they were told or advised by their legal advisers. The former is a matter for the tribunal to decide and take a view on, and the latter is privileged.
7. Do not attempt to coach witnesses in advance. Even more importantly, do not ask them to deal with matters on the day which you have not covered in the statement. Witnesses must be dealt with fairly and understand what they can assist the tribunal with before they enter the witness box. Note that this is quite different from a witness who strays off the point while giving evidence and begins to offer additional information. At that stage there is very little that you can do but see how things progress!
8. Finally, do not expose your witness to unnecessary and cruel cross-examination. A poorly prepared statement, or one which does not cover all the matters on which the witness may be asked to give evidence, means that your adversary will go over all possible ground to establish their client's case in cross-examination or will attempt to push the witness to go further. An example of this would be an organisation giving evidence about an unfair dismissal in which a number of managers or functions was involved. Each witness should be clear about their function in the organisation, their role in the process of dismissal, and which documents they either prepared or saw.

Witness orders

A tribunal can issue an order for a witness to attend and/or produce certain documents for the purposes of giving evidence under r.10. Employers will often need to arrange for their employees to be ordered to attend as a way of releasing them from work and getting paid. Public servants usually need to be served with a witness order.

If either party requires a witness to be ordered to attend to assist in the presentation of the case, that party will have made an application to the tribunal under r.11 for an order to be made under r.10(2). This must not be left to the last minute as the request will usually be dealt with as part of a tribunal judge's administrative business at the end of the day and will be competing with other business, which may necessitate some matters being held over until the following day. Note that the other party does not need to be informed of the request for a witness order.

The tribunal will also need to serve the order (or if you have indicated that you want to serve it yourself, the tribunal will need to return it to you for service) and allow time for the witness to be warned to attend. For all these reasons it is suggested that any application for a witness order should be made at least two weeks before the Hearing date. Consider carefully before you apply for a witness order. If the witness is willing and helpful and only needs an order to show to an employer, that may cause no problems. An unwilling witness may not give the evidence you hope and expect, so such a witness should only be called if the evidence is necessary.

A witness may give evidence for whomever they choose. So if you find out that someone who you thought would be of assistance to your case is now going to appear for the other side, there is nothing you can do about it. The effect will be that the witness will prepare their evidence for the other side and the only opportunity you will have will be to cross-examine (if that might prove helpful to your client's case).

A witness ordered to attend by a tribunal can still be examined by the party who asked for them to be called. The tribunal will require the witness's attendance and it may impose the relevant fine (if it so decides) should the witness fail to attend. If you have not been able to speak to or take a statement from that witness prior to seeking a witness order, you will have no prior knowledge of what the witness will say in the witness box.

Be wary, therefore, of calling evidence by seeking a witness order where you have not met the witness or taken a statement. Even if you think that the witness may be helpful to you (perhaps on your client's recommendation), it may turn out not to be the case. Furthermore, the witness may well feel threatened by being ordered to attend the Hearing and may respond by being reluctant to speak, having a sudden attack of amnesia, or saying the exact opposite of what you expected them to say.

9.4 CHRONOLOGY AND SKELETON ARGUMENTS

A chronology and skeleton argument are now frequently required by the tribunal as part of the orders made in advance of the Hearing.

A chronology

This simply sets out the sequence of events to assist the tribunal in seeing how the case unfolded. A chronology should, in any event, be prepared by the parties' advisers at an early stage, initially by the claimant's adviser. It does not have to be in any particular form and as long as it does not bias the events it will just recite what happened in date order. Do not include in the chronology any contentious matters or any matter not known to the other party (e.g. '1 October – manager deliberately excludes claimant from staff meeting' or '5 November – claimant obtains legal advice and decides to issue proceedings'). If the tribunal has ordered a chronology, the parties must ensure it is agreed within the required time limits and should place it in the bundle or have a set available for the Hearing. The tribunal may or may not wish the opening party to begin by going through the chronology. The tribunal may prefer to be pointed to the chronology and refer to it as evidence is being given.

Skeleton argument

The skeleton argument is a short outline of the facts of the case, the legal issues, and then sets out proposals as to how the law applies to each issue and how it should be interpreted (usually by reference to case law) to support a party's case. This will be prepared by the person doing the advocacy in relation to their own case, whether this person is counsel or a solicitor or adviser. It is less commonly called for as part of the case management orders. However the preparation of the skeleton argument is to be recommended as it can assist the party preparing for the Hearing to focus on the case and it can often assist the tribunal. The ingredients of the skeleton argument are:

- Setting out the issues.
- Stating what the law is in relation to each issue.
- Stating how in your opinion the issue will go in your favour and/or against your opponent's, referring in summary to the law and the evidence.
- Referring to any cases helpful to your client's case to support your arguments (with full case law references provided). Take to the Hearing copies of any cases referred to. If they have been reported in a set of Law Reports, take a copy of the case report. Make sure that copies are also available for your opponent. Tribunals can also take notice of *Harvey on Industrial Relations and Employment Law* (LexisNexis Butterworths) if it contains references as to how the law should be interpreted in relation to your case.

It should be noted that this document is prepared in advance and does not therefore take any account of any changes to the way the case looked before evidence was given, in comparison to how it looks at the end of the Hearing. Nevertheless the skeleton argument should be prepared in advance.

Some representatives take a laptop to the Hearing and adjust their prepared skeleton arguments just prior to summing up the case and presenting submissions. Others will rely on the skeleton argument already prepared, point this out to the tribunal and then state orally where they wish to deviate in the light of the evidence presented at the Hearing. Either way, it is quite common for amendments to be made to the skeleton argument as the Hearing draws to a close.

The point of preparing the skeleton argument in advance is partly to ensure that nervousness does not prevent the representative from ensuring all of the strongest points are highlighted when summing up their case. In addition, it will focus the attention of the representative once again on the basic issues of the case. This may well be necessary if the case preparation has gone on for several months and there are a lot of documents and much correspondence which may have obscured the main issues in the case.

9.5   DEALING WITH THE CLAIMANT'S SCHEDULE OF LOSS

The schedule of loss will be prepared by the claimant's adviser. Tribunals now tend to require it to be sent to the respondent's representative at a fairly early stage as part of paper or oral orders (see **4.4** for the first draft of the schedule of loss for our case study, Molly). In preparing the schedule the claimant's adviser should have an understanding of the remedies which are appropriate to the claim being pursued including the duty to mitigate loss (see **12.2**). The schedule should therefore deal with:

1. Income earned at the point of dismissal.
2. Current income including benefits being paid. All benefits may be under discussion between the parties if the claim is to settle, but only Income Support and Jobseeker's Allowance will be relevant for the purposes of the Hearing because of the Recoupment Regulations (see **12.2**).
3. Evidence of attempts to obtain employment, what type of employment is being sought and the results of these efforts.

Case study: Molly Martin's schedule of loss

Assuming that Molly's case is heard in September, about ten weeks after she has had her baby in June, her adviser will update her schedule of loss just before the Hearing. The chart begun in **Chapter 4** would, by September, perhaps look like this.

Date	Income/ Source of income	No of weeks after dismissal	Loss	Job applications	Result of job application
20 Dec	Nil/None	1	£300 (1 week's net pay)	2 applications via local paper for waitressing jobs	Told 'no vacancies for part-timers'
11 Jan	Nil/None	3	£900 (3 weeks' pay)	1 application for receptionist job at local taxi firm	Told 'no relevant experience'
11 Mar	Nil/None	7	£2,100 (7 weeks' pay)	No jobs applied for – not well	N/A
11 Mar – SMP period	Nil/None	16	6 weeks @ £270 – 90% net pay (£1,620) + 33 weeks at SMP rate of £X (current rate)	No jobs applied for – not well	N/A

Injury to feelings (discrimination claims)

Where the claim is for hurt feelings alone, a schedule of loss would not be appropriate. However, if the claimant has expert evidence to support any evidence of injury to feelings from, for example, a GP or counsellor, this should be disclosed to the respondent as soon as possible. Note that this is not necessarily the same as the medical evidence required to support a personal injury claim arising out of discriminatory behaviour (see **12.3**). In our example, Molly has a claim for discrimination which the tribunal will be asked to calculate in accordance with the guidelines in the case of *Vento* (see **12.3**) and her adviser may prepare submissions on how much they think she should be awarded.

Dealing with loss in the witness statements

It should be noted that it is quite common for tribunals to have a 'split hearing', especially where the issues are complex. They will decide on the substantive (or liability) issues first and then list a separate remedy hearing. It is therefore common for the claimant to deal with loss at the end of the statement of fact or to provide a separate statement dealing with loss and referring to the schedule of loss.

144

The tribunal may not decide until the day whether or not there will be a separate remedy hearing. For this reason the claimant's representative must be fully prepared to deal with loss on the date of the main Hearing and the respondent should be alerted to the loss claimed and should be ready to deal with mitigation or other factors concerning remedy.

9.6 BRIEFING COUNSEL

Counsel may be involved at various stages of preparation.

In some cases, as an adviser you may have had little involvement in your client's preparation for the Hearing and may have been instructed shortly before the Hearing date, mainly to brief counsel to attend the Hearing and present the case.

In these circumstances you should prepare a brief which not only has the bundle and witness statements fully prepared but also indicates the strengths and weaknesses of your client's case and the opposition's case and/or alerts counsel to any special features or difficulties in the case.

Be prepared, even at this late stage, for counsel to advise on possible further preparation or tactics even though the case is virtually ready for a Hearing and case management orders have all been complied with. The client should be alerted to the possibility of the advocate advising on new and alternative strategies at a relatively late stage.

The opposite end of the spectrum is where counsel is involved from an early stage to advise on the merits, settle the grounds to the claim or response form and advise on the contents of and/or assist in drafting witness statements with the key witnesses. They may also advise on what documents are relevant and/or should be disclosed.

Either way, where counsel is to represent the client at the Hearing, counsel will usually prepare the skeleton argument and possibly also advise on or settle a chronology.

The brief for the Hearing should include:

- any previous advice given by counsel;
- a copy of the final bundle;
- all the witness statements;
- any correspondence concerning contentious matters which may come up at the Hearing;
- copies of any directions or orders made by the tribunal.

9.7 PREPARING THE CLIENT AND OTHER WITNESSES FOR THE HEARING

The best practical advice to offer claimants is that they should view a tribunal Hearing in advance of their own. It should be suggested to them that they ring the day before and indicate that they would like to observe a Hearing. With rare exceptions Hearings will be open to the public. If they are unprepared for how the tribunal operates in a Hearing they may be thrown by the apparent formality of the tribunal and in particular by cross-examination. Other witnesses of fact for either claimant or respondent would also be well advised to view a case.

Furthermore witnesses should be advised that it will not be possible for them to fully prepare for cross-examination. Their best (and only) tactic will be to tell the truth or to stick with what they know and/or have already dealt with in chief. Other tips for witnesses are:

- Don't look at the questioner when speaking in the witness box – always look at the panel. This will calm nerves and also ensure that the tribunal hears what you are saying.
- Remember that the person cross-examining is doing a job – they are not there to make personal attacks on witnesses, but they may sometimes be required to attack the witness's credibility to assist their own client, as will the witness's own advocate when cross-examining.
- Don't ask questions in the witness box – just answer them (if able to).
- Remember that the members of tribunal will not have had very much time to familiarise themselves with the background or the issues. Members of the tribunal need to take it all in and be spoken to clearly, slowly and courteously. They may also have questions to ask.

9.8 CONTACT WITH THE OTHER PARTY

It is important to keep in regular contact with your opponent and to establish, if at all possible, a professional working relationship. Some representatives will be on first-name terms, but this still allows them to keep a professional distance and demonstrate to their client that their own clients' interests come first. However, a client will not thank you for appearing to be very familiar or friendly towards your opponent.

On the other hand, there is little merit in being unpleasant or combative towards your opponent or making the preparation for the case a battleground. Think carefully if you are tempted to refuse to co-operate with your opposite number in requests for reasonable extensions or for documents or information, bearing in mind the overriding objective.

Remember that the costs rules will always apply (see **Chapter 13**) and that the costs rules mean that parties' representatives are themselves at risk on costs where they have acted unreasonably in the conduct of the case (with the exception of advisers in the voluntary sector).

9.9 PREPARING FOR THE MAIN HEARING

The adviser

Many employment tribunal Hearings are lengthy affairs. Busy advisers will have numerous other demands on their time and other cases to handle. There will be an issue of time management whenever a case is listed for a Hearing.

If you are representing the client yourself, you must devote time to preparation of the case. By this stage all the steps in this and previous chapters will have been undertaken by you on behalf of your client, and prior to the Hearing you will need to spend time preparing cross-examination and making sure that you are absolutely familiar with the documents.

At the Hearing you will not only have the conduct of your client's case, but you may well also need to be a calming influence on the client and/or other witnesses. If possible, avoid allowing yourself to be distracted by other work until the end of each day. In any event, you will need to find time to prepare for the next day.

If counsel or another member of your work team is representing the client at the Hearing, try to attend at least the start of the Hearing, as clients often feel that they have been left at the door with a representative or advocate with whom they have not yet had a chance to build up a relationship. You may also be needed to deal with any unexpected developments, such as preliminary applications made by the opposing party, or settlement negotiations.

Even if you are not there for the whole Hearing, make sure you keep in touch with the client and/or your advocate at least once a day. Discuss with your client the options for a settlement and try to establish whether the client would be willing to instruct the advocate to negotiate on his or her behalf if settlement was to become a possibility during the Hearing.

The well-prepared client

As well as recommending that a key witness or a claimant goes to a tribunal Hearing in advance of their own, there are other issues for which you can help prepare them.

Stamina

The experience of having to concentrate hard on their evidence and the documents while in the witness box can be very tiring for a witness. Before the Hearing, remind your witnesses to rest, and to avoid late nights and alcohol so that their minds are alert and clear.

Food and drink

Many tribunals are at some distance from places where food or drink can be bought. Only a few have their own canteen facilities. Advise those attending the Hearing to bring a snack and/or a drink with them to ensure that they keep up their stamina.

Talking to the press

Claimants in particular should be aware that there will often be a reporter at a tribunal Hearing who may approach them. The parties need to know if a restricted reporting order has been made or applied for (see **7.5**) which will limit what the press can print about a case.

Parties should consider whether they wish the press to be involved and why. Will publicity help their case? Some litigants may wish to approach the press in any event. They should decide what they wish to say and why. As an adviser, you should be wary of clients who want to have 'trial by journalism' and you should attempt to keep control of any contact with the press, to avoid the other party alleging that your client has prejudiced the conduct of a fair Hearing, which could even lead to a costs order for unreasonable conduct.

The parties should now be ready for the Hearing. Good luck!

CHAPTER 10

The main Hearing

10.1 INTRODUCTION

The main purpose of this chapter is to give guidance on the main Hearing. This might be called the 'merits' Hearing, the 'substantive' Hearing, or the 'full' Hearing, to distinguish it from those hearings which take place before the Hearing to determine all (or most) outstanding issues. **Chapter 8** deals with those hearings which take place earlier in the process, including case management discussions and pre-hearing reviews, and **Chapter 14** deals with reviews.

The starting point should be r.14 and rr.26–7 of the 2004 Rules which specify that there may be more than one hearing which may deal with 'liability, remedies, costs or preparation time'. In practice, the tribunals try to list cases to deal with all those issues together but this is not always possible, particularly where the case is complex or where an application for costs is made at the end of the decision on liability.

We have assumed that you have decided to attend the full Hearing but do remember there is no obligation to do so. The main problem with non-attendance is that the tribunal may need oral evidence given on oath. If there are witnesses who can give this sort of evidence it is not possible to challenge it unless you attend. However, particularly if this is a 'short track' case (see **Chapter 7**) you may send written representations instead. If you do, r.14(5) says that you must make sure the tribunal office has them not less than seven days before the Hearing and that you must copy them to the other party. In circumstances where a party does not attend and does not send any written representations, the tribunal may still determine the claim in accordance with r.27(5) and (6):

(5) If a party fails to attend or to be represented (for the purpose of conducting the party's case at the Hearing) at the time and place fixed for the Hearing, the tribunal may dismiss or dispose of the proceedings in the absence of that party or may adjourn the Hearing to a later date.

(6) If the tribunal wishes to dismiss or dispose of proceedings in the circumstances described in paragraph (5), it shall first consider any information in its possession which has been made available to it by the parties.

Considering the previous similar but not identical r.11(3), the EAT in *Cooke v. Glenrose Fish Co Ltd* [2004] IRLR 866 made it clear that, contrary to the earlier decision of *London Borough of Southwark* v. *Bartholomew* [2004] ICR 358, there was no obligation on the employment tribunal to try to discover the whereabouts of an absent party. However, in the normal course of events, an application for review from such an absent party would usually be allowed.

If you have decided not to attend, inform the tribunal of that fact and send in your written representations. If you attend and the other party does not, you should assist the tribunal with any information you have. If it is your understanding that the other party was to attend, it might be better to suggest that there is an attempt to contact them. This may well prove to be less inconvenient than having to attend another day for a review hearing.

Rules 14 and 27

Rules 14(2) and (3) say this:

(2) So far as it appears appropriate to do so, the judge or tribunal shall seek to avoid formality in his or its proceedings and shall not be bound by any enactment or rule of law relating to the admissibility of evidence in proceedings before the courts.

(3) The judge or tribunal (as the case may be) shall make such enquiries of persons appearing before him or it and of witnesses as he or it considers appropriate and shall otherwise conduct the hearing in such manner as he or it considers most appropriate for the clarification of the issues and generally for the just handling of the proceedings.

Rule 27(2) states:

(2) Subject to rule 14(3), at the Hearing a party shall be entitled to give evidence, to call witnesses, to question witnesses and to address the tribunal.

As can be seen, this gives the employment tribunal, usually through the judge, a wide discretion as to how the Hearing will proceed, although there are many common patterns and practices which most tribunals adopt, which are outlined below. Bearing in mind also the overriding objective in reg.3 and the right to a fair trial in Art.6 of the European Convention on Human Rights, the tribunal's powers concerning how the Hearing is run are not unlimited.

Private Hearings

It is possible that you, the other party or the judge may feel that a private Hearing is necessary. In all other cases, it will be in public (r.26(3)) although, in many cases, there are no members of the press or public present. Quite often the concern is whether the press will be present. This can be dealt with, in some circumstances as set out in the rules, by an application for a restricted reporting order (see **7.5**). There is sometimes a question as to what might be said to be 'in public' where a tribunal room without easy access to the public is used (see *Storer* v. *British Gas plc* [2000] IRLR 495) but, as general rule, the main Hearing will be in a well-marked tribunal room which should state that it is 'in public'. Apart from the situation where a restricted reporting order is in place, there are a few limited circumstances when consideration may be given to holding part or all of the Hearing in private. These are set out in r.16(1) and is where the evidence may involve the person giving it in contravening a statutory enactment, or it was obtained in confidence, or it would cause substantial injury to the person's undertaking. It may also be for reasons of national security and there is no discretion for those reasons if there is a Minister's certificate to that effect. Because the use of these powers is limited and it is a departure from the very well entrenched common law principle that 'justice must be seen to be done', it must be exercised in accordance with Art.6 of the European Convention on Human Rights and reasons must be given. The decision to hold all or part of this Hearing in private will almost certainly have been made at an earlier point as part of the case management process. If it has not been, you should make an application as soon as possible, quoting the rule and facts relied upon.

Split Hearings

Although most tribunals will make the substantive Hearing one which will deal with all outstanding issues of liability and remedy, there are some circumstances where it will be decided to have split Hearings. Again, it is helpful to have decided this before the Hearing begins so that parties can prepare for the necessary parts. If you think that the best course is for the tribunal to make a judgment only on liability, you will need to raise this during case management, the most likely place being the case management discussion. It is only likely to be granted where the issues on remedy are complex and the tribunal or judge can be convinced that a great deal of potentially unnecessary work and preparation will have to be done. If the contested issues on remedy, for example, are whether re-instatement or re-engagement should be ordered, where there are complex financial calculations because of pension loss or share options and similar benefits, the tribunal might agree that that Hearing should take place only if the claimant succeeds on liability. In that case, it is wise to list both Hearings at the same time so that parties, representatives and the tribunal can all have them diarised at an early stage. In some cases, if this is not done, it can be many months before the matter can be re-listed which causes obvious difficulties. If you attend at the Hearing and have come to the conclusion that a split Hearing is a good idea, possibly because you have seen the case at a late stage or because something has changed since the listing of the case, raise it at the commencement of the Hearing after you have tried to obtain the other party's consent to that idea. Guidance from the case of *Iggesund Converters Ltd* v. *Lewis* [1984] ICR 544 makes it clear that the tribunal has to give some direction on which parts of the evidence it will deal with at which Hearing as some aspects are relevant for both aspects, for instance where a conduct dismissal might also lead to a reduction for contributory fault under ERA 1996, ss.122 and 123. Where there are split Hearings or where the only Hearing is a remedy Hearing because of a default judgment, guidance is given at **10.8** on how to prepare for remedy Hearings.

Substantive Hearings

For this, the main Hearing of the claim, there will be a full tribunal unless it is a case where the judge may sit alone (see **Chapter 1**). Obviously, this Hearing is of great importance. This Hearing is where the case will finally be decided, except in the unlikely event of a review or an appeal. Whether you are representing a claimant, an individual or corporate respondent or it is your own case, this is where the majority of your preparation will bear fruit.

This means that you must be ready to deal with all the issues, including remedy if that has been listed at the same time. You will need to be able to address the tribunal orally and possibly in writing, examine and cross-examine witnesses and answer questions put to you by the judge from time to time. In addition to this, you will need to know the facts of the case, where the factual disputes are, the law and how to deal sympathetically with witnesses.

This chapter will consider the progress of the case step-by-step from last minute preparation to the point where the tribunal will decide.

10.2 BEFORE THE HEARING BEGINS

On the first day of the Hearing, it is extremely important to ensure that you have all relevant people with you at the tribunal Hearing centre, at the very latest, half an hour before the Hearing is due to start (which will probably be 10am). It is preferable to be there as early as you can manage. One hour before would be reasonable, as this would allow time to arrange to see people for last-minute matters in a straightforward one- or two-day case.

If you are not familiar with the venue, locate the waiting room, conference room and toilets, and check that your opponent has arrived. It is a good idea to introduce yourself to your opponent and to the member of the administrative staff who will be acting as the clerk. The Hearing list is usually displayed in a prominent place in a public area near the waiting and hearing rooms. Be sure to check who the members of the tribunal will be in case of any perceived conflict of interest. If there is a possible conflict of interest question (see **Chapter 1**), this should be brought to the attention of the clerk, who will raise it with the judge or tribunal. It will then usually be dealt with either by the Regional Judge arranging a swap, if that is possible and correct, or at the commencement of the Hearing.

Of course, all relevant documents should be in the joint bundle. However, if any are missing you should give copies of the new documents to your opponent and the clerk as soon as possible. You will have to ask for permission to refer to them, and permission may be contested. If you have any other written materials, such as a witness statement if there has been no exchange, a chronology, case law or closing argument, make sure that you have enough copies and give one to your opponent.

Parties often leave it until this point to talk about a possible settlement. Obviously, this is not the best approach, and with fixed periods of conciliation, it should not have happened. However, if there is a suggestion that you may be able to reach agreement, do not assume that the tribunal will allow you time to talk without making an application to the tribunal for that time. Many tribunals are very busy and will have 'floaters', that is cases that have been listed but not allocated a tribunal. The tribunal may be anxious to deal with those cases and may well ask you to explain why the discussion is taking place so late in the process. Do remember that a party or a party's representative may be ordered to pay costs (see **Chapter 13**) and this may be a consideration.

If you are acting as a representative, this is your last opportunity to speak to the party and witnesses about the Hearing. It is a good idea to explain the outline of the procedure including details such as where they will be sitting, and whether they can leave the hearing room or ask for a break if they need to. You should not 'coach' a witness (including the party you act for). This means you should not suggest what their answer to any questions should be, but they can be advised generally on their conduct at the witness table. This might include speaking sufficiently clearly and loudly, answering with short answers where possible, always listening carefully to the questions, and answering honestly as they will be on oath or affirmation. It is also wise to tell all those attending the tribunal with your party (including any supporters who are not witnesses) that it is a formal process, that they should be quiet, polite and avoid both facial and oral expressions whilst the evidence is being given. Tribunals and particularly tribunal wing members will notice any signs of intimidating behaviour. Loud sighs, whispers, laughing and giggling will be frowned upon and may lead to a person being excluded from the tribunal room.

You will be taken to the tribunal room by the clerk. It is important that everyone is in or out of the room at the same time. You should therefore make sure that all your witnesses, the party and those of the opposing party enter at the same time. When the tribunal adjourn, if they stay in the room, you should leave promptly and together. This is so that there can be no suggestion that anything has been said without a party. Some witnesses may not need to be present throughout and they can certainly leave to use the bathroom or for other reasons. They can also leave after they have given evidence unless the tribunal thinks it may need to hear from them again.

10.3   PRELIMINARY MATTERS BEFORE THE TRIBUNAL

The most common procedure will be for the judge to commence the Hearing by introducing the tribunal and checking the names of the parties and/or representatives.

The issues

The judge will then check whether there are any preliminary matters to be dealt with and outline the issues. This is a very important part of the process. If the issues have not been agreed or outlined before, either within the case management process generally, at a case management discussion, or pre-hearing review, they must now be agreed so that everyone is aware of what the tribunal will determine that day. If you feel that an issue has been omitted, this should be raised so that there can be discussion on that issue. You should have checked to see whether there has been a previous agreement or direction on the issues. If not, you should consider what the issues are and ask to add any if you feel they have not been adequately covered. An example of the issues in our case study (Molly Martin's case) appears at **8.2**. Further examples may be, in a direct discrimination case, identifying any comparators or, in an indirect discrimination case, identifying the pool for comparison. If the parties are legally represented, it will be very difficult, if not impossible, to raise new issues later in the Hearing, which should rather have been raised at the commencement of the Hearing, unless they have emerged unexpectedly during the hearing of the evidence.

As far as preliminary matters are concerned, these may include the admissibility of a witness or a document, timetabling, or any special requirements, such as excluding a witness from the tribunal room. An unusual request such as the wish to submit video or tape-recorded evidence should be raised at this point if necessary, although, again, it is much more likely to be dealt with properly if it has been raised earlier in the process. There may be issues of confidentiality or regarding the right to privacy and family life under the Human Rights Act 1998 which may be argued where video or tape-recorded evidence has been gathered (see, for instance, *XXX* v. *YYY and ZZZ* [2004] EWCA Civ 231, CA). You should also be aware that the employment tribunal hearing centre may not have the facilities to transmit such evidence and, on a practical level, you should check with the office and if necessary arrange to provide the necessary equipment.

If one of the parties is representing themselves or they have an unqualified representative the judge will almost certainly explain the procedure for the Hearing. Even if you are legally qualified, you should be aware that different regions, judges and tribunals have different practices so do request clarification wherever necessary.

Admissibility

One of the questions that might arise is where a dispute has arisen between the parties on admissibility of some piece of evidence, either oral or in documentary form. The dispute may well have arisen during the course of the parties complying with case management orders so there may not have been sufficient time for it to be resolved before the Hearing. If there is enough time, it is a good idea to warn the tribunal and the other party, in writing, that you will be raising the issue at the commencement of the Hearing. Do be aware that r.14(2) provides for tribunals to admit evidence that is not normally admissible in other courts. This would include 'hearsay', written statements and documents which might be privileged, for example correspondence marked 'without prejudice'. The tribunal can deal with the possible unfairness or admitting that sort of evidence by putting less weight on it than on first-hand direct oral evidence. It does happen that there are arguments at the commencement of the Hearing and that these sometimes reflect the complexity of the rules applied in the civil courts. You might wish to consider that a tribunal will often deal with matters pragmatically and try to avoid getting bogged down on time-consuming technicalities, particularly if they are at the start of a tightly time-tabled Hearing. If you decide that you wish to argue to exclude or include evidence that the other party has not agreed to, guidance on some of these issues can be found in *Digby* v. *East Cambridgeshire DC* [2007] IRLR 585 concerning whether evidence about a previous final warning would be relevant. For some discussion on the admissibility of evidence with respect to settlement discussions see *Brunel University and anor* v. *Vaseghi and anor* [2007] IRLR 592.

Remember, above all, that the evidence must be relevant to the issues. Where there is dispute about it, consider its relevance with great care. It may be that there is a central issue which relies on the credibility of a witness. This generally happens where important facts are in dispute. Although it is tempting for some legally qualified representatives to argue that contentious evidence should be admitted because it 'goes to credibility', you may well be asked to explain how that aspect will affect the tribunal's determination of the facts.

Timetable

The length of the Hearing will have been indicated on the Notice of Hearing. Rule 27 deals with fixing the time and place of the Hearing and requires notice to be given to the parties with information and guidance on the procedure. There will have been an early indication during case management of an assessment of how long the case will be listed for and, if there have been no representations on that estimate and no significant changes, this will be the time allocated. It will vary from an hour to half a day, one or more days.

Broadly speaking those matters which have been allocated to the short track will be listed for something between one and two hours to a day. Those in the standard track are listed usually for a day-and-a-half to around three days for a 'straightforward' unfair dismissal. More complex cases, usually including a discrimination claim may be listed for anything from three or four days to 20 or 30 days, the maximum to date being a race discrimination claim which ran for over 100 days, although this is, of course, most unusual.

If you get to the Hearing and at that point consider that there may not be long enough to deal with the matter, you are likely to be given very short shrift. If the matter genuinely cannot be dealt with within the allocated time, you might have to ask for an adjournment and, depending who is to blame for not having considered this earlier, either or both parties and/or their representatives may well be looking at a costs or preparation time order under rr.40, 44 or 48.

In general, it is expected that the matter will be dealt with within the time allocated and the parties and their representatives will be expected to co-operate in working to achieve that end. If a case management discussion has included an agreement on the allocation of time for the main Hearing you should refer to this and prepare accordingly. If you feel that the time estimate needs amendment you should raise it as soon as possible. Matters such as this which have been agreed between the parties or their representatives are sometimes quite difficult to change without a very good reason.

If the case has not been timetabled at a case management discussion, you may find that it will be done at the commencement of the Hearing. This is especially true of longer cases or those where it appears that it is going to be difficult to deal with all the evidence within the allocated time. Some tribunal regions and some judges now have a practice of allocating time within the Hearing for the majority of the case, so you should give some thought to how you will get through the evidence. Remember that the Hearing is not just to hear the evidence but time will also be required for oral submissions, tribunal deliberations and the giving of an oral judgment and remedy if the claimant succeeds. Remember also that the length of a tribunal day is around four-and-a-half to five hours after short breaks and lunch breaks. As a broad rule of thumb, there will need to be as much time for aspects of the case which do *not* relate to the giving of oral evidence as to the oral evidence itself. After consultation, it is highly likely that the judge will indicate that they will allow fixed time for each party's case and any closing speeches. In particular, closing speeches especially might be time restricted. In most tribunal Hearings you can expect the preliminary matters to include an indication on the time allowed. An example of the timings in our case study can be found at **10.7**.

Opening speeches

An opening speech is not usually necessary as the issues will have been agreed before this point in discussion with the judge or at a case management discussion. Only if there are unusual elements or a new or rarely used legal principle arises will it be worth considering. Be aware that if you do make an opening speech, you may not be allowed to make any closing statements. You may, however, use this opportunity to introduce the bundle of documents. If there are contentious or very long documents, for example, minutes of disciplinary meetings, the tribunal can consider when to read them. In some longer cases, the tribunal may take some time, a morning or even longer, to read documents.

10.4   THE FIRST PARTY'S EVIDENCE

Rule 27(3) and (4) of the 2004 Rules states:

(3)   The tribunal shall require parties and witnesses who attend the Hearing to give their evidence on oath or affirmation.

(4)   The tribunal may exclude from the Hearing any person who is to appear as a witness in the proceedings until such time as they give evidence if it considers it in the interests of justice to do so.

Generally, the tribunals in England and Wales expect all witnesses, parties and representatives to come into the tribunal room together and stay throughout the Hearing, although witnesses who are not parties may well attend only to give evidence. In Scotland the practice has been to exclude witnesses until they give their evidence. If you request that the tribunal excludes a witness in England or Wales, you will need to explain why it is in the interests of justice to do so.

Who goes first?

Who is heard first will depend on the type of case. The general rule is that the person who has the burden of proving the first issue will go first. The normal sequence is therefore as follows.

Respondent to start:

- Unfair dismissal where dismissal is admitted and no issue regarding right to claim.
- Where making any application.

Claimant to start:

- All discrimination claims.
- Where there is an issue regarding the right to claim, for example, is the claimant an employee, does the claimant have the requisite length of service, was the claimant dismissed?
- Breach of contract.
- Unpaid wages.
- Where making any application.

Although it looks from this list as though the claimant starts more often, the majority of claims are actually unfair dismissal with admitted dismissal. As the respondent has the burden of satisfying the tribunal that there was a potentially fair reason for dismissal, the respondent will start.

Many claims are combined unfair dismissal and other claims. It may still make sense for the respondent to go first if the other issues and claims are really subsidiary to that. If the other claims are discrimination linked, consider which is the best way for the tribunal to hear the evidence and discuss with the other party beforehand. If there is any doubt, raise this with tribunal at the beginning of the Hearing.

The description below assumes that the respondent's witnesses give evidence first. General advice given with respect to the first witness applies also to subsequent witnesses.

First witness

The first witness is very important as this witness may well set the scene and the tone for the rest of the case. In a dismissal the first witness may be the dismissing officer or possibly the first person who dealt with the issue. Most people appearing before an employment tribunal as witnesses will not have any previous experience of this or any other formal court appearance. They may never have taken the oath and this, in itself, can make people nervous. Make sure you have spoken to your witness about the level of formality that can be expected.

Witnesses will normally be required to stand to take the oath unless it is difficult for them to do so. This can be done on any of the holy books of the world's major religions. Alternatively they can affirm. Everyone in the tribunal room should be still and silent whilst the oath or affirmation is administered.

Evidence-in-chief

This evidence is usually done by submitting a typed witness statement (see **9.3**). Witness statements may have been exchanged and they may be 'taken as read' or read aloud to the tribunal. Lay members in particular often prefer the statement to be read aloud. In at least one tribunal region, though, the practice is for the witness statements to be 'taken as read' and few if any extra questions allowed. However in the majority of regions and before most judges, the witnesses will be reading their statements aloud, and you should warn them to expect this. The witness should be encouraged to read the statement before giving evidence and should check it carefully. Although this may sound like superfluous advice, do check that witnesses fully understand what they will be reading aloud and that they may be asked detailed questions on it. They must know exactly what it is they are reading and it must be in the sort of language that they would use in ordinary speech. If the witness is for your case you may want to settle them in by asking some non-contentious questions, such as their name, address and so on. This will probably be the tribunal's first introduction to the documents as the first witness is giving their evidence, so it may be slow. Even if they have signed the statement, witnesses may find, when they read the statement before going into the tribunal room or as they are reading it, that there is something they wish to change. A tribunal would prefer a witness to be honest about a mistake made in the statement and it is better that the witness mentions it rather than face difficult cross-examination later.

Hopefully everything of relevance (and no more) will be in the statement. It may be best to ask the witness to pause at the end of each paragraph to go to any particular part of the bundle of documents. Try not to interrupt too often as it can stop the flow and may irritate the tribunal. If there are a large number of documents relating to one witness's evidence, you may suggest the tribunal takes a break to read them.

Further questions

You may possibly be allowed to ask extra questions after the end of the prepared statement. If the statements have been exchanged, the other party (or their representative) may object as there has been no warning of any matters outside the statement. Some judges are quite strict and will not allow extra questions, so be ready for that and ready to argue that the points you are asking about are directly relevant to the issues. There may have been an order on this point so do check.

You should avoid asking 'leading questions' of your own witnesses as much less weight will be put upon the answers. A leading question is one where the answer is implied in the question.

Example of leading and open questions

LEADING QUESTION

'You left work at 5pm, didn't you?' or 'Did you leave work at 5pm?' This question invites agreement.

OPEN QUESTION

If there is an issue about what time the person left work, the question should be: 'What time did you leave work?'

This is an 'open' question as the answer is not implied. For example, it cannot be answered with a 'Yes' or a 'No'.

No such rule about leading questions applies to cross-examination and it is an aspect of representing that often confuses people, not just those who are not legally qualified. You should ask leading questions, or 'lead' as it sometimes called, only when cross-examining.

Make sure that you look after your witnesses. As they approach the witness table, make sure that everything they need is there so that they do not need to search through papers on the table to find a copy of their statement.

If you are the opponent or the opponent's representative be careful about your behaviour whilst the opposing party's witnesses are being asked questions. Be alert and polite. If there is some confusion about a document and you can assist, do so. Your body language should make it clear that you are listening and you should certainly not make facial expressions or any noise. If some of their evidence takes you by surprise, you should try to avoid taking instructions whilst the witness is giving evidence. Either wait or ask for a break.

Cross-examination

The first witness will then be cross-examined. One of the purposes of cross-examination is to put your (or your party's) case. This means that where there is a dispute over the facts, you should ask questions. Another purpose of cross-examination is to secure an 'admission' from that witness. This means that you hope that the witness will admit one of the facts that is important for your case.

If you are cross-examining there are some basic rules. You should be polite. Do not act aggressively or bully the witness. Speak clearly and loudly in language that all in the room will understand. You will have already heard this witness and should therefore have assessed, to some extent, the witness's educational level. But you also have to consider the tribunal, parties, other witnesses and maybe some members of the public who should all be able to follow what is being said.

Have some questions ready, especially if you have seen the statement before. Only ask those questions which are relevant to the issues. Ask questions that are capable of being answered. This usually means making them as short as possible. Do not ask more than one question at a time and do wait for the answer. Accept the answer even if it does not concord with your case unless you believe that further questions will elicit a different answer – they hardly ever do. The judge has to take a note of the evidence. Whilst there have been typed witness statements, for any evidence-in-chief given outside the statement and for cross-examination, a handwritten note is now taken (although some judges use computers) and the evidence may therefore need to be somewhat slower.

There is a so-called 'golden' rule of cross-examination well known to lawyers: do not ask a question if you do not already know the answer. This is worth bearing in mind, but cannot always be achieved. Be aware you do not have to ask questions in cross-examination if the witness has said nothing contrary to your case and be ready to leave matters when you have an answer. Do not get involved in an argument with a witness. Occasionally you may have to suggest that a witness is lying or has fabricated some evidence. Tread cautiously, as your allegation may amount to an allegation of perjury or contempt of court. You might choose to use words which suggest that you do not accept what they say, for example that they may be 'mistaken' or similar euphemisms, unless it is a central piece of the evidence and the witness's credibility is in issue.

Questions from tribunal

You have little control over the questions raised by the tribunal. You cannot object unless the questions are clearly outrageous, but listen and see if you can understand any concerns they may have. They may indicate what the tribunal is thinking but they may well not have had any discussions at this point so do not jump to any conclusions. Some judges and lay members ask lots of questions and some none or hardly any. It may or may not be an indication of anything very significant. More experienced representatives will make a point of learning the names of the lay members and referring to any points they have raised when they ask questions. This may well impress that particular lay member but it may be difficult to be even-handed about it.

Re-examination

This is the opportunity for the party or their representative to clear up matters which have arisen in cross-examination or questions from the tribunal. If you have genuinely forgotten to raise an important matter with the witness and it has not arisen from cross-examination or the tribunal's questions, seek permission to ask it now as this will almost certainly be your last opportunity with this witness. In limited circumstances the tribunal may be prepared to re-call a witness but it is not good practice.

The witness's oral evidence may possibly run over adjournments, most usually lunchtime or overnight. The judge will usually remind witnesses that, as they are in the middle of giving evidence, they should not discuss it with anyone else until they have finished. If the judge does not do this, do remind the witness yourself. For this reason, if for no other, it is highly unsatisfactory if a witness's evidence is interrupted by a long adjournment if the case goes 'part heard'.

That is then the end of this witness's evidence. The witness, unless also a party, can usually be 'released'. If the judge does not mention this, remember to check so that the witness can leave if they wish.

Second and subsequent witnesses

Check whom you need to call. The number (and even the names) of witnesses may have been arranged at a case management discussion. If witness statements are exchanged it may become clear that some witnesses are not needed after all. Do not call unnecessary witnesses, for example 'character' witnesses. This is a fact finding exercise by the tribunal and it will generally only expect to hear those who can give direct (or occasionally expert) evidence if at all possible.

The same procedure as above now follows with examination-in-chief, cross-examination, questions from the tribunal and re-examination for all witnesses, although occasionally there may be nothing beyond the evidence-in-chief. As the Hearing progresses, witness evidence may get shorter as the disputes become clearer. Be flexible. You may have started the Hearing denying dismissal but, if your best witness has not given evidence to support your case, consider whether you should make what is known as a 'concession'. Think your strategy through very carefully and, if you are representing a party, make sure you take clear instructions on any concessions. You are likely to find that the judge makes a note of any concession so that the outstanding issues are clear. If this does not happen you may want to suggest it so that it can be agreed. It is extremely hard, if not impossible, to withdraw a concession made in the proceedings, particularly where there has been legal representation.

No case to answer?

At the end of the first party's evidence, it is theoretically possible to make a submission of 'no case to answer'. For example, if the claimant's evidence has been that he had six months' service and his unfair dismissal claim is not one of those for which no qualifying service is needed, a submission, at this stage, that the tribunal has no jurisdiction may be accepted. A 'no case to answer' submission is only likely to be entertained where, on the claimant's own case, it will be virtually impossible for him to succeed. In *Logan* v. *Commissioners of Customs and Excise* [2004] ICR 1, the Court of Appeal agreed with earlier case law that suggested that such a submission would rarely be accepted at the end of the first party's case.

10.5 THE SECOND PARTY'S EVIDENCE

The same procedure as above applies to the second party's evidence. Build on what you might have gained from other side. You may have to adapt some evidence as matters have proceeded. So, for instance, if you or the other party has made a concession, it will not be necessary to give evidence on that point.

This may mean that sections of the witness statements can be removed (or, more likely crossed out) which will save time. Except where we mention some special factors below, the advice above on the first party's evidence also applies here.

Evidence-in-chief

If the respondent has given evidence first, it is likely that the claimant will be the first witness for the claimant's case. If there is another witness from whom it is necessary to hear first for a particular reason, explain this to the tribunal who will, in most cases, be expecting to hear from the claimant.

The claimant will almost certainly be the most nervous witness, although this may not be obvious to all observers. Remember that, for the most part, the respondent's witnesses have given evidence regarding a relatively minor proportion of their working lives. For claimants it is likely to be much more significant. The case will be of great importance to them and many will have spent a considerable amount of time and perhaps money on preparing for the Hearing. Their investment will have been significant. The claimant may become upset and find this particular part of the process the hardest part. Some of the respondent's witnesses may well have been to an employment tribunal before, but this will most likely be the claimant's first case. If you are representing the claimant, be aware of this and do what you can to put the claimant at ease.

The claimant will still use the prepared witness statement but, of course, some matters may have emerged during cross-examination of the respondent's witnesses. You may well wish to ask questions in evidence-in-chief on those matters. Ask for permission to do this, particularly if there has been a direction that the statements will be taken as read.

Cross-examination

If you are to cross-examine the claimant, be aware of the claimant's probable vulnerability. Take note of the advice above on cross-examination and the particular care needed in dealing with the claimant. In most cases, claimants will have lost their jobs. Whilst the claim may not succeed, an element of genuine sympathy will not go amiss. Use language that the claimant can understand but do not be condescending or patronising.

If there are other witnesses for the claimant treat them with respect. Be aware that if claimants represent themselves they may bring witnesses whose evidence is not completely relevant. If their evidence is likely to be short, it may not be worth complaining about this. The judge and tribunal may have taken the view that, as someone has attended the tribunal, they should hear from them. You do not have to ask any questions if there is no relevant evidence.

10.6 SUBMISSIONS

Written representations

Rule 14(5) and (6) of the 2004 Rules deal with the possibility of written representations:

> (5) If a party wishes to submit written representations for consideration at a Hearing (other than a case management discussion) he shall present them to the Employment Tribunal Office not less than 7 days before the Hearing and shall at the same time send a copy to all other parties.
> (6) The tribunal or judge may, if it or he considers it appropriate, consider representations in writing which have been submitted otherwise than in accordance with paragraph (5).

It is sometimes the case that the time remaining at a Hearing has become too short for oral representations and the tribunal, usually with the agreement of the parties and their representatives, will ask for written representations to be forwarded. This is usually stipulated to be within a certain time so that they can be exchanged with the other party, supplementary submissions made and the tribunal can receive the representations by the time it comes to deliberate and make its judgment.

Submissions are sometimes referred to as 'skeleton arguments' (see **9.4**), especially by legally qualified representatives, but they really amount to submissions or representations. The representative may put in written representations and make an oral statement. If you do this, do not read out what is in writing but highlight those important parts or add to it.

Oral representations

There is also the opportunity to address the tribunal orally as mentioned in r.27(2) (see above) and this remains the commonest form of closing address. Prepare beforehand as it may be expected that you address the tribunal immediately at the end of all the evidence. If you need time, ask for it, but you may find that the time available is quite limited. Base your closing address on the issues as defined and (if you have prepared one) on your skeleton argument.

The order of closing speeches usually depends upon whose evidence was given first. The general expectation is that the party who started will finish. However, this is often changed, especially where parties have represented themselves, when a legally qualified opponent may well make oral representations first.

Content of submissions

Remember the tribunal judgments will be based on the facts as found on the evidence before it. The main purpose of submissions, representations or the closing address is to suggest to the tribunal how to find facts, particularly where they are disputed, and how those facts fit into the legal framework.

In a sense you are hoping to guide the tribunal towards the right answer. If you are able to make concessions, do so. For instance, you might be inclined to accept that not all aspects of disciplinary procedure were followed but argue that those omissions are not sufficient to amount to unfairness. Be prepared to amend what you planned to say to accord with the evidence as given rather than what you hoped would be given.

It may be that you wish to refer to precedents or other case law. Exercise caution here. Employment tribunals can only be bound by a superior court judgment, that is, from the EAT, Court of Appeal or House of Lords (or where there has been ECJ guidance). Judgments from other courts or tribunals may be persuasive but, as a general rule, you would not refer to them. Those judgments from higher courts which are binding tend to be well known to the tribunal. So, for instance, in a misconduct dismissal the tribunal will be very well aware of the principles set out in *British Home Stores* v. *Burchell* [1980] ICR 303 and when considering injury to feelings in a discrimination compensation will know that the guidelines in *Chief Constable of West Yorkshire* v. *Vento* [2003] IRLR 102 should be applied and you therefore will not need to produce copies. Where the relevant case is a little less well known and particularly where it is a very recent judgment, copies should be brought for all the tribunal members and the other party. It is very often the case that there is a feature of the two cases which means the higher court judgment can be distinguished but it may still be of persuasive value. If the tribunal feels that a judgment is relevant, the judge should inform the parties so that they can consider it. In some cases, the judge will refer to a recent case and should be prepared to have copies handed to the representatives for them to consider.

Again, do not argue bad points and do not include irrelevant information. There may have been a previous order or agreement with the tribunal about the length of time that closing speeches will take. If not, you will probably find the judge asking you how long you will be. Do try to be accurate in your estimate of time as there is sometimes an expectation that the length of time used by each representative or party should be roughly equal and you will annoy and antagonise the tribunal by 'running over' by more than a very few minutes. The majority of straightforward one or two-day cases may not need closing speeches of anything longer than 15 to 20 minutes. In a case that has taken a number of days and includes more complex legal points, closing speeches may be closer to an hour but should very rarely be longer than that. Do not take longer than you estimate and be prepared for the possibility that the judge may ask you to reduce the length of your speech.

10.7 JUDGMENT

At the end of submissions the tribunal will normally retire to begin its deliberations. In most cases the tribunal will attempt to come to a judgment on liability first, and to do so on the day of the Hearing. The judge may attempt to give an indication as to how long it might take and suggest that those involved take a break and return at an appointed time. The tribunal may decide that it will 'reserve' the judgment and send all concerned away to wait for it. Again, an indication may be given of when the tribunal will be meeting and how long the delay is likely to be. If you are waiting in the tribunal building this can be a very nervous time for all parties. See **Chapter 11** for more on the judgment itself.

Case study: outline of hearing timetable

Molly Martin v. Just in Time – two-day Hearing, 18 and 19 September

FIRST DAY

9.30am	All parties, representatives and witnesses are present in their waiting rooms.
10.00	Representatives ask clerk to ask for time to try to settle.
10.05	Tribunal asks reps and parties to come into tribunal room to explain why time is required. 10 minutes allowed.
10.15	No agreement reached. Hearing starts – judge refers representatives to orders given at pre-hearing review and asks if issues remain the same. Agreed. Molly's representative asks to exclude a respondent witness on grounds that Molly feels intimidated. Request refused. Molly's representative asks if there can be breaks in the Hearing for Molly to breastfeed the baby and if it can finish at 3pm so that she can collect her other children from school. Agreement reached on breaks and finish at 3pm with a start next day at 9.30am. Representatives agree to written submissions if insufficient time for oral submissions.
10.40	Molly reads from exchanged witness statement. No additional questions.
11.00	Cross-examination including questions on her 'lifestyle', that she is a single parent and acted 'irresponsibly' by becoming pregnant. The judge intervenes and does not require Molly to answer but she becomes upset. 5 minute break.
11.15	Questions from tribunal.
11.45	Molly's witness, Mary, reads from exchanged witness statement. Additional questions, cross-examined and questions from tribunal.
12.30pm	Short lunch agreed so Hearing can finish early.
1.15	Just in Time's first witness, Events Manager, reads from exchanged witness statement.
1.45	Break for baby feeding.
2.15	Cross-examined, including questions from tribunal and re-examination.
3.00	Finish for day – agree to start next day at 9.30am.

9.30am	Just in Time's second witness, the Managing Director, reads from exchanged witness statement. Cross-examined, questions from tribunal.
10.30	Babyfeeding break.
11.00	Closing speeches. Both reps hand in written representations and make short speeches – 15 minutes each.
11.30	Tribunal begins to decide and ask parties to return at 1pm.
1.00pm	Oral judgment given. Molly succeeds. She has been automatically unfairly dismissed as the dismissal was connected to her pregnancy and there was no adherence to the statutory disciplinary procedures; and there was direct discrimination on the grounds of sex because the reason for her treatment was on the grounds of pregnancy. The comment on her appearance and the changes to her shifts were also an act of direct sex discrimination. She fails in her claims for victimisation and harassment. Parties asked to return at 2pm for remedies.
2.00	Molly gives further evidence on attempts to find work and how the dismissal affected her. Her baby was born on 18 June and she is expecting to be unable to work for another two months. She receives statutory maternity pay from the Department for Work and Pensions but no other benefits. She will then start looking for work and hopes to find work within three months, although it has to fit into her more complicated childcare arrangements. She is cross-examined on her childcare arrangements and asked why the baby's father cannot assist. Molly's representative asks for break for Molly to ring to ask her mother to pick the children up from school as she would like to have judgment on remedies today.
2.30	Submissions on remedies.
3.00	Remedies judgment. (See judgment in **11.5**.)
3.15	Costs application made and opposed.
3.45	No costs order made.

10.8 REMEDY HEARINGS

If the Hearing that you are to attend is just to deal with remedies, take care to prepare for that only. In some circumstances it will be because there has been a default judgment under r.8 and in others it will be where there has been a Hearing on liability decided in the claimant's favour. If there is a judgment on liability, including a default judgment, read it with care as any remedy can only be based on what has been determined by the tribunal. Consider all aspects of potential remedy (see **Chapter 12**), not just compensation but whether re-instatement or re-engagement is to be considered, whether there might be any reductions or increases to awards for contributory conduct, failures to follow the statutory procedures, under s.98A(2) or a *Polkey* reduction. In discrimination claims, remember that the tribunal may also make a recommendation or declaration and that injury to feelings is usually awarded as well as damages for personal injury arising out of the discrimination.

CHAPTER 11

Orders and judgments

11.1 INTRODUCTION

Rule 28 of the 2004 Rules specifies the different sorts of orders and judgments that may be made by a tribunal or a judge whilst the case progresses. A number of the interim matters that arise have been discussed in previous chapters but here we will briefly cover orders made on interim matters before moving on to concentrate on those decisions which are finally determinative – now called judgments. Previously they were all called 'decisions' or 'orders', and summary or extended reasons were given depending on the type of case, any request of the parties, or at the judges' discretion. Rather than a distinction between summary and extended reasons, there is now a process for requesting written reasons within time limits. All judgments must be put into writing.

The Rules state that the judge may issue an order or judgment orally at the end of a Hearing or can reserve to a later date. It is also clear that the judgment may be made by a majority and, if it is a two-person tribunal, the judge has a casting vote. Please be aware that, where the judgment is a majority judgment, the minority member (which could be the judge) should be identified, with reasons both for the majority and minority judgments. Indeed, where there is to be a majority judgment and, particularly where it is the judge in the minority, the Court of Appeal have recommended that efforts are made to try to reach unanimity and extra time may be needed for this purpose (see *Anglian Home Improvements* v. *Kelly* [2005] ICR 242). Majority judgments are quite rare and often form the basis of an appeal.

11.2 DECISIONS ON INTERIM MATTERS INCLUDING ORDERS

Most of these will be decided by a judge alone dealing with a matter of case management, a case management discussion, or a pre-hearing review (covered in **Chapters 7** and **8**). Those orders will be contained, in most cases, within a relatively short document requiring a person to do or not to do something. There are examples of orders, one at **7.4** and another which is a judgment with an order, as in our case study at **8.2**.

Rule 30(1) states that reasons must be given for orders if a request is made *before* or at the Hearing. Again, reasons may be given orally or reserved. If you are involved in a matter at an interim stage and believe that the decision which will be made is one of some importance and that you may consider asking for a review or making an appeal (see **Chapter 13**) remember to ask, before or at the Hearing, for reasons to be given.

Unless orders

By the 2004 Rules (see rr.10(3) and 13(2)) a judge can now make what is known as an 'unless order'. This will state, in terms, that something must be done by a certain date by one of the parties or the claim or response may be struck out *without further consideration of the proceedings or the need to give notice or hold a pre-hearing review*. The order may have been made upon application by a party or on the judge's own motion. It is generally made where there has been a previous failure to comply with a particular order. So, read any orders you receive carefully and note the following:

- Which party has to comply, claimant or respondent or both?
- What do they have to do?
- When do they have to do it by?

If you are the party ordered to do something and you cannot comply or cannot do so by the date specified, make an application immediately, either for the order to be set aside or for more time. If you cannot comply, for instance if you do not have the document ordered to be produced, you should say so. The case of *Coles* v. *Barracks* [2006] EWCA Civ 1041 makes it clear that it is wrong to make an unless order in these circumstances. Note that there has been some debate about whether such an unless order can be reviewed and the EAT judgment in *Uyanwa-Odu and Adeniram* v. *Schools Office Services Ltd and Caxton Islington Ltd* (unreported, UKEAT/0941/05) states that an unless order should be considered to be a 'conditional judgment' and is therefore capable of review. You must have good reasons to make such an application and, if you are a legal representative, you must comply with r.11(4) by giving notice to the other party. If you are the other party and there has been no compliance with the order, you may wish to write and ask whether the claim or response has been struck out.

11.3 JUDGMENTS

This section concentrates on decisions which dispose of the case or an issue in the case, usually after the main Hearing. However, such a decision may have been made at an earlier point, for instance at a pre-hearing review on an issue about the right to claim. Rule 28(1)(a) defines a judgment thus:

... a final determination of the proceedings or of a particular issue in those proceedings; it may include an award of compensation, a declaration or recommendation and it may also include orders for costs, preparation time or wasted costs.

In most cases the tribunal will come to its judgment on the last day of the Hearing or if the Hearing has lasted a day or shorter than a day, at the end of the case. The judge will usually inform the parties of the judgment in open tribunal after the tribunal has retired to deliberate. How long it may take the tribunal to decide and how the judge informs the parties will depend much upon the length of the case, the complexity of the facts or law and whether there is sufficient time within the allocated Hearing.

As outlined in **Chapter 10**, the parties' participation in the Hearing usually ends with the representatives' submissions. The tribunal will then retire to consider the judgment while the parties wait. Sometimes the wait may be for minutes and sometimes for considerably longer. The judge may be prepared to give an indication of the likely wait, especially if a party or representative has an important commitment. This can be a very difficult time for the parties (and, indeed, the representatives) and they may want to discuss the probable outcome. Unless it is very clear what this is going to be, either because of some piece of clear evidence or a strong indication from the tribunal, too much speculation at this stage could be unwise. It is, however, worth reviewing the range of possible outcomes so that you are prepared to deal with matters that arise from the judgment, such as remedy or costs. It may be that the judgment on liability will mean the matter can be settled.

You will then be called back into the hearing room for the judgment, and the judge will announce the judgment orally. It is common practice for many judges to give the judgment and reasons orally and for this to be recorded on tape so that it forms the basis of the written judgment. Alternatively, some judges give an oral judgment which is a summary of the tribunal's decision and, generally, a summary of the reasons. The first approach may take some time and it is not always easy for the parties to sit through, especially the losing party. If a client is not used to legal procedures, it could even be that after listening to a judgment given in this way the client might have no idea at the end of the judgment whether he or she has won or lost, although this really should not happen. Judgments may be reserved and then will contain written reasons. If there is any doubt, ask for clarification.

Rule 30(1) and (2) gives some clarity as to the procedure although there remains some discretion for the tribunal or judge. It is clear that a tribunal or judge must give reasons for any judgments and that 'Reasons may be given orally at the time of issuing the judgment . . . or they may be reserved to be given in writing at a later date'.

What is different from the previous 2001 rule is contained in r.30(3) which states:

Written reasons shall only be provided:

(a) in relation to judgments requested by one of the parties within the time limit set out in paragraph (5); or
(b) in relation to any judgment or order if requested by the Employment Appeal Tribunal at any time.

The time limit set out at r.30(5) is either orally at the Hearing or within 14 days of the date the judgment is sent to the parties.

It may happen that a judge has noticed a mistake in the oral judgment before the written judgment (when correcting the draft, for instance). In that case, depending on the significance of the error, you may be asked if you wish to address the tribunal further, possibly in writing but also possibly at a further hearing (see *Hanks* v. *Ace High Productions Ltd* [1978] ICR 1155).

If the giving of the judgment is the end of the substantive matter (for instance if the claimant has lost or if it already includes the remedy), there still may be some other matters that need to be dealt with by the tribunal. These range from small administrative points (such as the return of documents, requests for written reasons, and witness expenses) to matters which require the exercise of judicial discretion, usually an application for costs (see **Chapter 13**). If not, the parties, representatives and any other persons who attended the Hearing are expected to collect their belongings and leave promptly, especially as the tribunal may well have another case to hear.

Reserved judgments

If it seems appropriate to the tribunal, it may choose to reserve its judgment. This will most commonly occur where there has been a large amount of evidence, usually given over a number of days. It can also happen where there have been disputes of facts or where the tribunal has simply run out of time on the day.

The announcement that the tribunal intends to reserve its judgment can come at any time during the progress of the case, and may even be at the end of the parties' submissions. However, sometimes the judge may indicate at the end of evidence that written submissions will be acceptable. This will usually be accompanied by orders for directions in respect of exchange and replies.

11.4 WRITTEN REASONS

If there is a reserved judgment or it has been given orally and reasons have been requested, the written document should be received within about a month. The internal Tribunal Service target is for written judgments to be sent to the parties within 28 days and the statistics indicate that this is achieved in the vast majority of cases. In cases where the Hearing has been longer than a few days, the written reasons or reserved judgment may well take longer. If there is a long delay, it may be necessary to write to the regional judge who will bring their influence to bear. It is clear that unreasonable delay can be an infringement of the parties' rights to a fair trial under Art.6 of the European Convention on Human Rights and, in the case of *Somjee* v. *United Kingdom* [2002] IRLR 886, the UK Government was ordered to pay costs and damages to an applicant whose employment tribunal claims were very substantially delayed over a number of years. More recently there has been guidance from the EAT on employment tribunal delays. In four conjoined cases under the lead case of *Kwamin* v. *Abbey National plc* [2004] IRLR 516, the suggestion was made that a reserved judgment should be sent to the parties within three-and-a-half months of the submissions. Although any delay longer than that is not, of itself, a reason to set the judgment aside, it clearly leaves the judgment more open to challenge on those grounds. If you face significant delays, it might be worth reminding the regional judge of this guidance.

The information which must be contained within written reasons for a judgment is now set out at r.30(6) and you can expect all judgments which include reasons to contain the following:

(a) the issues identified as relevant;
(b) if some issues have not been determined, what they were and why they were not determined;
(c) any findings of fact relevant to the issues;
(d) a concise statement of the applicable law;
(e) how those findings of fact and applicable law have been applied to determine the issues; and
(f) where there is an award of compensation, a table showing how the amount has been calculated.

Always check the written document carefully when it arrives. It will state the date when the judgment was sent to the parties and should be signed by the judge, although there are provisions in r.31 if the judge is incapacitated.

Checklist: written judgments

1. Does it accord with what you were told orally?
2. Does it comply with r.30(6)?
3. Are the names of the parties, witnesses and representatives correct?
4. Are the dates and sums of money correct?
5. What is the date it was sent to the parties?
6. Are there further matters outstanding – remedy or costs?
7. Are there grounds for a review?
8. Are there grounds for an appeal?
9. What must you do now?

Minor errors

Minor errors can either be ignored or, if a party or representative feels it is important, they can dealt with by the 'slip rule'. This is covered in r.37 which gives the judge (or the President, Vice-President or regional judge) power to correct clerical or accidental mistakes by drawing up a signed certificate. For example, there may be a misspelling of a name or an incorrect calculation which it would be better to have corrected. A polite letter to the tribunal office outlining the mistake and asking for correction will usually clear up the matter.

More important errors

Where the error cannot be corrected using the slip rule, you may wish to consider applying for a review under rr.34–6 (see **14.3**). There are time limits and this procedure should not be used if you believe that the 'error' is really one of law.

Errors of law

This is the right time to consider an appeal under s.21 of ETA 1996 (see **Chapter 14**). Again, there are strict time limits for lodging an appeal. In most cases, appeals to the EAT can be on a point of law only and will not be a re-hearing but legal argument only. Consider the possible outcomes, including costs and delay, when deciding whether to launch an appeal.

Going back for remedy or further matters?

It may be that the written judgment is on liability only and, if the claimant has been successful, there will need to be a further hearing for remedy. This will probably be covered in a letter accompanying the written judgment or it may have been arranged earlier. It is usual practice for the tribunal to have agreed a provisional date for a remedy hearing or to ask for available dates of all parties. If you have been given a date, immediately check the issues with the client and any witnesses. Remember, questions on remedy may include mitigation, the reasonable practicability of reinstatement, the job market and so on (see **Chapter 12**). You may well need further documentation or evidence and witness statements may be useful. The judgment on liability may well contain orders that need to be complied with before the remedy hearing. These will most commonly be an up-to-date schedule of loss, witness statement exchange and a joint bundle of documents. If this has not happened and you want the judge to consider further orders, write to the tribunal office and follow the guidance on case management contained in **Chapter 8**. This may also be an opportunity to settle the matter. Avoid the temptation of being so angry at losing or happy at winning that you forget that the level of compensation may still be relatively low. The services of ACAS remain available to both parties in discrimination cases and should be used if possible to avoid the costs of a further hearing.

If, when you have considered the judgment, you want to apply for orders for costs, preparation time or wasted costs, on any of the grounds set out in rr.38–48 (see **13.2**) you will need to write to the tribunal to ask for a hearing.

Remember that for both the above matters and for any review the tribunal will be the same as the tribunal that dealt with the hearing on the merits, except in some cases where the regional judge can appoint a tribunal. This means that securing a hearing date may be difficult and the more flexible you can be the better.

11.5   CASE STUDY: JUDGMENT IN MOLLY MARTIN'S CASE

As discussed in **Chapter 10**, in our case study claimant Molly Martin was successful at the main Hearing. **Chapter 12** deals with remedies and you should be aware of the principles to be applied when awards are considered. You will also see from **Chapter 10** that there was an application for costs and wasted costs orders and the written judgment deals with all those issues decided on at the main Hearing. For those of you who have not seen a tribunal final judgment an example of what it might look like in Molly's case is provided. Most is in outline only, as we have not, for instance, rehearsed all the relevant facts. The example includes headings for those areas that r.30(6) indicates should be covered but remember that this is an example only. Judgments are written by judges who all have different styles, and the content of the judgment will vary considerably depending on the circumstances. In the example we have drafted, for illustrative purposes only, what might be recorded in writing for the judgment itself, the issues, conclusion and remedies. It is relatively short and often judgments will be longer than this. Those parts of the judgment that are in bold are similar in style and language to an employment tribunal judgment in a case like this. The other parts are a rough guide to what might be included. Copies of actual judgments are available from the central office in Bury St Edmunds although a case name and number will be needed. In many ways, employment tribunal judgments are similar to EAT judgments, which may be viewed on the EAT website (**www.employmentappeals.gov.uk**).

The figures for remedy used in the examples have been kept relatively simple by using round numbers where possible. It will be important to double check any statutory amounts as these may alter in the future. This example shows how the calculation might look in a case where the period of loss was quite short. You should be aware that, where possible, assumed net figures have been used.

175

Case study: judgment

In the South West Employment Tribunal Case No 33333/00

Molly Martin	Just in Time Catering Limited
Claimant	**Respondent**

Before Ms X Judge
Mr Y and Mrs Z Members   On 18 and 19 September

Representation
For claimant: Ms C, Solicitor X Advice Centre

For respondent: Mr B, Consultant Employment and Discrimination
Law Direct

Judgment

1   The claimant was dismissed and that dismissal was for a reason connected to her pregnancy and is therefore unfair.

2   There has been no compliance with the statutory discipline and dismissal procedure and the dismissal is also unfair on those grounds. It is just and equitable to apply an uplift to the awards made to the claimant of 50%.

3   The claimant was also discriminated against on the grounds of her sex when she was dismissed for a reason connected to her pregnancy.

4   The claimant was less favourably treated on the grounds of sex when Mr Jones made comments about pregnant employees and when her shifts were changed.

5   The claimant carried out a protected act when she complained about Mr Jones' comments but was not subjected to less favourable treatment as result. Mr Jones' comments did not amount to harassment of the claimant.

6   The respondent is ordered to pay the following sums to the claimant:

Basic award – £1,550

Compensatory Award – £17,116.87

Injury to feelings – £7,869

TOTAL = £26,535.87

Reasons

INTRODUCTION AND ISSUES

1   The claimant worked for the respondent's catering firm for over 5 years. She claims sex discrimination and unfair dismissal. The respondent disputed that she was an employee within the definition contained within the Employment Rights Act 1996 but that issue was decided at a pre-hearing review on 11 March with the decision being that the claimant was an employee. The claimant's claims for unpaid wages were also resolved at that hearing.

2   *[Reference may be made here to the issues as clarified at the end of the PHR (see 8.2) or there may be a summary to this effect.]*
The remaining issues are therefore to decide whether the claimant was less favourably treated on the grounds of her sex if a comment was made about her appearance at work when pregnant or about other pregnant employees, when there were changes to her shifts and whether they were because she had complained about the events manager's comments, whether the claimant was dismissed which is

denied by the respondent, and, if she was, what was the reason for that dismissal. The claimant alleges that the principal reason for the dismissal was on the grounds of pregnancy and therefore automatically unfair. If the tribunal so finds, that dismissal would also amount to less favourable treatment on the grounds of the claimant's sex. The tribunal must also consider whether there was any failure to follow the statutory dispute resolution procedures and, if there was, whether to apply an increase to any award. If the claimant succeeds in her claim the tribunal must also consider what is the appropriate remedy, including any uplift and injury to feelings.

3   Facts

    [*The relevant facts would be listed here. For instance, the details of the conversation between Molly and Mr Jones and where there is a dispute, which version is preferred by the tribunal and why.*]

4   The law

    [*The relevant legal provisions would be listed here. There would be reference to ERA 1996, s.95 for the question as to whether there was a dismissal, ERA 1996, ss.98 (including s.98A for failures to follow the statutory procedures) and 99 for the unfair dismissal claim and EA 2002, s.31 for the uplift and SDA 1975 for the sex discrimination claim. There may also be reference to case law where that is appropriate and has been referred to for any part of the decision. For instance, it is likely that this tribunal will refer to* Vento v. Chief Constable of West Yorkshire *[2003] IRLR 102 (see* **12.3**) *for the amount of damages for hurt feelings and* Igen v. Wong *[2005] EWCA Civ 142 on the burden of proof in discrimination cases. As there has been an application for costs the judgment will refer to the provisions of rr.38–48 of the Employment Tribunals (Constitution and Rules of Procedure) Regulations 2004 (see* **13.2**).]

5   Submissions

    [*The judgment may record in outline the submissions made by the representatives.*]

6   Conclusions

6.1 The tribunal is satisfied that the conversation which the claimant had with Mr Jones was one which contained elements of discrimination on the grounds of sex. His comment on her appearance was one which is clearly linked to his perception of how a pregnant waitress would appear to customers. That comment could not have been made to a man, as men are never pregnant, and to the claimant's detriment. His comments on other pregnant employees was also less favourable treatment. The changes to the claimant's shifts were because she was pregnant, was to her detriment and less favourable treatment on the grounds of sex. The claimant's claims for direct sex discrimination succeed.

6.2 The tribunal is also satisfied that the claimant was dismissed on that day and that she understood and Mr Jones meant her to understand that she was no longer required. That dismissal was clearly on the grounds of her pregnancy as the respondents were otherwise content with her work and raised no complaint about it. The claimant's claims for automatic unfair dismissal and sex discrimination succeed. As there was no attempt to follow the statutory dismissal procedure, the dismissal is also unfair on that ground.

6.3 The tribunal are also satisfied that the claimant's letter of complaint was a protected act but have found no link between that and the change in shifts. We do not accept that the acts of discrimination set out at 6.1 above amount to harassment as defined. The claimant's claims for victimisation and harassment under the SDA therefore fail.

7   Remedy

    The claimant does not wish the tribunal to consider reinstatement or re-engagement. She has not secured employment since her dismissal partly because she was unsure about her position and partly because she was heavily pregnant and then a new mother. Her baby was born on 18 June and the tribunal is confident that she will secure employment within 10 weeks from the time she will commence looking for employment when the baby is four months old as she has already arranged childcare. We believe it is just and equitable to increase the relevant awards (the compensatory award and injury to feelings) by 50% as there was a complete failure to complete any of the statutory procedures. The tribunal believes that the acts of discrimination were relatively serious and had a detrimental effect on the claimant. Not only was she dismissed, which of itself is serious enough, but adverse comments were also made about her appearance which the tribunal accepts were discriminatory and offensive. We assess the injury to feelings at the top of the lower band of *Vento* (above) and, taking everything into account, award the sum of £5,000 under that head.

8   The calculation of her financial loss is as follows:

Unfair dismissal

1   Basic award – 5 years × maximum weekly pay £310 = £1,550
2   Compensatory award

Loss of earnings

a) Loss of earnings from dismissal to the date when the claimant would have commenced maternity leave – 16 weeks net pay £300 × 16 = £4,800
b) Loss of 90% statutory maternity pay 6 weeks @ 90% × 270 = £1,620
c) Loss of statutory maternity pay @ £112.75 to Hearing 5 × 112.75 = £563.75
d) Loss of statutory maternity pay for a further 10 weeks × £112.75 = £1,127.50
e) Loss of earnings from end of maternity leave until she is expected to find employment 10 weeks × 300 = £3,000

Total loss of earnings (a+b+c+d+e)	£11,111.25
Loss of statutory rights	£300
Total	£11,411.25
+ 50%	£5,705.62
TOTAL COMPENSATORY AWARD	£17,116.87
Sex discrimination	
Injury to feelings	£5,000
+ 50%	£2,500
+ interest at 6% from date of discriminatory act	
(6 December to Hearing £1.23 per day × 300)	£369
TOTAL INJURY TO FEELINGS	£7,869

9   Costs

The claimant's representative applied for a costs order and a wasted costs order on the grounds of the respondent's unreasonable behaviour in arguing that the claimant was not an employee and their representative's improper line of cross-examination at the Hearing. We have considered that application seriously and heard the respondents' representative's objection to both applications. We do not accept that it was unreasonable or misconceived for the respondent to dispute the claimant's employment status. Though the claimant succeeded there was an arguable case that she was not an employee. The tribunal does believe that the questioning of the claimant about her private life at the Hearing was disruptive and abusive but the judge intervened quickly and the claimant was not required to answer. We therefore make no order for costs or wasted costs in this case.

[*The judgment will then be signed by the judge and dated on the day when it was sent to the parties.*]

CHAPTER 12

Remedies

12.1 REMEDY HEARINGS

The employment tribunals are given a statutory power to award compensation to successful claimants in tribunal Hearings. Much of the unfair dismissal award can be estimated in advance by an adviser as it is quantifiable by reference to ERA 1996. In unfair dismissal claims the basic award can usually be precisely calculated and the compensatory award can be prepared for based on existing and likely future losses.

Tribunals usually ask the claimant to provide a schedule of loss as part of the case management orders for the preparation for the main Hearing. Further orders may require an update of the schedule to be prepared for the tribunal and the respondent nearer to the date of the Hearing (see **Chapters 6** and **9**). This assists in looking at what financial loss can be attributable to the dismissal. In any event an up-to-date schedule of loss should have been prepared by the claimant in advance of the main Hearing. At all times in the preparation for the Hearing the claimant's adviser should be focussing on remedy and on what the client is likely to recover should he or she be successful. Claimants should also ensure that they are mitigating their loss by doing whatever they can to replace the loss of income consequent on a dismissal.

Discrimination claims are less easy to quantify but can be reasonably predicted by reference to average and median awards reported: see especially the Equal Opportunities Review which provides an annual update. Case law guidance will also assist (see below).

Remedies can be awarded by the tribunal immediately following the main Hearing where the employee's claim is successful, and claimants must be in a position to quantify their loss and address the tribunal on remedy.

The remedy may be decided on and awarded at a later remedy hearing but it will be difficult to predict whether the tribunal will decide to take this approach. The tribunal may only decide on that point once the Hearing is concluded or when it is ready to give judgment. The claimant must be fully aware of the appropriate remedy and how it should be calculated and should be prepared to present the calculation as soon as it is requested.

After the claimant has outlined in evidence the financial losses in relation to the matter or matters claimed (and we shall see how different claims carry their own remedy), the respondent can challenge any perceived failure on the claimant's part to mitigate the loss by, for example, asking the claimant about efforts to find work and/or by bringing evidence to the Hearing of job vacancies which would be suitable for the claimant.

This chapter will outline the remedies available in all the main tribunal jurisdictions and how these are calculated by the tribunal.

12.2   UNFAIR DISMISSAL REMEDIES

The remedies for unfair dismissal are calculated under the powers given to the employment tribunals in ERA 1996, ss.112–27. There are three options. The first two are that the tribunal will order that the successful claimant is either reinstated or re-engaged by the respondent, with all lost earnings and associated payments made to the employee in addition. The third alternative (which must be made if there is no order for reinstatement or re-engagement) is an order for compensation.

Reinstatement or re-engagement

An order for reinstatement is to allow the employee to return to work with all pay and conditions preserved as though there had never been any break. The effect of an order for re-engagement is to start the employee back in employment with the employer either in the old job or a suitable alternative.

Neither of these orders will be considered by the tribunal unless the employee has expressed a desire for such an order (see ERA 1996, s.113). In the ET1 at point 5.7, the claimant will have been asked to state whether the remedy of reinstatement or re-engagement was being sought.

The order for reinstatement carries with it a far more stringent requirement on the employer to comply than the order for re-engagement, as the employee must be returned to the same job as if the employee had not been away during the period of time which elapsed since the dismissal.

The tribunal may order that the employee is to be reinstated, with any reduction in wages to allow for benefits paid whilst awaiting the outcome of the tribunal claim, or any wage increases or benefits that would have been received in the same period (see ERA 1996, s.114).

The order for re-engagement is more flexible. It does not have to be with the same employer but could be with a successor or an associated employer and the job does not have to be the same job as long as it is a suitable alternative. The loss of pay and benefits calculation is the same as for reinstatement (see ERA 1996, s.115).

181

Steps to making the order for reinstatement

In deciding whether to make one or other of these orders the tribunal has first to consider whether it should make an order for reinstatement. In doing that it will take into account the following factors which are set out in ERA 1996, s.116:

- whether the claimant wishes to be reinstated;
- whether it is practicable for the employer to comply with such an order;
- whether, where the claimant has caused or contributed to the dismissal, it would be just to make this order.

The question of practicability is one which has been the subject of dispute. There are often issues regarding whether good industrial relations have been irrevocably damaged arising out of the circumstances which existed prior to the employee's dismissal or arising out of the dismissal itself. Usually the tribunal will not make the order if there is some evidence to support this type of breakdown or if it is persuaded that it would be wholly inappropriate to reinstate, perhaps due to the nature of the offence (see *ILEA* v. *Gravett* [1998] IRLR 497: swimming instructor who had regular contact with the public found guilty of indecent assault on young people). More recently in the case of *Johnson Matthey plc* v. *Watters* (unreported, EAT 0236-38/06) the employer attempted to resist such an order on the basis that the relationship of mutual trust had broken down. The tribunal found that the issue between the employer and the employee which led to the dismissal was not that serious (although the employee succeeded in showing that the dismissal was not within the band of reasonable responses). The employer would have to 'swallow its pride' and accept the order.

Steps to making the order for re-engagement

Having followed the above steps, if it decides against an order for reinstatement the tribunal will move on to decide if it should instead order re-engagement. In coming to this decision the tribunal will take into account:

- whether the claimant has expressed a wish to be re-engaged;
- whether it is practicable for the employer or a successor or associated employer to comply with the order;
- whether the claimant contributed in any way to the dismissal.

Even if the tribunal decides that the employee did contribute to his or her dismissal (by an act of misconduct) the order can still be made but the employee may suffer a reduction in the amount received (see later for contributory fault).

However, the tribunal in considering the question of practicability can take conduct into account.

Otherwise the tribunal must award sums which will place the employee in the same position as if the employee had never lost that job, just as for reinstatement.

There is no obligation for employees to show that they have mitigated their loss in the period of unemployment leading up to an order for reinstatement or re-engagement. However, in making either order the tribunal can reduce the sum payable by the employer by any wages paid to the employee by another employer in the interim period.

Practicability and permanent replacements

In considering reinstatement or re-engagement, ERA 1996, s.116 makes specific provision for where the employer has found a permanent replacement for the dismissed employee. The employer cannot rely on the fact that a replacement has been found as an example of impracticability unless the employer can show that the job could not be done without appointing a permanent replacement or that the employer has not heard from the employee indicating a wish to be reinstated and that appointing the permanent replacement was the only way to get this particular job done.

If orders are made for reinstatement or re-engagement and the employer fails to comply, the tribunal will, as well as awarding the compensatory award (see below) make an additional award of compensation to the employee of between 26 and 52 weeks' pay (see ERA 1996, s.117).

The statutory procedures

If the tribunal finds that the employer has failed to follow the statutory procedure in relation to an employee's dismissal they can make a finding of automatic unfair dismissal. This is provided for in ERA 1996, s.98A and for the employee there is a requirement of a minimum of a year's service to qualify. Once such a finding is made the tribunal will then calculate the employee's loss. When calculating the basic award, the tribunal will award the claimant a basic award of a minimum of four weeks' gross pay (calculated in line with the statutory limit on a week's pay – see below), unless it would cause injustice to the respondent. See ERA 1996, s.120(1A) and (1B). If the employee would have received less due to shorter service the award is increased to four weeks but there is no additional basic award where the calculation leads to an award of four weeks or more. The calculation is set out below.

In addition, EA 2002, s.31(3) provides for adjustments to awards where the employer has failed to complete a statutory disciplinary and dismissal procedure (DDP). The employee's compensation can be increased by between 10 and 50 per cent unless the tribunal considers that there are 'exceptional circumstances' for not doing so. This is usually referred to as the employee's 'uplift'. Under EA 2002, s.31(2), if the fault for not completing a procedure lies with the employee, the employee may suffer a reduction of between 10 and 50 per cent to the compensatory award (not the basic award).

Principles of calculation: the basic award

In most unfair dismissal cases the tribunal remedy will not be for reinstatement or re-engagement but will be compensation. The way in which this is calculated is set out in ERA 1996, ss.119–22.

The basic award is calculated on the same principles as a statutory redundancy payment. The factors which are used to calculate the sum are:

- age of the employee;
- length of service of the employee;
- reference to a week's gross pay; and
- a maximum of 20 years' service is factored in.

The calculation is set out in ERA 1996, s.119.

The differences between the calculation of the basic award and the statutory redundancy payment are that the employee can receive a basic award where the employee is under 18 (unlike the statutory redundancy payment). In addition, in certain circumstances (for example, dismissal for being a member of a trade union, or in health and safety unfair dismissal cases, or automatically unfair dismissal for failure to use the statutory disciplinary and dismissal procedures (DDP)) there will be a statutory minimum basic award. Furthermore, as we shall see later, the basic award can be subject to a reduction.

There is a statutory limit on a week's gross pay which is reviewed and uprated annually in February. In 2008, the limit on a week's gross pay is £310 per week, which will be reviewed in February 2009. The successful claimant receives:

1. $\frac{1}{2}$ a week's pay for each full year worked for that employer up to the age of 22;
2. 1 week's pay for each full year worked year while aged 22–40;
3. $1\frac{1}{2}$ weeks' pay for each full year worked while aged 41 and over – subject to the maximum of 20 weeks

The calculation must be in relation to a full year and the reckoning is done backward from the date of dismissal.

Reductions

In certain circumstances a reduction will be made to the basic award. These are:

- Where the claimant has already received a contractual or statutory redundancy payment or any other payment in respect of a dismissal procedure operating under the contract.
- Where the tribunal finds that the claimant has unreasonably refused an offer of employment by the respondent which would, if accepted, have had the same effect financially as if the claimant had been reinstated, the tribunal may reduce the basic award by any amount it considers to be just and equitable.
- Where the tribunal finds that the claimant has contributed to the dismissal by his conduct (called 'contributory fault'). The amount to be reduced is whatever the tribunal considers to be 'just and equitable' (see ERA 1996, s.122(2)). This amount is calculated on a percentage basis of the full basic award and can be up to a 100 per cent deduction. It can include a deduction to take into account misconduct which occurred prior to dismissal but which may not have come to light until after dismissal (see *Devis* v. *Atkins* [1977] IRLR 314).

Principles of calculation: the compensatory award

The compensatory award is not to punish the employer or enrich the employee. The adjustments under EA 2002, s.31 do, however, have a somewhat punitive aspect. In general, the guiding principle is to aim to compensate the employee financially for losses incurred as a result of being unfairly dismissed. The tribunal will always be guided by what is 'just and equitable' (see ERA 1996, s.123(1)) and will take into account:

- the fact that financial loss is occasioned by the dismissal (i.e. is the loss attributable to action by the employer?);
- benefits which the employee might have had but for the dismissal;
- the effort made by the employee to find other work ('duty to mitigate').

There is a statutory limit on the compensatory award which is reviewed and uprated annually in February. The limit from 1 February 2008 (for dismissals which occurred on or after that date) is a maximum of £60,600. The salary element of the compensatory award is in relation to net pay, in contrast with the basic award where the calculation is based on a week's gross pay.

Heads of loss

Tribunals will award under the following heads of loss.

1. *Loss of salary.* Salary loss actually occasioned by the dismissal, including anticipated bonuses or increases in salary which have been introduced in the workplace by the time the Hearing takes place. When calculating what would have been due to the employee during the notice period the

tribunal will award whatever actual payments the employee would have received in that period. So if the employee would have been on a reduced sick pay in that period for example, that is the level of pay he or she will receive. (See *Burlo* v. *Langley* [2007] IRLR 145.)

2. *Loss of future salary.* The tribunal will decide how far into the future to go. Where the claimant has found a new job prior to the Hearing date, the tribunal will calculate loss up to that date. Where the new job pays less than the old the tribunal will attempt to ascertain a period of time in which it would be just and equitable to award the claimant the differential. This may depend on the skill level of the claimant or the skill level the claimant is now working at, and the claimant's efforts to mitigate (see below).

3. *Loss of fringe benefits.* These are 'extras' which the employee received and may be benefits such as a company car or a free nursery place.

4. *Loss of pension rights.* These are sometimes difficult to calculate, but it should be noted that the claimant's adviser should do this calculation. A good guide to calculating pension loss, which you can also expect the tribunal to use, can be found in an HMSO handbook *Compensation for Loss of Pension Rights: Employment Tribunals* published by the Stationery Office in November 2003.

5. *Loss of statutory rights.* This is usually a nominal sum of around £200–£300 to compensate for the fact that the claimant will need to work for a new employer for 12 months in order to acquire the right to be able to claim unfair dismissal and two years in order to gain redundancy protection.

6. *Expenses.* This means expenses occasioned by the dismissal. Examples would be an ex-employee who had to travel some distance in order to find work as a result of the unfair dismissal.

Mitigation

The duty to mitigate places an obligation on claimants not to sit back and wait for the tribunal Hearing but to make every reasonable effort to reduce their loss by finding other employment. Under ERA 1996, s.123(4), tribunals are obliged to consider the main court rules concerning the victim's duty to mitigate loss in ascertaining the claimant's losses.

The claimant should be encouraged from the outset to provide proof of efforts to mitigate loss. This will usually take the form of a record of attempts made to find alternative employment.

The tribunal will expect claimants to fully mitigate their loss. Where the claimant has applied for work of a commensurate level, and has not been successful, the claimant will be expected also to apply for lower paid or lower skilled work. If no effort to mitigate can be demonstrated, the tribunal will have to try to ascertain when the claimant might have obtained work and at what salary level.

Note that although the onus is on the claimant to mitigate, where the respondent asserts that the claimant has failed to do so it will be up to the respondent to prove that this is so (see *Bessenden Properties Ltd* v. *Corness* [1974] IRLR 338, CA).

The manner of the dismissal

For many years it has been understood that an employment tribunal could not award a sum for compensation for the manner of dismissal. The case of *Dunnachie* v. *Kingston Upon Hull County Council* [2004] UKHL 26 finally decided this point and that does indeed remain the position. Financial loss therefore is all that can be awarded in unfair dismissal claims.

Approach to calculating unfair dismissal remedy: Employment Rights Act 1996, s.98A

Section 98A(1)

It is likely that subsection (1) of s.98A will be repealed under the new legislation (the Employment Bill 2007), which will review the current regime whereby internal disputes procedures are linked to the jurisdiction of the tribunals to hear claims and to the way in which remedy is looked at (see **Chapter 1**).

The current position is that the tribunal will look at the parties' use of the statutory disputes procedures as part of calculating the unfair dismissal remedy.

In unfair dismissal claims, as we have seen, a failure on the part of an employer to complete a DDP in circumstances where it should have done so will result in a finding of automatically unfair dismissal. The minimum basic award will be four weeks' gross pay, calculated according the statutory limit of a week's pay. The tribunal will have no obligation to examine fairness under ERA 1996, s.98(4), as is usually the case. Case law (*Venniri* v. *Autodex Ltd* (unreported, UKEAT 0436/07)) has indicated that the tribunal should look to see if the statutory disciplinary and dismissal procedure has been followed by the employer as a preliminary step in looking at the appropriate way to approach the unfair dismissal (and thus the appropriate approach to remedy) unless the employee has specifically conceded that he or she is satisfied that the statutory procedures have been followed. This confirms the correct approach for the tribunal in assessing unfair dismissal remedy, as set out in the case of *Software* v. *Andrews*, discussed in further detail below.

In looking at s.98A(1) therefore, a tribunal may decide that the dismissal is automatically unfair and award the appropriate basic award as referred to above. It will then look at the appropriate compensatory award, examining the heads of loss set out above, and any mitigation carried out by the employee.

The tribunal will also exercise its powers to increase the compensatory award by between 10 and 50 per cent where they find the employer has failed to complete the statutory disputes procedure – dismissal or grievance (which the employee will have commenced in a constructive dismissal claim). There is no guidance for tribunals as to the factors which are relevant in deciding on the amount of the uplift. In some cases they may penalise an employer who pleads ignorance of the statutory disputes procedures. In other cases they will minimise the increase for the same reason (see *Cex Ltd* v. *Lewis* (unreported, UKEAT 0013/07)).

Once the tribunal has decided that s.98A(1) bites it can then look at the question of whether, had there been a procedure followed, the principles known as the *Polkey* reduction can be applied. Under this sub-section the tribunal can look to see whether the employee would have been dismissed if the statutory DDP had been followed. If it decides that the dismissal would have occurred in any event, it can reduce the amount of the compensatory award to whatever level it believes to be appropriate. The tribunal can look to see if the chances of a dismissal occurring in any event were anything between 0 and 100 per cent, and award compensation accordingly. The *Polkey* reduction applies to a case where the dismissal has only become unfair by virtue of a failure to follow the statutory procedure and where that has been found to have been the reason for the unfair dismissal, following the case of *Polkey* v. *AE Dayton Services Ltd* [1998] ICR 142. The compensatory award may only be limited to how long (possibly a matter of weeks) it would have taken the employer to follow the statutory procedure.

Section 98A(2)

Section 98A(2) of ERA 1996 will come into play in assessing fairness and remedy once the tribunal has decided that s.98A(1) will not apply; that is, once it has decided that the statutory DDP has been followed by the employer. Where the DDP has been used, the tribunal will then examine any other aspects of procedure which might lead to a finding of unfair dismissal. The tribunal can look at any procedural defect (see *Kelly-Madden* v. *Manor Surgery* [2007] IRLR 17) to decide if the decision to dismiss was procedurally flawed in the general sense.

If it finds flaws it will then look to see whether, in spite of those flaws, there was more or less than a 50 per cent chance that the dismissal would have occurred in any event. If the tribunal finds that the chances of a dismissal occurring in any event are less than 50 per cent, the dismissal will be unfair. If, in spite of a procedural flaw, the chances of dismissal having occurred using a fair procedure are more than 50 per cent, the dismissal may be upheld as being nevertheless fair. This is known as the partial *Polkey* reversal.

Where the finding is one of unfair dismissal, the *Polkey* calculation will once again apply and a reduction to the full award made to reflect the time it would have taken to dismiss following a proper and fair procedure. However, in this case the reduction will never be below 50 per cent as this is the threshold for the difference between a fair and unfair dismissal in looking at the fairness of procedures used.

There are some useful guidelines for how the tribunal should generally approach the question of calculating compensation, including factoring in the *Polkey* reduction, in the case of *Software 2000* v. *Andrews* [2007] ICR 825:

(1) In assessing compensation the task of the Tribunal is to assess the loss flowing from the dismissal, using its common sense, experience and sense of justice. In the normal case that requires it to assess for how long the employee would have been employed but for the dismissal.

(2) If the employer seeks to contend that the employee would or might have ceased to be employed in any event had fair procedures been followed, or alternatively would not have continued in employment indefinitely, it is for him to adduce any relevant evidence on which he wishes to rely. However, the Tribunal must have regard to all the evidence when making that assessment, including any evidence from the employee himself. (He might, for example, have given evidence that he had intended to retire in the near future).

(3) However, there will be circumstances where the nature of the evidence which the employer wishes to adduce, or on which he seeks to rely, is so unreliable that the tribunal may take the view that the whole exercise of seeking to reconstruct what might have been is so riddled with uncertainty that no sensible prediction based on that evidence can properly be made.

(4) Whether that is the position is a matter of impression and judgment for the Tribunal. But in reaching that decision the Tribunal must direct itself properly. It must recognise that it should have regard to any material and reliable evidence which might assist it in fixing just compensation, even if there are limits to the extent to which it can confidently predict what might have been; and it must appreciate that a degree of uncertainty is an inevitable feature of the exercise. The mere fact that an element of speculation is involved is not a reason for refusing to have regard to the evidence. An appellate court must be wary about interfering with the Tribunal's assessment that the exercise is too speculative. However, it must interfere if the Tribunal has not directed itself properly and has taken too narrow a view of its role.

(5) The s.98A(2) and Polkey exercises run in parallel and will often involve consideration of the same evidence, but they must not be conflated. It follows that even if a Tribunal considers that some of the evidence or potential evidence to be too speculative to form any sensible view as to whether dismissal would have occurred on the balance of probabilities, it must nevertheless take into account any evidence on which it considers it can properly rely and from which it could in principle conclude that the employment may have come to an end when it did, or alternatively would not have continued indefinitely.

(6) Having considered the evidence, the Tribunal may determine

(a) That if fair procedures had been complied with, the employer has satisfied it – the onus being firmly on the employer – that on the balance of probabilities the dismissal would have occurred when it did in any event. The dismissal is then fair by virtue of s.98A(2).

(b) That there was a chance of dismissal but less than 50%, in which case compensation should be reduced accordingly.

    (c)   That employment would have continued but only for a limited fixed period. The evidence demonstrating that may be wholly unrelated to the circumstances relating to the dismissal itself, as in the O'Donoghue case.

    (d)   Employment would have continued indefinitely.

However, this last finding should be reached only where the evidence that it might have been terminated earlier is so scant that it can effectively be ignored.

Other adjustments to the compensatory award – a substantively unfair dismissal

It will be seen from the preceding sections that the tribunal will initially focus on the question of procedure when looking at unfair dismissal remedy and the compensatory award. If there is no question of an unfair procedure there will be no consideration of a reduction in relation to the time it would have taken to follow a fair procedure, statutory or otherwise. Sometimes it will be hard for the parties and the tribunal to untangle the difference between a procedurally and a substantively unfair dismissal in terms of the correct approach to remedy, and one effect of s.98A appears to be that unfair dismissal remedy focusses now much more on the question of procedure.

Where procedural and substantive issues are being factored in as part of calculating remedy it will be useful to note that a number of factors will be taken into account in adjusting the claimant's award for unfair dismissal. There are also guidelines for the order in which the adjustments should be made.

(1) *Just and equitable.* The tribunal is given the discretion to assess the both the basic and the compensatory award on just and equitable principles and this may mean a reduction in the award. For example if misconduct comes to light after the decision to dismiss the employee was known, it cannot be relied on to resist the unfair dismissal claim but if there is a finding of unfair dismissal it may be a factor in reducing compensation (see *Devis* v. *Atkins* [1977] ICR 622).

(2) *Contributory fault.* The tribunal can deduct a part of the compensatory award (using the just and equitable maxim) in circumstances where it believes that the employee has contributed to his dismissal by virtue of his conduct. Section 123(6) of ERA 1996 states:

> Where the tribunal finds that the dismissal was to any extent caused or contributed to by any act of the complainant, it shall reduce the amount of the compensatory award by such proportion as it considers just and equitable having regard to that finding.

The basic award can also be reduced in relation to 'any conduct' of the employee (see ERA 1996, s.122(2)). Note the difference between any 'act' and any 'conduct', which gives the tribunal a broader scope for reduction of the compensatory award.

The reduction in the compensatory award for a failure on the employee's part to complete the statutory procedures under ERA 2002, s.31 will be made *before* any reduction in the compensatory award based on the employee's contributory fault. In addition any reduction of a redundancy payment to the statutory level where the employee has received a more generous contractual payment is made before the contributory fault reduction. See ERA 1996, s.124A.

Where the tribunal is considering both the *Polkey* reduction in relation to the use of procedures and the question of the contributory fault, it will therefore adjust the award firstly to reduce compensation to the level to reflect the fact that an employee would have been dismissed anyway, say within three weeks, and then look at the contributory fault reduction, which as we have seen can apply to both the basic and compensatory awards with slightly different tests for each.

The principles and the process of deduction are summarised in guidelines in the case of *Digital Equipment Co Ltd* v. *Clements (No.2)* [1997] IRLR 140, CA. However that case preceded the introduction of EA 2002 and the deductions now calculated for incomplete use of the statutory procedures. So taking those factors into account, the order of deductions will be as follows.

(1) The tribunal must give full credit for any sums already paid by the employer to the employee for the dismissal. This sum can now take into account any contractual severance payments (e.g. contractual notice pay) which have been made (see *Hardy* v. *Polk (Leeds) Ltd* [2004] IRLR 420).

(2) Deducting any sums for an employee's failure to mitigate his or her loss (e.g. turning down job offers) or where the employee has partly mitigated his or her loss, by for example taking less well paid work following their dismissal.

(3) Deduction for any failure to complete the statutory procedures (EA 2002, s.31 deduction).

(4) Deduction for any contractual redundancy payment in excess of the basic award.

(5) Any *Polkey* reduction for where the dismissal would have occurred in any event had a fair procedure been followed.

(6) Any contributory fault reduction.

(7) Reduce down to the statutory cap. If the award is now above the statutory cap currently in force, a reduction will be made at this stage.

(8) Decide if an award should be made.

Finally, given the overriding principle that an award should be made in such amount as it considers just and equitable, the tribunal will have the discretion to decide if an award (as calculated in the above manner) or no award at all should be made. An example of where no award would be made may be where the tribunal subsequently discovers the claimant has behaved very badly in relation to the respondent (e.g. theft, assault).

The Recoupment Regulations

Under the Employment Protection (Recoupment of Jobseeker's Allowance and Income Support) Regulations 1996, SI 1996/2349, the employment tribunal is enabled to reduce a part of the award to the claimant who has been in receipt of either of these two benefits. These Regulations operate so as to order the respondent to pay back to the Benefits Agency the amount paid to the claimant between the date of dismissal and the date of the Hearing, and the balance is then paid to the claimant. The tribunal will send out a detailed breakdown of how it applies the Recoupment Regulations and how they are to be applied in that particular case when it sends out its judgment.

The employment tribunal will serve a notice on the Benefits Agency at the Job Centre where the claimant is registered for the benefit payment. The Benefits Agency is required to inform the employer of the amounts paid in benefit to the claimant during the relevant period set out by the tribunal award, i.e. the period during which compensatory award for loss of wages was calculated.

Having received the notice, the employer must repay to the Benefits Agency the amount paid out to the claimant by way of benefits, and pay the balance of the award to the claimant.

Note that the Recoupment Regulations do not apply to all state benefits. For example, they do not apply to housing benefit (see *Savage* v. *Saxena* [1988] IRLR 182). There are various conflicting EAT decisions as to whether they apply to incapacity benefit. It is arguable that they do not as this benefit is not by way of income but is more akin to a provision to compensate for ill health (and as such is more like an insurance benefit than a source of income).

Finally it should be noted that there is no obligation to have any regard to the Recoupment Regulations when settling a case.

Increases of award under the Employment Act 2002

The tribunal can reduce an award where the employee has failed to follow the statutory procedures. In addition there are circumstances where the tribunal can increase the award:

1. Where there has been a finding that the employer failed to give a statement of employment particulars under ERA 1996, s.1. This award is between two and four weeks' pay.
2. Where the employer has failed to follow either of the statutory procedures (for no allowable reason as provided for in the Dispute Resolution Regulations) and there is a finding of automatic unfair dismissal, at least four weeks' basic award pay must be awarded. This may have the effect of increasing a basic award or an award made on reinstatement or re-engagement.
3. Where, as we have seen, the employer has failed to use the statutory procedures, the compensatory award can be increased by between 10 and 50 per cent.

4. If the failure to follow either the statutory DDP or the GP is found to be due to the harassment or threat of harassment on the part of the other party (one of the situations in which the parties are exempted from the requirement to follow a procedure), the fault will be attributable to that other party when calculating the increased or reduced award of between 10 and 50 per cent under EA 2002, s.31.

Case study: calculating Molly's award

Molly has calculated her basic award to be five weeks' pay for each of the five full years she worked for Just in Time @ £310 per week = £1,550.

On the basis that Molly wins her unfair dismissal claim the following facts are inserted to show how her compensatory award might be calculated

COMPENSATORY AWARD

Loss of net income: 16 weeks' loss of income up to the date when she would have started her maternity leave @ £300 per week = £4,800

Loss of statutory maternity pay

(i)   90 per cent of her actual net pay for the first six weeks – £270 × 6 = £1,620
(ii) Actual SMP rates – Molly is claiming 5 weeks up to the date of the Hearing and then 10 weeks thereafter @ £112.75 (2007/08 rates) = £1,691.25

Future loss of earnings: she estimates will take another three months to get a job after she is ready to return to work, say 10 weeks @ £300 = £3,000

ADJUSTMENTS

She has looked at what these may be and in what order they may be made and her summary is as follows:

(1) No notice pay or contractual severance pay was paid.
(2) Mitigation. Molly did not seek work at all from the end of February as she became ill and then would have started her maternity leave by early April – so she believes the tribunal will agree that there was no failure to mitigate by not seeking work once she was better by the end of March.
(3) Failure to use the statutory disputes procedures. She wants the tribunal to find that the employer failed to use a DDP in dismissing her and had also failed to respond to her Step 1 grievance statement and she will claim an uplift to her awards (unfair dismissal and discrimination) of 50 per cent. The tribunal does so – see judgment in **11.5**.
(4) Any payments of contractual redundancy pay – N/A.
(5) Any *Polkey* reduction. She believes none will be deducted as Molly would have worked up to the date her maternity leave was due to start had her employment not been terminated.
(6) Contributory fault. Molly does not believe this will impact on her award (and indeed this is what the tribunal found – see judgment in **11.5**).
(7) Added sum for loss of statutory rights – £300.
(8) The Recoupment Regulations will apply as Molly received Income Support from 1 April to the date the baby was born. She then received Maternity Allowance. The employer will repay payments to the benefits agency and they will be deducted from Molly's final compensatory award.

> **THE REMEDY**
>
> How the tribunal approached and calculated Molly's unfair dismissal award and her discrimination award (see below) is set out at **11.5**.

12.3 DISCRIMINATION REMEDIES

Damages in discrimination claims are regarded as tortious (see *MOD* v. *Cannock* [1994] IRLR 509). A breach of a discrimination statute is a statutory tort. Like personal injury claims, which are also tortious, the injured party is entitled to be paid compensation for his or her foreseeable loss which will include loss of earnings and prospects as well as injury to feelings. The principle of 'just and equitable' does not apply when assessing discrimination damages.

The six discrimination enactments (dealing with age, race, sex, sexual orientation, disability and religion and belief) all have similar provisions stating that compensation is to be calculated (and can include a sum for injury to feelings) in the same way as it would be in the county court.

The measure of damages for hurt feelings

There is no limit on the amount which the tribunals can award for hurt feelings and it will be for the claimant to provide evidence of the degree of hurt and distress suffered.

However in the case of *Vento* v. *Chief Constable of West Yorkshire Police* [2003] IRLR 102, the Court of Appeal provided financial guidelines to assist tribunals in assessing injury to feelings compensation. They prescribe that these awards are likely to fall into three bands:

1. £15,000–£25,000 for the most serious cases, where for example there has been a long campaign of harassment proved;
2. £5,000–£15,000 for the middle range;
3. £500–£5,000 for the lower range, for example an isolated incident.

The guidelines recommend that awards of less than £500 should not normally be made. It would be 'exceptional' to award a sum higher than £25,000. Note, however, that this case is now a number of years old and tribunals may look to go above the maximum band.

Other heads of damage

In addition to hurt feelings the tribunal can award other heads of damages which take into account the foreseeable loss by the claimant for the discriminatory treatment.

Loss of earnings

This will include loss to date and future earnings. In *Essa* v. *Laing Ltd* [2004] IRLR 1313 it was held that foreseeability was irrelevant in assessing the extent of the claimant's injury and loss; only causation need be established. The tribunal will not, however, award loss of earnings twice where it has already been required to assess a compensatory award for an unfair dismissal claim brought as part of the same proceedings (see ERA 1996, s.126).

Aggravated damages

Where the tribunal believes that the behaviour of the respondent is particularly reprehensible, it can award a sum for aggravated damages: see e.g. *HM Prison Service* v. *Johnson* [1997] IRLR 162. This award may reflect (as in the case of *Johnson*) a failure to investigate what was clearly a serious campaign of discriminatory harassment. The aggravated damages element may also refer to the behaviour of the respondent in conducting the proceedings (see *Zaiwalla and Co* v. *Walia* [2002] IRLR 697).

Personal injury

Where claimants allege that the discriminatory treatment has adversely affected their health and caused them to suffer a personal injury, the claimants must have their claim heard, and damages for the personal injury assessed by the employment tribunal annexed to the claim for discrimination (*Sheriff* v. *Klyne Tugs (Lowestoft)* [1999] IRLR 481, CA).

Preparation for this aspect of the claim must take place at an early stage and medical evidence is likely to be called, if not agreed between the parties. The employment tribunals are not normally expected to conduct themselves in the same way as the civil jurisdiction of the courts, but in these circumstances they must do so.

Other awards

In addition to assessing all damages which flow from the statutory tort, the employment tribunals can make other awards on the finding of discriminatory treatment.

Declaration

They can, in addition or instead of awarding compensation, make an order declaring the rights of the claimant, for example not to suffer unlawful discrimination.

Recommendation

They can also make a recommendation that the respondent takes certain steps to alleviate the effects of the discrimination or to improve procedures in the workplace.

Specific provision for indirect discrimination awards

Note that all discrimination enactments (except the Disability Discrimination Act 1995) have a concept and a definition of indirect discrimination. Note that under the Race Relations Act 1976, where the act was indirect and unintentional, no compensation will be awarded. Under SDA 1975, the Employment Equality (Religion or Belief) Regulations 2003, SI 2003/1660, and the Employment Equality (Sexual Orientation) Regulations 2003, SI 2003/1661, the tribunal is given a discretion to make an award for unintentional indirect discrimination, if it believes it is 'just and equitable' to do so.

12.4 REMEDIES FOR OTHER CLAIMS

Claims are, of course, brought under a whole range of statutes in the employment tribunals and these statutes will carry with them the appropriate remedies available to successful claimants.

These should be carefully researched whilst preparing for the tribunal Hearing. It will not be possible in this book to go into the range of awards and remedies available but advisers should make themselves aware of the provisions of the relevant statute. Specific remedies are set out, for example, in the National Minimum Wage Act 1998, the Working Time Regulations 1998, SI 1998/1833, the Transfer of Undertakings (Protection of Employment) Regulations 1981, SI 1981/1794 (failure to consult), and the Equal Pay Act 1970.

Breach of contract

It is now well established that a breach of contract claim can be brought in the employment tribunal by an employee upon the termination of employment. Respondents may counterclaim for a breach of contract claim. Note that there is a financial limit for these claims of £25,000 (see the Employment Tribunals Extension of Jurisdiction (England and Wales) Order 1994, SI 1994/1623).

It was formerly thought that if the breach of contract claim was worth more than £25,000, the correct approach was to pursue the claim in the tribunal up to the £25,000 limit and then pursue the balance in the High Court. However the case of *Fraser* v. *HLMAD Ltd* [2007] 1 All ER 383 declared that any claim for wrongful dismissal brought in an employment tribunal would have the effect of 'merging' a High Court action for a claim in excess of the tribunal limit of £25,000. For this reason wrongful dismissal claims worth over £25,000 should be commenced in the High Court .

Interest

Interest is not an award, but the capacity of the tribunal to add interest on to awards for damages for discrimination should be noted. Interest will be referred to in the judgment and will be calculated from the date of the act of discrimination, for loss of earnings from a mid-point and for injury to feelings from the date of the act. See the judgment in our case study, Molly Martin's case, at **11.5,** for an example of that calculation. Interest on tribunal awards for other jurisdictions runs from six weeks after the date the judgment was made. At the time of writing, the rate of interest is 6 per cent.

CHAPTER 13

Costs, allowances and expenses

13.1 HISTORY OF COSTS

In the early days of employment tribunals it was felt that there should be only very limited cases where costs might be awarded. Rule 14 of the 1967 Rules stated that 'a tribunal shall not normally make an award in respect of costs or expenses' but went on to say that where a party has acted frivolously or vexatiously an order might be made.

That was amended in 1993 to include the words 'otherwise unreasonably' and the addition of a limit of the 'fixed' sum to £500.

In 2001, the rule was further changed in a number of significant ways:

- the words 'shall not normally make an award' were omitted;
- the word 'frivolously' was omitted;
- the word 'misconceived' was added;
- the limit on the tribunal's powers to award assessed costs rose from £500 to £10,000.

According to the Tribunal Service Annual Report for 2006/07, between April 2006 and March 2007 a total of a little over 500 costs orders were made, a slight reduction on previous years. Although the average award of costs was £2,000 and the median £1,000, the figures do not seem to include costs orders where the county court was to assess the costs and would therefore be over £10,000. As there has been power to order an assessment in the county court over £10,000, some costs orders may be substantial. (See, for instance, *Kovacs* v. *Queen Mary and Westfield College* [2002] IRLR 414 where the costs after assessment in the county court amounted to £62,000 and *Alasdair McPherson* v. *BNP Paribas* [2004] IRLR 558 where assessed costs were over £90,000 without the matter going to a full Hearing – this was said to be by Lord Justice Mummery 'very large, by tribunal standards'.) In 2006/07 the largest cost award was £65,000.

The 2004 Rules reflect the provision in EA 2002 for additional costs powers. They include the power to award costs against a party's representative and costs for 'preparation time' for parties who are not legally qualified. For those who have been practising for some time in employment tribunals, it will mean considering whether to apply for, or how best to oppose, a costs application in a greater proportion of cases. It will be vital to read and understand the Rules carefully and be ready to make representations. The relevant rules are between r.38 and r.48 of the 2004 Rules. There is considerable overlap, with some identical wording, but you should read those which apply in your own case to ensure they are clear.

13.2   RULES 38–48

The rules with respect to costs (rr.38–41) and preparation time (rr.42–5) have a number of similarities, particularly with respect to the serving of notice, the provision that the judge or tribunal may have regard to the party's ability to pay, to provide written reasons if requested and, importantly, the circumstances in which a costs or preparation time order will be considered. Rules 46 and 47 are common to both costs and preparation time orders. The rules on costs and preparation time will be discussed separately as they will apply in different circumstances, dependent on whether a party is legally represented at the Hearing. Rule 48 is the rule on wasted costs and is framed very differently from those dealing with costs and preparation time. Again, it is dealt with below.

Rules 38–41 and 46–7

These rules reflect, to a large extent, the previous costs r.14 mentioned above but with some alterations and clarification.

In limited circumstances awarding costs is mandatory and it is worth mentioning these relatively rare circumstances now. Rule 39 makes special provision for the mandatory award of costs where there has been an adjournment caused by the respondent's unreasonable failure to adduce evidence of available jobs where the claimant has asked for reinstatement or re-engagement on a complaint of unfair dismissal. For this part of the rule to apply the claimant must have given seven days' notice of the wish to be reinstated or re-engaged.

Secondly, where a party has been ordered to pay a deposit at a pre-hearing review (see **Chapter 8**), r.47 makes it mandatory for the tribunal to consider a costs order (although not necessarily to make one!). Rule 47 provides more detail on deposits.

More often, you will be dealing with the tribunal's discretionary power, so that parties and their representatives must be alive to the possibility and be ready with arguments for and against the making of an order. Rule 38 sets out the powers and procedure. Costs orders can be made upon application by either party or by the tribunal considering it 'of its own motion', that is without prompting by a party. Usually, it is considered on application, most often, but not exclusively, by the successful party. It can be made orally at the end of the Hearing or in writing within 28 days from the date of the judgment. Note that if the judgment is given at the end of the Hearing orally, the 28 days will be calculated from that date and not the later date when written reasons are sent to the parties. Only if the judgment is reserved will the date from which the 28 days run be the date on which the written judgment is sent.

Written notice of any application or consideration of costs must be sent to the party against whom a costs order is sought so that representations can be made unless the opportunity to address the tribunal orally has already been given. Of course, it is possible for there to be a number of applications for costs emanating from different parts of the process and it is not uncommon for there to be 'cross applications' where both parties apply for costs and accuse the other party of unreasonable conduct.

It is now made clear that a costs order under this part of the Rules can only be made where the party in whose favour the order is sought has been legally represented at the Hearing, or if there has been a determination without a Hearing, if the party was represented at the point of determination. If that party has not been legally represented the tribunal may consider a preparation time order (see below). It also defines 'costs' as 'fees, charges, disbursements or expenses' (r.38(3)) and legal representation as solicitors or barristers (r.38(5)).

Rule 40 sets out the criteria upon which the tribunal will decide whether to award costs. The following circumstances will lead to consideration of a costs order.

1. Where the paying party 'has in bringing the proceedings, or he or his representative has in conducting the proceedings, acted vexatiously, abusively, disruptively or otherwise unreasonably, or the bringing or conducting of the proceedings by the paying party has been misconceived' (r.40(3)).
2. Secondly an order may be made where there has been a postponement or adjournment or a party has not complied with an order or practice direction (r.40(1) and 40(4)).

Note that the wording of r.40(3) at 1 above is almost identical to the 'old' costs r.14. It is the case that the judge or tribunal 'shall' consider a costs order if the circumstances at 1 above apply and then 'may' make an order (r.40(2)), making that decision a two-stage process.

It may be worth considering what the wording at 1 above may mean. Some cases assist us, so that for the tribunal to accept that the conduct has been 'vexatious' there should be some evidence of *mala fides* or improper motive (see *ET Marler Ltd* v. *Robertson* [1974] ICR 72). There is very little case law on what 'abusive' or 'disruptive' mean so it must be assumed that their dictionary definitions would be considered. It may well be common sense to the tribunal and the parties what the words mean. Furthermore, because the consideration of costs also comes about if there has been unreasonable conduct, it is likely that tribunals will not spend too long worrying about the details of fitting into any more stringent test.

The tribunal, again, will consider the ordinary English meaning of 'otherwise unreasonable'. It is a fairly wide test and will include matters such as withdrawal at the last minute, changing the nature of the claim, making the case longer than it need be and arguing bad points. The case of *Alasdair McPherson* v. *BNP Paribas* [2004] IRLR 558 is very helpful with regard to unreasonable conduct. The Court of Appeal was considering an award of costs made by the employment tribunal under the previous but identical r.14. Mr McPherson had withdrawn his claim some two weeks before the full Hearing but the respondents applied for costs and the employment tribunal made the order. The Court of Appeal confirmed the making of the order, accepting that the tribunal had properly exercised its discretion. The court did allow the appeal to the extent that Mr McPherson did not have to pay the full extent of the costs, but only from a point in time after which, according to the court, his conduct had been unreasonable, which was after an application to the tribunal to adjourn an earlier Hearing.

'Misconceived' was added in 2001 and is defined in reg.2(2) of the new regulations as including 'having no reasonable prospects of success'. This can be difficult to assess because if a party has been unsuccessful at the Hearing, this might suggest that there had been no reasonable prospect of success. However this is, of course, not the case. A tribunal will consider whether the claimant (or the respondent) pursued a claim or response that was clearly hopeless. If it was an arguable but weak case, this does not mean it was misconceived.

The amount of any costs order, again, replicated from the 'old' 2001 Rules is set out at r.41. There are, in effect, three possibilities:

(a) fixed sum, assessed by the tribunal, not more than £10,000;
(b) agreed by the parties, no limit;
(c) assessed by the county court under the Civil Procedure Rules 1998 (or sheriff court fees in Scotland), no limit.

Preparation time orders (rr.42–5 and 46–7)

This is a new concept introduced after consultation. It is intended to make some recompense to those parties who have not been legally represented at the Hearing and therefore cannot (and could not under the 'old' Rules), recover costs. In many ways the rules here mirror those for the consideration of a costs order (above). But they relate specifically to time spent on preparation rather than the Hearing itself (r.42(3)). There are identical provisions in r.42 with respect to the giving of notice, the time period to apply after judgment (28 days) and the giving of written reasons for the decision on preparation time if requested.

Similarly, r.43 sets out the mandatory consideration of a preparation time order for postponement where reinstatement has been asked for (see above). Rule 44 is identical to r.40 above in the circumstances where an order shall be considered and the tribunal may make an order. The consideration is mandatory where in the bringing or conducting the proceedings, there has been vexatious, abusive, disruptive or otherwise unreasonable behaviour or the bringing of the proceedings has been misconceived. If there has been a postponement request or a failure to comply with an order, a preparation time order may be made.

The calculation will be on a tribunal's assessment of number of hours spent in preparation, based on information from the party and the tribunal's own assessment. To that will be applied a set rate set initially at £25 per hour increasing yearly from April 2006 by £1 per hour: thus it is £27 per hour at the time of writing, and will increase to £28 per hour from April 2008, and so on.

Rule 46 makes it clear that a costs order and a preparation time order cannot be made in favour of the same party in the same proceedings and provides for a tribunal or chairman to make an order, before the end of a case, that either a costs or a preparation time order will be made and the tribunal or chairman may decide at the end of the case which to make.

Rule 47 covers the circumstances where a deposit has been ordered at a pre-hearing review. It makes it clear that a tribunal must consider whether to make a costs or preparation time order where that party has subsequently been unsuccessful but stipulates that the tribunal must look at the document under r.20 (see **8.2**) which records the reasons for the deposit having been ordered. A costs or preparation time order can only be made on these grounds if the reasons for the finding against that party were 'substantially the same as the grounds recorded in that document for considering that the contentions of the party had little reasonable prospect of success'.

Wasted costs

Rule 48 is an attempt to deal with one of the concerns raised by organisations when responding to the DTI consultation paper. As there is no requirement that representatives are legally qualified and there are an increasing number of employment law consultants, it was thought wise to encourage responsible representation by introducing this rule.

Rule 48 is widely drafted and gives power to the tribunal to 'disallow, or order the representative of a party to meet the whole or part of any wasted costs of any party, including an order that the representative repay to his client any costs which have already been paid' (r.48(2)(a)).

As with the costs orders mentioned above there is also the power to make a representative pay the Secretary of State (r.48(2)(b)).

Rule 48(3) defines 'wasted costs' as any costs incurred:

(a) as a result of any improper, unreasonable or negligent act or omission on the part of any representative, or
(b) which, in the light of any such act or omission occurring after they were incurred, the tribunal considers it unreasonable to expect that party to pay.

A representative in this rule may be a legal or other representative but it does not include a representative who is *not* acting in pursuit of profit. This would seem to include most legally qualified representatives except for those in the voluntary sector such as law centres, Citizens Advice or advice centres. It would also include employment law consultants even where they are acting on a 'conditional fee arrangement' (r.48(4)). Please note that unqualified advisers are now regulated with respect to claims management services under the Compensation Act 2006 which prohibits the provision of these services without authorisation, exemption or a waiver from the Ministry of Justice. Breach of this provision is a criminal offence. Further information on this can be found on the Ministry of Justice website (**www.justice.gov.uk**) and on its claims management regulation website (**www.claimsregulation.gov.uk**). There are a number of regulations, and registration involves payment of a fee and the need to show various safeguards are in place such as insurance and a code of practice. There will also be the Claims Management Services Tribunal to consider and oversee registration. However, these restrictions would seem not to apply to the family friend or general employment tribunal expert who offers assistance *without payment* within the community.

There is no restriction on the amount to be ordered, simply that the amount must be specified, that there must be written reasons if requested within 14 days and that the representative must be given 'a reasonable opportunity to make oral or written representations'. The tribunal may have regard to the representative's ability to pay.

13.3 GOOD PRACTICE

Because it has, until relatively recently, been unusual for the tribunal to award costs, if you are to make an application, you may need to tread carefully. A number of judges and lay members have been sitting for many years and have never made an award of costs and it is still the case that an application should only be made in a minority of cases, where there has been, at the very least, unreasonable conduct. The checklist below makes some suggestions that may improve your chances of succeeding in an application or successfully defending one.

Under the previous costs rule, it was decided by the EAT that the rule known as the '*Calderbank*' rule in the civil courts (from the case of *Calderbank* v. *Calderbank* [1975] 3 All ER 333) can be used in employment tribunal proceedings. Although the rule does not apply strictly as it is contained within Part 36 of the Civil Procedure Rules 1998, it nevertheless is a factor that can be taken into account. Essentially, this rule relates to circumstances where a reasonable offer has been made and rejected, and that offer, marked 'without prejudice save as to costs' could be referred to and relied upon in an application for costs (see *Kopel* v. *Safeway Stores plc* [2003] IRLR 753). Note, however, that the issue must still be decided on the basis of the relevant costs rule, that is, that the party's behaviour must be unreasonable or misconceived. Therefore in cases where offers to settle have been made by either party, it is useful to have that offer and the warning of a costs application available for the tribunal.

Checklist: good practice

Applying?	Defending?
Are you applying for costs, preparation time or wasted costs?	Are you a legal representative?
Do rr.40(3), 44(3) or 48 apply?	Are you from a non-profit organisation?
All or part of the costs?	Act reasonably throughout.
Breakdown of time, schedule of costs.	Explain any delays, failure to comply.
Warn other party by careful, non-threatening letter.	Be ready to argue size of award, time and hourly rate.
Do not apply until end of case.	Have evidence of financial means of party.

13.4 ALLOWANCES AND EXPENSES

Under ETA 1996, s.5, parties and witnesses are entitled to claim expenses and allowances from the Tribunals Service. If the representative is unpaid the representative may also claim, but there is no provision for paid representatives, whether legally qualified or not. The expenses cover certain travel costs *over* £5 which includes public transport, or car or motorcycle at the rate of 15p per mile. Taxi fares are only payable in exceptional circumstances and necessary air fare will be limited to tourist class and previous permission must be sought. Overnight expenses, where essential, up to a limit of £81 in London and £71 outside London may be claimed or you may claim up to £21 for staying with friends or relatives. Loss of earnings allowance up to a maximum, currently £45 per day, and a carer's allowance of up to £5 per hour can be paid upon proof of the cost or loss of wages. All of these allowances and expenses must have receipts or invoices.

A fee can also be paid if an interpreter is needed and you should contact the tribunal office to arrange this. The usual practice is for the Tribunals Service to book an interpreter from an approved list rather than use someone known to a party. You may also be able to claim some travel and loss of earnings expenses (up to £45 per day currently) if you need a helper to attend with you.

If you have a claim under the Disability Discrimination Act 1995 or where medical evidence has been ordered by the judge (usually in an order), repayment of the cost of the report can be made in line with BMA rates. It is wise to check these beforehand and clearly inform the medical expert what the rate of payment will be. The regional secretary will have details of these rates and leaflets explain the position. The rates above may change but have been in place for some time.

Case study: costs

Molly Martin has been told that she was successful at the Hearing.

Molly Martin was represented at the Hearing by a legally qualified adviser from an advice centre, acting on a not-for-profit basis. At the end of the Hearing Molly Martin's representative applies for costs and wasted costs.

She says that the respondent added time and expense in pursuing the argument that Molly was not an employee and that the pre-hearing review was unnecessary and amounted to unreasonable behaviour. She also says that the behaviour of the respondent's representative in the Hearing in asking questions about Molly's lifestyle were disruptive and abusive. She also asks for a wasted costs order against the representative because the questioning was improper.

The respondent is asked to comment on the application. The respondent was represented at the Hearing by an employment law consultant who is registered under the claims management services provisions.

The respondent's representative disagrees vehemently and says it was arguable that Molly was not an employee and that all questions asked were relevant to the issues.

The application is considered at the end of the Hearing with the tribunal hearing arguments from both parties including evidence of the financial situation of Just in Time and the means of the employment law consultant.

The tribunal decides that the questions about Molly Martin's lifestyle were disruptive and abusive. Bearing in mind that the questioning was stopped quickly by the judge and the claimant was able to deal with the questions the tribunal decides to make no order for wasted costs. It also decides that there was an arguable case on whether Molly was an employee and that the pre-hearing review was not unnecessary and so that behaviour was therefore not unreasonable. The tribunal makes no order for costs.

Ex gratia payments from the Tribunals Service

There are some circumstances in which parties can request that an ex gratia payment be made where there has been administrative error which has caused financial loss. For instance, there may have been an error if the tribunal office has neglected to inform a respondent that a claimant has withdrawn and the respondent has attended at the tribunal. Where there has been a significant loss and inconvenience, a party should write, in the first instance, to the regional secretary at the office dealing with the case. The regional secretary will check whether there has been, in fact, an administrative error. If there has, the secretary will pass it on to the customer services manager for consideration of an ex gratia payment.

CHAPTER 14

Reviews and appeals

14.1 INTRODUCTION

Apart from asking for a correction certificate to an order or judgment for minor errors, you may wish to consider applying, or find your opponent has applied, for a review or an appeal, challenging the substance of an order or judgment or some aspect of it. This chapter deals with how to make or defend any such application. Either route should be considered carefully as it is possible that you will not be successful and that you might find yourself in a worse position. Of course, there are costs implications, given the narrow grounds for either a review or an appeal. Not all decisions can be challenged by review and an appeal is only available, in the vast majority of cases, where there is an arguable point of law. Weigh up carefully the pros and cons of prolonging the case further.

14.2 REVIEW OF DEFAULT JUDGMENTS

Because of the relatively new power to make default judgments (see **5.5** and **7.2**), there is also a new and specific procedure for review of default judgments at r.33. Either the claimant or the respondent can apply to have a default judgment reviewed. The application must be made within 14 days of the date the order or judgment is sent to the parties. It must be in writing and must state the reasons for asking for the judgment to be varied or revoked.

> In our case study, the respondents, Just in Time, were late filing their response form; they did not give reasons for the delay as required by r.4 and default judgment was entered under r.8. They applied to have that default judgment reviewed and were successful in that application (see **Chapter 8** for an outline of the review process).

If you are the respondent and applying for review of a default judgment, you must also provide the proposed response as a default judgment can only be made where there has been no response or it has been sent out of time. You must also apply for an extension of time to present the response. The hearing will usually be conducted by a judge alone in public and both parties will have the opportunity to make oral or written representations. You may find that the tribunal contacts the claimant to find out whether he or she consents to the review, as guidance from the EAT has suggested that applications to review should normally be granted where there is a defence and a reason (not necessarily a 'good' reason – see below) given for the late response. In those circumstances, if it seems likely that the review will be granted and you are acting for the claimant, it might be wise to save the cost and expense of attending a hearing.

The judge may refuse an application to review, vary the default judgment, revoke all or part of it, or confirm it. There are some circumstances in r.33(5) where a default judgment must be revoked. Essentially this is where the whole of the claim has been satisfied or is settled. It may be revoked or varied if the respondent has a reasonable prospect of successfully responding to the claim or there is some other 'good reason'. (But see *Barrosso and others* v. *Fahy* (unreported, UKEAT 558/06) on the consideration of a 'good reason'.) The case of *Kwik Save Stores Ltd* v. *Swain* [1997] ICR 47 remains good law for the tests to be applied.

14.3 REVIEW OF DECISIONS, ORDERS, AWARDS OR JUDGMENTS

For other decisions, orders, awards or judgments, r.34(3) contains the five grounds upon which a review can be granted. As with applications under any of the Rules, read it carefully before advising a client or making the application. It is worth setting the rule out here to emphasise the circumstances when such an application may be worthwhile.

> (3) ... decisions may be reviewed on the following grounds only:
>
> (a) the decision was wrongly made as a result of an administrative error;
> (b) a party did not receive notice of the proceedings leading to the decision;
> (c) the decision was made in the absence of a party;
> (d) new evidence has become available since the conclusion of the hearing to which the decision relates, provided that its existence could not have been reasonably known of or foreseen at that time; or
> (e) the interests of justice require such a review.

Note that r.35(1) imposes a time limit of 14 days from the date the decision was sent to the parties. An application may also be made at the Hearing, although that may be unwise unless you know clearly what the reasons for the decision or judgment are and that it is reviewable. As 14 days are available, we suggest you use that time to consider the best course of action.

Not all decisions which are made in the course of a matter proceeding are reviewable. In particular, many of those made by a judge in case management (see **Chapter 7**) will not be. What can be reviewed are decisions on the non-acceptance of a claim or response, orders or judgments made at a pre-hearing review, judgment made at a Hearing or an award (including costs and preparation time). This means many of the decisions (usually made by way of directions or orders) in case management such as to make or refuse witness orders, postponements and so on cannot be reviewed. But, as long as there is a point of law and the other circumstances described under **14.4** apply, they can be appealed.

Review applications are a two-stage process. First, the application is considered. It may be refused either by the judge who heard the matter or, if that is not practicable, by the regional judge, another judge nominated by the regional judge or the president. In the vast majority of cases, it is dealt with by the judge who decided the issue (perhaps with lay members). The grounds for refusal at this stage are that there are none of the five grounds set out in r.34(3) (above) or 'there is no reasonable prospect of the decision being varied or revoked' (r.35(3)).

If it is not refused by the judge, there will be further consideration. If the matter was decided without a hearing, the review can also be without a hearing. In the majority of cases there will have been a hearing, and another hearing will be arranged to decide whether to grant the application. If there is a hearing of the application which is successful, it will be followed by the review itself again, by the same tribunal or judge who heard the original matter, unless another tribunal is appointed by the regional judge. That tribunal or judge can confirm, vary or revoke the decision. The hearing of a review application will be listed generally with the review itself to follow on immediately thereafter if the request is allowed. You must be prepared to address the tribunal on why there should be a review and then, if your application is granted, the review will be considered.

So, the first question for the tribunal is whether any of the grounds above apply. For instance, has there been an administrative error? If it decides that there has been such an error, the next question is whether to confirm, vary or revoke the earlier decision. This may well mean re-hearing some of the evidence, especially where some was not available at the earlier hearing. In this situation, deal with it as you would at the main Hearing and follow the advice in **Chapter 10**. The tribunal may well again come to the same judgment, or there may be a variation. Of course, if it is a complex case, the tribunal may consider adjourning the review and make case management orders so that further preparation can be made.

14.4 APPEALS

A small proportion of employment tribunal cases and interim matters are appealed to the Employment Appeal Tribunal (EAT). Appeals can only be made on a point of law, see below for details.

A question of law is where there has been a 'misdirection, misapplication or misunderstanding of the law'. The EAT cannot interfere with an employment tribunal's decision on the facts unless it is unsupported by the evidence or is 'perverse'. It can be very hard to define what is a point of law or a fact in any given decision or judgment. Remember that it is the judgment or decision that you are appealing so it is what is recorded there that is important. Generally speaking, how a statutory provision is interpreted will be a question of law, whereas whether A said something to B is likely to be a question of fact, unless the tribunal heard no evidence that A spoke to B at all! Some useful guidance was supplied by the former President of the EAT, Mr Justice Browne-Wilkinson in *Ellett* v. *Welsh Products Ltd* (unreported, UKEAT 652/82) as follows:

> there is no error of law where there is some evidence pointing in one direction and some evidence pointing in the other direction and the tribunal has preferred one set of evidence to the other. A finding contrary to the weight of the evidence is not a question of law.

The vast majority of matters which come before the employment tribunal can be (but most are not) appealed on a point of law to the EAT. These include claims under the ERA 1996 (including unfair dismissal, unpaid wages and a number of 'family friendly' rights), the anti-discrimination statutes, and collective disputes under the Trade Union and Labour Relations (Consolidation) Act 1992. A very few claims would be appealed to the High Court with the same time limit of 42 days, or by way of judicial review within three months where the usual conditions apply. In practice, these are extremely rare so we will concentrate in this chapter on the EAT.

To bring the EAT in line with employment tribunal changes there are EAT Rules. The current Rules are the Employment Appeal Tribunal Rules 1993, SI 1993/2854, which are commonly referred to as the 'EAT Rules 1993'. These are amended by the Employment Appeal Tribunal (Amendment) Rules 2004, SI 2004/2526 which came into force at the same time as the employment tribunal rule changes on 1 October 2004. There were later minor amendments in 2004 on information and consultation and in 2005 concerning national security cases.

The key points to note are these.

1. An overriding objective for the EAT.
2. Clarification of the time limit for submitting an appeal which will be 42 days from date of the judgment or order. This may be the date the written judgment is sent if it is reserved but may also be the date of the oral judgment. If written reasons are given on request at a later date, 42 days will run from the date when it is sent to the parties.
3. Provision for the 'weeding out' of parts of appeals by the registrar or judge and a 28-day time limit for the appellant to complain about that.
4. Temporary restricted reporting orders.

5. Costs changes – no cap of £10,000 but otherwise in line with the Rules although there is no provision for costs to be awarded where the bringing of the appeal has been misconceived, presumably because appeals can only be on a point of law.

Time limits for appeal

The appeal must be lodged at the EAT within 42 days from the date of the order or judgment. It was thought that the previous deadline was quite strict. Rule 3 of the EAT Rules 1993 covers the time limit, and many of the principles in respect of the time limit will remain the same. The Practice Direction referred to below gives helpful guidance in the Introduction.

a. For the purpose of serving a valid Notice of Appeal under Rule 3 and para 3 below, when an Employment Tribunal decision is sent to the parties on a Wednesday, that day does not count and the Notice of Appeal must arrive at the EAT on or before the Wednesday 6 weeks (i.e. 42 days) later

b. When a date is given for serving of a document or for doing some other act, the document must be received by the EAT or the relevant party by 4.00pm on that date

c. All days count, but if a time limit expires on a day when the central office of the EAT or the EAT office in Edinburgh (as appropriate), is closed, it is extended to the next working day

Our advice would be to count the day of the judgment, if given orally, as Day 1 and make sure that the notice of appeal is with the EAT by the forty-second day thereafter. The previous time limit rule was considered in *Aziz* v. *Bethnal Green City Challenge Co Ltd* [2000] IRLR 111, CA and suggested a strict approach to the time limits, stating that 'the time limit laid down in the rules will be relaxed only in rare and exceptional cases where the EAT is satisfied that there is a full, honest and acceptable explanation for the delay'.

The more recent case of *Peters* v. *Sat Katar & Co Ltd* [2003] IRLR 574, CA suggested a more relaxed approach where the appellant claimed that documents had been lost in the post. Paragraph 3 of the practice direction says that any notice of appeal 'served after 42 days must be accompanied by written application for an extension of time, explaining clearly and concisely the reasons for delay'. See also *Kanapathiar* v. *LB of Harrow* [2003] IRLR 571 where the then President of the EAT made it clear that that requirement is 'not intended to be wholly prescriptive and exclusive' but goes on to emphasise that it will only be relaxed in rare and exceptional cases.

Public funding

Public funding through the Legal Services Commission (LSC) may be available for matters in the EAT, subject to the rules and criteria set by the LSC. For more information on this visit the LSC website (**www.legalservices.gov.uk**).

Notice of appeal

A precedent notice of appeal can be found in Form 1 of Sched.1 to the EAT Rules 1993. It can easily be accessed by visiting the EAT website (**www.employmentappeals.gov.uk**). The information required is the name and address of the appellant, the decision or judgment appealed (date and place), the parties to the proceedings and their names and addresses and the grounds of appeal. A copy of the decision, judgment or order must be enclosed as well as a copy of the claim form and response. Do remember to name all interested parties if there has been more than one respondent or claimant. It goes without saying that, unless the grounds identify an appealable point of law, the appeal will be rejected at the first stage (see below).

Practice direction

There is a 2008 Practice Direction in force which parties should be aware of for the likely progress of their case. It can be read in full on the EAT website (**www.employmentappeals.gov.uk**). This new practice direction makes some changes to time limits, usually by reducing. Please check carefully that you read this practice direction rather than the earlier 2004 one.

A list of the sections of the practice direction appears below:

1. Introduction – including overriding objective.
2. Institution of appeal.
3. Time for serving appeals.
4. Interim applications.
5. Right to inspect register and copy.
6. Papers for use at hearing.
7. Evidence before ET.
8. Fresh evidence and new points of law.
9. Case tracks.
10. Respondent's answer and directions.
11. Complaints about the conduct of ET hearing.
12. Listing of appeals.
13. Skeleton arguments.
14. Citation of authorities.
15. Disposal of appeals by consent.
16. Appellant's failure to present response.
17. Hearings.
18. Handing down judgments.
19. Costs.
20. Review.
21. Appeals from EAT.
22. Conciliation.

Perhaps most importantly for the progress of appeals, it should be noted that there are now in place four 'tracks' as in item 9 and cases will be allocated to one of these after the initial sift. This is consistent with the newer case management initiatives in the court system and employment tribunals (see **Chapters 7** and **8**). The four tracks are set out in the practice direction at direction 9 as:

1. *Rule 3(7) cases.* Where there is no jurisdiction to hear the appeal. Summary reasons will be given.
2. *Preliminary hearing.* Until 2002, all cases at the EAT had to pass through a preliminary hearing. This is no longer the case. A preliminary hearing will determine whether the grounds in the notice of appeal raise a point of law which gives the appeal a reasonable prospect of success or if there is some other compelling reason for a hearing, for example a human rights point, or to test the law by going to a higher court or the European Court of Justice.
3. *Full hearing cases.* These are cases that can go forward without the need for a preliminary hearing. It should be obvious from the notice of appeal that there is a reasonable prospect of success. Listing categories of 'P' indicating that it will be heard by the President or 'A' indicating a complex case or one of public importance or 'B' other cases, are now applied. Directions will be given.
4. *Fast track full hearing cases.* These may be where it is an appeal on an interim point and the employment tribunal case is stayed pending appeal or where there appear to be a large number of cases and the legal position is unclear and should be clarified as soon as possible.

On 1 June 2007 ACAS conciliation was introduced into the EAT and there is an accompanying protocol which can be viewed on the website and has caused some consequential changes to procedure. It allows the EAT judge to consider whether to give a direction that the parties consider conciliation and allows for the papers to be sent to ACAS.

The appeal

Anyone considering an appeal should read the practice direction and follow the guidance given there. Should you be successful enough to be allowed a preliminary or a full hearing, there are a number of important factors to bear in mind. First, the onus will be on the person bringing the appeal to show that the employment tribunal's order or judgment is, in some significant way, defective. Secondly, the EAT will not generally hear any evidence. What it decides will be based on the papers before it, essentially the order or judgment challenged, any case law and statutory provisions and oral argument by representatives. Thirdly, the outcome can vary from a refusal of the appeal, allowing part or all of it, and then the matter may be 'remitted' (sent back) to either the original or a different tribunal.

In some cases the EAT may reverse the order or judgment of the employment tribunal although this is less common because the EAT understands that the employment tribunal is the forum for the hearing of oral evidence (see *O'Kelly* v. *Trusthouse Forte plc* [1983] IRLR 369). If you are the respondent to an appeal you may choose not to attend a preliminary hearing but you should be prepared to give an estimate of time for any full hearing if you want to defend any appeal. You may take the view that the employment tribunal's decision or judgment cannot be disturbed and, in that case, you do not need to appear or be represented. Few respondents to EAT appeals take that risk and you should only do so after taking advice.

Grounds – bias, irregularity or insufficient reasons appeals

The number of appeals alleging bias or other irregularity on the part of the tribunal or the judge have increased over the last few years. There are some aspects of irregular procedure that are more likely to succeed than others. Alleging bias without sufficient evidence is not one of them. Unrepresented losing parties sometimes feel aggrieved and occasionally express their sense of injustice by alleging bias. Note that Art.6 of the European Convention on Human Rights requires a 'fair and public hearing within a reasonable time'. If there has been serious delay, that may amount to a good ground for appeal but much will depend on the length and reason for the delay. (See *Kwamin* v. *Abbey National plc* at **11.4** on the question of a delayed judgment.)

Where an appellant wishes to raise the possibility of bias, para.11 of the Practice Direction gives guidance on this. It requires the provision of affidavits (sworn statements) upon which the tribunal or judge may comment and warns the party about the risk of costs. You should only pursue such a ground of appeal where your evidence is clear. Paragraph 11 refers specifically to the overriding objective and to the extensive powers that the judge has on case management.

If you are complaining about the inadequacy of the reasons given for the order or judgment, the leading case to consider remains *Meek* v. *City of Birmingham District Council* [1987] IRLR 250. This, of course predated r.30 which set out what written reasons must contain, but it remains good law. The EAT does have a procedure where it invites the tribunal to clarify the reasoning. This is known as the *Burns* procedure after the case of *Burns* v. *Royal Mail Group plc (formerly known as Consignia)* [2004] IRLR 425, which has been approved by the Court of Appeal. This avoids the need to remit if there can be clarification before the appeal is heard.

The EAT hearing

The EAT hearing will be in public with the EAT having a similar power to the employment tribunals to regulate its own procedure. As a general rule, new evidence (that was not before the employment tribunal) will not be allowed. In some limited circumstances new evidence will be allowed if certain pre-conditions are met but you will have to apply for leave to have the new evidence admitted. There is also the question of whether new points of law can be argued that were not argued before the employment tribunal. This is a matter of discretion for the judge hearing the case and it is clear there needs to be some flexibility because of the high numbers of unrepresented parties who appear before employment tribunals. The EAT is unlikely to allow new arguments on the law where it would require new consideration of facts that had not been found by the employment tribunal. Where there is a question of the employment tribunal's jurisdiction (i.e. was the employment tribunal entitled to hear the case or not?) or where subsequent Court of Appeal or ECJ judgments affect the correctness of the employment tribunal judgment, the EAT is more likely to allow new points of law; however, this is unusual. See *Secretary of State and others* v. *Rance and others* (unreported, UKEAT 60/06) for guidance on when this is likely to be allowed.

14.5 FURTHER APPEALS

An unsuccessful appellant (or respondent) from an EAT case can consider whether to take matters further. Again, further appeal can be on a point of law only to the Court of Appeal (or the Court of Session in Scotland). Leave to appeal must be sought from the EAT within 28 days and, if it is refused, an application for leave to appeal must be made to the Court of Appeal within 14 days.

From the Court of Appeal (or the Court of Session) further appeal is to the House of Lords but only with leave and where the grounds of appeal raise a point of law of general public importance. If a point of European law has been identified it is also possible to refer a question to the European Court of Justice (ECJ). Whilst this can, theoretically, be done by any of the courts (or tribunals) in the progress of a case, it has tended to be the higher courts that frame and ask the questions. This process can be very slow and should only be embarked upon where the point at issue is of some importance to the parties.

14.6 OTHER CHALLENGES

Where there is no possibility of a review or appeal because the decision or judgment is not subject to either process, it may be necessary to attempt to challenge a decision by way of judicial review. This is a remedy available for questions of public law. It may include a decision to grant, or not to grant a restricted reporting order, for instance, though it is invariably better to apply for a review first and consider an appeal. However, an application for leave to move for judicial review should not be made where there is another remedy available, so tread carefully when considering this option. Although public funding aid may be available, there may also be significant costs risks attached to such an application.

Case study: challenging the judgment

The respondent in our case is outraged at the judgment and want advice on how it can challenge it. Just in Time does not agree with the employment tribunal's finding that Molly was dismissed and definitely does not believe that it discriminated against her. It also believes that the award of compensation is too high, that the tribunal has given too long a period of loss of earnings and that the injury to feelings award is excessive. Just in Time says that there is another witness who might have overheard the conversation between Molly and Mr Jones and it now wants the employment tribunal to hear from her.

It may be possible for Just in Time to ask for a review or consider an appeal. The following factors should be considered:

The new witness. Can Just in Time apply for a review on the grounds of wishing to introduce new evidence? Not if the existence of that evidence could have reasonably been known of at the time. Not very likely and liable to be refused.

Finding of dismissal. The tribunal states that there was a dismissal on the facts it found. Can this be challenged? It is not possible to challenge the facts but possibly they could challenge whether the right test has been applied to deciding whether there was a dismissal under ERA 1996, s.95.

Finding of sex discrimination. There are two findings of sex discrimination. One is linked to the dismissal which the tribunal found was on the grounds of Molly's pregnancy. Can this be challenged? No challenge as the law is settled on that issue. The other sex discrimination finding concerns the comments which Mr Jones was found to have made and the shift changes. It is not possible to challenge the fact that he made such comments or that shifts were changed but was the tribunal entitled to find it was to her detriment and/or for a reason relating to her written complaint? Not a good challenge.

Finding on loss of earnings. The tribunal has allowed the claimant 10 weeks to find employment after the baby is three months old. Is that within its discretion and was it properly exercised? It does not seem excessive.

Finding on injury to feelings. The tribunal has placed the claimant's injury to feelings at the top of the lower band of *Vento* (see earlier chapters). Is that excessive? It is probably within its discretion. It does not seem excessive.

Considering all of the above, the costs of a possible appeal and the range of outcomes, it may seem unlikely that Just in Time would ask for a review or appeal. If Just in Time does appeal it would be the appellant in the EAT and the claimant (Molly Martin) would become the respondent.

To bring matters to a conclusion for all parties and their representatives, Just in Time pays Molly the compensation awarded and she finds employment at the time when the employment tribunal estimated she would. Just in Time have reviewed its procedures including written terms and conditions and procedures dealing with disciplinary and grievance matters. It has also reviewed its equal opportunities policy and the managers have been on a training courses in all these areas.

Employment Act 2002 (Dispute Resolution) Regulations 2004, SI 2004/752

1. Citation and commencement

These Regulations may be cited as the Employment Act 2002 (Dispute Resolution) Regulations 2004 and shall come into force on 1st October 2004.

2. Interpretation

(1) In these Regulations –

'the 1992 Act' means the Trade Union and Labour Relations (Consolidation) Act 1992;

'the 1996 Act' means the Employment Rights Act 1996;

'the 1999 Act' means the Employment Relations Act 1999;

'the 2002 Act' means the Employment Act 2002;

'action' means any act or omission;

'applicable statutory procedure' means the statutory procedure that applies in relation to a particular case by virtue of these Regulations;

'collective agreement' has the meaning given to it by section 178(1) of the 1992 Act;

'dismissal and disciplinary procedures' means the statutory procedures set out in Part 1 of Schedule 2;

'dismissed' has the meaning given to it in section 95(1)(a) and (b) of the 1996 Act;

'employers' association' has the meaning given to it by section 122 of the 1992 Act;

'grievance' means a complaint by an employee about action which his employer has taken or is contemplating taking in relation to him;

'grievance procedures' means the statutory procedures set out in Part 2 of Schedule 2;

'independent trade union' has the meaning given to it by section 5 of the 1992 Act;

'modified dismissal procedure' means the procedure set out in Chapter 2 of Part 1 of Schedule 2;

'modified grievance procedure' means the procedure set out in Chapter 2 of Part 2 of Schedule 2;

'non-completion' of a statutory procedure includes non-commencement of such a procedure except where the term is used in relation to the non-completion of an identified requirement of a procedure or to circumstances where a procedure has already been commenced;

'party' means the employer or the employee;

'relevant disciplinary action' means action, short of dismissal, which the employer asserts to be based wholly or mainly on the employee's conduct or capability, other than suspension on full pay or the issuing of warnings (whether oral or written);

'standard dismissal and disciplinary procedure' means the procedure set out in Chapter 1 of Part 1 of Schedule 2;

'standard grievance procedure' means the procedure set out in Chapter 1 of Part 2 of Schedule 2;

and a reference to a Schedule is a reference to a Schedule to the 2002 Act.

(2) In determining whether a meeting or written communication fulfils a requirement of Schedule 2, it is irrelevant whether the meeting or communication deals with any other matter (including a different matter required to be dealt with in a meeting or communication intended to fulfil a requirement of Schedule 2).

3. Application of dismissal and disciplinary procedures

(1) Subject to paragraph (2) and regulation 4, the standard dismissal and disciplinary procedure applies when an employer contemplates dismissing or taking relevant disciplinary action against an employee.

(2) Subject to regulation 4, the modified dismissal procedure applies in relation to a dismissal where –

(a) the employer dismissed the employee by reason of his conduct without notice,

(b) the dismissal occurred at the time the employer became aware of the conduct or immediately thereafter,

(c) the employer was entitled, in the circumstances, to dismiss the employee by reason of his conduct without notice or any payment in lieu of notice, and

(d) it was reasonable for the employer, in the circumstances, to dismiss the employee before enquiring into the circumstances in which the conduct took place,

but neither of the dismissal and disciplinary procedures applies in relation to such a dismissal where the employee presents a complaint relating to the dismissal to an employment tribunal at a time when the employer has not complied with paragraph 4 of Schedule 2.

4. Dismissals to which the dismissal and disciplinary procedures do not apply

(1) Neither of the dismissal and disciplinary procedures applies in relation to the dismissal of an employee where –

(a)   all the employees of a description or in a category to which the employee belongs are dismissed, provided that the employer offers to re-engage all the employees so dismissed either before or upon the termination of their contracts;

(b)   the dismissal is one of a number of dismissals in respect of which the duty in section 188 of the 1992 Act (duty of employer to consult representatives when proposing to dismiss as redundant a certain number of employees) applies;

(c)   at the time of the employee's dismissal he is taking part in –

      (i)   an unofficial strike or other unofficial industrial action, or

      (ii)   a strike or other industrial action (being neither unofficial industrial action nor protected industrial action), unless the circumstances of the dismissal are such that, by virtue of section 238(2) of the 1992 Act, an employment tribunal is entitled to determine whether the dismissal was fair or unfair;

(d)   the reason (or, if more than one, the principal reason) for the dismissal is that the employee took protected industrial action and the dismissal would be regarded, by virtue of section 238A(2) of the 1992 Act, as unfair for the purposes of Part 10 of the 1996 Act;

(e)   the employer's business suddenly ceases to function, because of an event unforeseen by the employer, with the result that it is impractical for him to employ any employees;

(f)   the reason (or, if more than one principal reason) for the dismissal is that the employee could not continue to work in the position which he held without contravention (either on his part or on that of his employer) of a duty or restriction imposed by or under any enactment;

(g)   the employee is one to whom a dismissal procedures agreement designated by an order under section 110 of the 1996 Act applies at the date of dismissal; or

(h)   the reason (or, if more than one, the principal reason) for the dismissal is retirement of the employee (to be determined in accordance with section 98ZA to 98ZF of the 1996 Act).

(2)   For the purposes of paragraph (1) –

'unofficial' shall be construed in accordance with subsections (2) to (4) of section 237 of the 1992 Act;

'strike' has the meaning given to it by section 246 of the 1992 Act;

'protected industrial action' shall be construed in accordance with section 238A(1) of the 1992 Act;

and an employer shall be regarded as offering to re-engage an employee if that employer, a successor of that employer or an associated employer of that employer offers to re-engage the employee, either in the job which he held immediately before the date of dismissal or in a different job which would be suitable in his case.

5.   Circumstances in which parties are treated as complying with the dismissal and disciplinary procedures

(1)   Where –

(a)   either of the dismissal and disciplinary procedures is the applicable statutory procedure in relation to a dismissal,

    (b)   the employee presents an application for interim relief to an employ-ment tribunal pursuant to section 128 of the 1996 Act (interim relief pending determination of complaint) in relation to his dismissal, and

    (c)   at the time the application is presented, the requirements of para-graphs 1 and 2 or, as the case may be, paragraph 4 of Schedule 2 have been complied with but the requirements of paragraph 3 or 5 of Schedule 2 have not,

the parties shall be treated as having complied with the requirements of paragraph 3 or 5 of Schedule 2.

(2)   Where either of the dismissal and disciplinary procedures is the applicable statutory procedure in relation to the dismissal of an employee or to relevant disciplinary action taken against an employee but –

    (a)   at the time of the dismissal or the taking of the action an appropriate procedure exists,

    (b)   the employee is entitled to appeal under that procedure against his dismissal or the relevant disciplinary action taken against him instead of appealing to his employer, and

    (c)   the employee has appealed under that procedure,

the parties shall be treated as having complied with the requirements of paragraph 3 or 5 of Schedule 2.

(3)   For the purposes of paragraph (2) a procedure is appropriate if it –

    (a)   gives the employee an effective right of appeal against dismissal or dis-ciplinary action taken against him, and

    (b)   operates by virtue of a collective agreement made between two or more employers or an employers' association and one or more independent trade unions.

6. Application of the grievance procedures

(1)   The grievance procedures apply, in accordance with the paragraphs (2) to (7) of this regulation, in relation to any grievance about action by the employer that could form the basis of a complaint by an employee to an employment tribunal under a jurisdiction listed in Schedule 3 or 4, or could do so if the action took place.

(2)   Subject to paragraphs (3) to (7), the standard grievance procedure applies in relation to any such grievance.

(3)   Subject to paragraphs (4) to (7), the modified grievance procedure applies in relation to a grievance where –

    (a)   the employee has ceased to be employed by the employer;

    (b)   the employer –

        (i)   was unaware of the grievance before the employment ceased, or

        (ii)   was so aware but the standard grievance procedure was not commenced or was not completed before the last day of the employee's employment; and

    (c)   the parties have agreed in writing in relation to the grievance, whether before, on or after that day, but after the employer became aware of the grievance, that the modified procedure should apply.

(4)   Neither of the grievance procedures applies where –

(a)   the employee has ceased to be employed by the employer;

(b)   neither procedure has been commenced; and

(c)   since the employee ceased to be employed it has ceased to be reasonably practicable for him to comply with paragraph 6 or 9 of Schedule 2.

(5)   Neither of the grievance procedures applies where the grievance is that the employer has dismissed or is contemplating dismissing the employee.

(6)   Neither of the grievance procedures applies where the grievance is that the employer has taken or is contemplating taking relevant disciplinary action against the employee unless one of the reasons for the grievance is a reason mentioned in regulation 7(1).

(7)   Neither of the grievance procedures applies where regulation 11(1) applies.

7.   Circumstances in which parties are treated as complying with the grievance procedures

(1)   Where the grievance is that the employer has taken or is contemplating taking relevant disciplinary action against the employee and one of the reasons for the grievance is –

(a)   that the relevant disciplinary action amounted to or, if it took place, would amount to unlawful discrimination, or

(b)   that the grounds on which the employer took the action or is contemplating taking it were or are unrelated to the grounds on which he asserted that he took the action or is asserting that he is contemplating taking it,

the standard grievance procedure or, as the case may be, modified grievance procedure shall apply but the parties shall be treated as having complied with the applicable procedure if the employee complies with the requirement in paragraph (2).

(2)   The requirement is that the employee must set out the grievance in a written statement and send the statement or a copy of it to the employer –

(a)   where either of the dismissal and disciplinary procedures is being followed, before the meeting referred to in paragraph 3 or 5 (appeals under the dismissal and disciplinary procedures) of Schedule 2, or

(b)   where neither of those procedures is being followed, before presenting any complaint arising out of the grievance to an employment tribunal.

(3)   In paragraph (1)(a) 'unlawful discrimination' means an act or omission in respect of which a right of complaint lies to an employment tribunal under any of the following tribunal jurisdictions (specified in Schedules 3 and 4) –

section 2 of the Equal Pay Act 1970;

section 63 of the Sex Discrimination Act 1975;

section 54 of the Race Relations Act 1976;

section 17A of the Disability Discrimination Act 1995;

regulation 28 of the Employment Equality (Religion or Belief) Regulations 2003;

regulation 28 of the Employment Equality (Sexual Orientation) Regulations 2003;

regulation 36 of the Employment Equality (Age) Regulations 2006.

8. (1) Where –

   (a) the standard grievance procedure is the applicable statutory procedure,
   (b) the employee has ceased to be employed by the employer,
   (c) paragraph 6 of Schedule 2 has been complied with (whether before or after the end of his employment); and
   (d) since the end of his employment it has ceased to be reasonably practicable for the employee, or his employer, to comply with the requirements of paragraph 7 or 8 of Schedule 2,

   the parties shall be treated, subject to paragraph (2), as having complied with such of those paragraphs of Schedule 2 as have not been complied with.

   (2) In a case where paragraph (1) applies and the requirements of paragraphs 7(1) to (3) of Schedule 2 have been complied with but the requirement in paragraph 7(4) of Schedule 2 has not, the employer shall be treated as having failed to comply with paragraph 7(4) unless he informs the employee in writing of his decision as to his response to the grievance.

9. (1) Where either of the grievance procedures is the applicable statutory procedure, the parties shall be treated as having complied with the requirements of the procedure if a person who is an appropriate representative of the employee having the grievance has –

   (a) written to the employer setting out the grievance; and
   (b) specified in writing to the employer (whether in setting out the grievance or otherwise) the names of at least two employees, of whom one is the employee having the grievance, as being the employees on behalf of whom he is raising the grievance.

   (2) For the purposes of paragraph (1), a person is an appropriate representative if, at the time he writes to the employer setting out the grievance, he is –

   (a) an official of an independent trade union recognised by the employer for the purposes of collective bargaining in respect of a description of employees that includes the employee having the grievance, or
   (b) an employee of the employer who is an employee representative elected or appointed by employees consisting of or including employees of the same description as the employee having the grievance and who, having regard to the purposes for which and method by which he was elected or appointed, has the authority to represent employees of that description under an established procedure for resolving grievances agreed between employee representatives and the employer.

   (3) For the purposes of paragraph (2)(a) the terms 'official', 'recognised' and 'collective bargaining' have the meanings given to them by, respectively, sections 119, 178(3) and 178(1) of the 1992 Act.

10. Where either of the grievance procedures is the applicable statutory procedure but –

   (a) at the time the employee raises his grievance there is a procedure in operation, under a collective agreement made between two or more employers or an employers' association and one or more independent trade unions, that provides for employees of the employer to raise grievances about the behaviour of the employer and have them considered, and

(b) the employee is entitled to raise his grievance under that procedure and does so,

the parties shall be treated as having complied with the applicable statutory procedure.

11. General circumstances in which the statutory procedures do not apply or are treated as being complied with

(1) Where the circumstances specified in paragraph (3) apply and in consequence the employer or employee does not commence the procedure that would otherwise be the applicable statutory procedure (by complying with paragraph 1, 4, 6 or 9 of Schedule 2), the procedure does not apply.

(2) Where the applicable statutory procedure has been commenced, but the circumstances specified in paragraph (3) apply and in consequence a party does not comply with a subsequent requirement of the procedure, the parties shall be treated as having complied with the procedure.

(3) The circumstances referred to in paragraphs (1) and (2) are that –

  (a) the party has reasonable grounds to believe that commencing the procedure or complying with the subsequent requirement would result in a significant threat to himself, his property, any other person or the property of any other person;

  (b) the party has been subjected to harassment and has reasonable grounds to believe that commencing the procedure or complying with the subsequent requirement would result in his being subjected to further harassment; or

  (c) it is not practicable for the party to commence the procedure or comply with the subsequent requirement within a reasonable period.

(4) In paragraph (3)(b), 'harassment' means conduct which has the purpose or effect of –

  (a) violating the person's dignity, or

  (b) creating an intimidating, hostile, degrading, humiliating or offensive environment for him,

but conduct shall only be regarded as having that purpose or effect if, having regard to all the circumstances, including in particular the perception of the person who was the subject of the conduct, it should reasonably be considered as having that purpose or effect.

12. Failure to comply with the statutory procedures

(1) If either party fails to comply with a requirement of an applicable statutory procedure, including a general requirement contained in Part 3 of Schedule 2, then, subject to paragraph (2), the non-completion of the procedure shall be attributable to that party and neither party shall be under any obligation to comply with any further requirement of the procedure.

(2) Except as mentioned in paragraph (4), where the parties are to be treated as complying with the applicable statutory procedure, or any requirement of it, there is no failure to comply with the procedure or requirement.

(3) Notwithstanding that if regulation 11(1) applies the procedure that would otherwise be the applicable statutory procedure does not apply, where that regulation applies because the circumstances in sub-paragraph (a) or (b) of

regulation 11(3) apply and it was the behaviour of one of the parties that resulted in those circumstances applying, that party shall be treated as if –

(a)   the procedure had applied, and

(b)   there had been a failure to comply with a requirement of the procedure that was attributable to him.

(4)   In a case where regulation 11(2) applies in relation to a requirement of the applicable statutory procedure because the circumstances in sub-paragraph (a) or (b) of regulation 11(3) apply, and it was the behaviour of one of the parties that resulted in those circumstances applying, the fact that the requirement was not complied with shall be treated as being a failure, attributable to that party, to comply with a requirement of the procedure.

13. Failure to attend a meeting

(1)   Without prejudice to regulation 11(2) and (3)(c), if it is not reasonably practicable for –

(a)   the employee, or, if he is exercising his right under section 10 of the 1999 Act (right to be accompanied), his companion; or

(b)   the employer,

to attend a meeting organised in accordance with the applicable statutory procedure for a reason which was not foreseeable when the meeting was arranged, the employee or, as the case may be, employer shall not be treated as having failed to comply with that requirement of the procedure.

(2)   In the circumstances set out in paragraph (1), the employer shall continue to be under the duty in the applicable statutory procedure to invite the employee to attend a meeting and, where the employee is exercising his rights under section 10 of the 1999 Act and the employee proposes an alternative time under subsection (4) of that section, the employer shall be under a duty to invite the employee to attend a meeting at that time.

(3)   The duty to invite the employee to attend a meeting referred to in paragraph (2) shall cease if the employer has invited the employee to attend two meetings and paragraph (1) applied in relation to each of them.

(4)   Where the duty in paragraph (2) has ceased as a result of paragraph (3), the parties shall be treated as having complied with the applicable statutory procedure.

14. Questions to obtain information not to constitute statement of grievance

(1)   Where a person aggrieved questions a respondent under any of the provisions set out in paragraph (2), those questions shall not constitute a statement of grievance under paragraph 6 or 9 of Schedule 2.

(2)   The provisions referred to in paragraph (1) are –

section 7B of the Equal Pay Act 1970;

section 74 of the Sex Discrimination Act 1975;

section 65 of the Race Relations Act 1976;

section 56 of the Disability Discrimination Act 1995;

regulation 33 of the Employment Equality (Religion or Belief) Regulations 2003;

regulation 33 of the Employment Equality (Sexual Orientation) Regulations 2003;

regulation 41 of the Employment Equality (Age) Regulations 2006.

15. Extension of time limits

(1) Where a complaint is presented to an employment tribunal under a jurisdiction listed in Schedule 3 or 4 and –

    (a) either of the dismissal and disciplinary procedures is the applicable statutory procedure and the circumstances specified in paragraph (2) apply; or

    (b) either of the grievance procedures is the applicable statutory procedure and the circumstances specified in paragraph (3) apply;

the normal time limit for presenting the complaint is extended for a period of three months beginning with the day after the day on which it would otherwise have expired.

(2) The circumstances referred to in paragraph (1)(a) are that the employee presents a complaint to the tribunal after the expiry of the normal time limit for presenting the complaint but had reasonable grounds for believing, when that time limit expired, that a dismissal or disciplinary procedure, whether statutory or otherwise (including an appropriate procedure for the purposes of regulation 5(2)), was being followed in respect of matters that consisted of or included the substance of the tribunal complaint.

(3) The circumstances referred to in paragraph (1)(b) are that the employee presents a complaint to the tribunal –

    (a) within the normal time limit for presenting the complaint but in circumstances in which section 32(2) or (3) of the 2002 Act does not permit him to do so; or

    (b) after the expiry of the normal time limit for presenting the complaint, having complied with paragraph 6 or 9 of Schedule 2 in relation to his grievance within that normal time limit.

(4) For the purposes of paragraph (3) and section 32 of the 2002 Act the following acts shall be treated, in a case to which the specified regulation applies, as constituting compliance with paragraph 6 or 9 of Schedule 2 –

    (a) in a case to which regulation 7(1) applies, compliance by the employee with the requirement in regulation 7(2);

    (b) in a case to which regulation 9(1) applies, compliance by the appropriate representative with the requirement in sub-paragraph (a) or (b) of that regulation, whichever is the later; and

    (c) in a case to which regulation 10 applies, the raising of his grievance by the employee in accordance with the procedure referred to in that regulation.

(5) In this regulation 'the normal time limit' means –

    (a) subject to sub-paragraph (b), the period within which a complaint under the relevant jurisdiction must be presented if there is to be no need for the tribunal, in order to be entitled to consider it to –

        (i) exercise any discretion, or

        (ii) make any determination as to whether it is required to consider the complaint, that the tribunal would have to exercise or make in order to consider a complaint presented outside that period; and

(b)   in relation to claims brought under the Equal Pay Act 1970, the period ending on the date on or before which proceedings must be instituted in accordance with section 2(4) of that Act.

16. National security

Where it would not be possible to comply with an applicable statutory procedure without disclosing information the disclosure of which would be contrary to the interests of national security, nothing in these Regulations requires either party to comply with that procedure.

17. Amendments to secondary legislation

[*Amending provisions*]

18. Transitional Provisions

These Regulations shall apply –

(a)   in relation to dismissal and relevant disciplinary action, where the employer first contemplates dismissing or taking such action against the employee after these Regulations come into force; and

(b)   in relation to grievances, where the action about which the employee complains occurs or continues after these Regulations come into force,

but shall not apply in relation to a grievance where the action continues after these Regulations come into force if the employee has raised a grievance about the action with the employer before they come into force.

APPENDIX 2

Employment Act 2002, ss.29–33 and Scheds 2–4

*****

PART 3
DISPUTE RESOLUTION ETC.

Statutory procedures

29. Statutory dispute resolution procedures

(1)   Schedule 2 (which sets out the statutory dispute resolution procedures) shall have effect.

(2)   The Secretary of State may by order –

(a)   amend Schedule 2;

(b)   make provision for the Schedule to apply, with or without modifications, as if –

(i)   any individual of a description specified in the order who would not otherwise be an employee for the purposes of the Schedule were an employee for those purposes; and

(ii)   a person of a description specified in the order were, in the case of any such individual, the individual's employer for those purposes.

(3)   Before making an order under this section, the Secretary of State must consult the Advisory, Conciliation and Arbitration Service.

30. Contracts of employment

(1)   Every contract of employment shall have effect to require the employer and employee to comply, in relation to any matter to which a statutory procedure applies, with the requirements of the procedure.

(2)   Subsection (1) shall have effect notwithstanding any agreement to the contrary, but does not affect so much of an agreement to follow a particular procedure as requires the employer or employee to comply with a requirement which is additional to, and not inconsistent with, the requirements of the statutory procedure.

(3)   The Secretary of State may for the purpose of this section by regulations make provision about the application of the statutory procedures.

(4)   In this section, 'contract of employment' has the same meaning as in the Employment Rights Act 1996 (c. 18).

31. Non-completion of statutory procedure: adjustment of awards

(1)   This section applies to proceedings before an employment tribunal relating to a claim under any of the jurisdictions listed in Schedule 3 by an employee.

227

(2) If, in the case of proceedings to which this section applies, it appears to the employment tribunal that –

    (a) the claim to which the proceedings relate concerns a matter to which one of the statutory procedures applies,

    (b) the statutory procedure was not completed before the proceedings were begun, and

    (c) the non-completion of the statutory procedure was wholly or mainly attributable to failure by the employee –

        (i) to comply with a requirement of the procedure, or

        (ii) to exercise a right of appeal under it,

it must, subject to subsection (4), reduce any award which it makes to the employee by 10 per cent, and may, if it considers it just and equitable in all the circumstances to do so, reduce it by a further amount, but not so as to make a total reduction of more than 50 per cent.

(3) If, in the case of proceedings to which this section applies, it appears to the employment tribunal that –

    (a) the claim to which the proceedings relate concerns a matter to which one of the statutory procedures applies,

    (b) the statutory procedure was not completed before the proceedings were begun, and

    (c) the non-completion of the statutory procedure was wholly or mainly attributable to failure by the employer to comply with a requirement of the procedure,

it must, subject to subsection (4), increase any award which it makes to the employee by 10 per cent and may, if it considers it just and equitable in all the circumstances to do so, increase it by a further amount, but not so as to make a total increase of more than 50 per cent.

(4) The duty under subsection (2) or (3) to make a reduction or increase of 10 per cent does not apply if there are exceptional circumstances which would make a reduction or increase of that percentage unjust or inequitable, in which case the tribunal may make no reduction or increase or a reduction or increase of such lesser percentage as it considers just and equitable in all the circumstances.

(5) Where an award falls to be adjusted under this section and under section 38, the adjustment under this section shall be made before the adjustment under that section.

(6) The Secretary of State may for the purposes of this section by regulations –

    (a) make provision about the application of the statutory procedures;

    (b) make provision about when a statutory procedure is to be taken to be completed;

    (c) make provision about what constitutes compliance with a requirement of a statutory procedure;

    (d) make provision about circumstances in which a person is to be treated as not subject to, or as having complied with, such a requirement;

    (e) make provision for a statutory procedure to have effect in such circumstances as may be specified by the regulations with such modifications as may be so specified;

    (f) make provision about when an employee is required to exercise a right of appeal under a statutory procedure.

(7)   The Secretary of State may by order –

    (a)   amend Schedule 3 for the purpose of –

        (i)   adding a jurisdiction to the list in that Schedule, or
        (ii)   removing a jurisdiction from that list;

    (b)   make provision, in relation to a jurisdiction listed in Schedule 3, for this section not to apply to proceedings relating to claims of a description specified in the order;

    (c)   make provision for this section to apply, with or without modifications, as if –

        (i)   any individual of a description specified in the order who would not otherwise be an employee for the purposes of this section were an employee for those purposes, and
        (ii)   a person of a description specified in the order were, in the case of any such individual, the individual's employer for those purposes.

32. Complaints about grievances

(1)   This section applies to the jurisdictions listed in Schedule 4.

(2)   An employee shall not present a complaint to an employment tribunal under a jurisdiction to which this section applies if –

    (a)   it concerns a matter in relation to which the requirement in paragraph 6 or 9 of Schedule 2 applies, and
    (b)   the requirement has not been complied with.

(3)   An employee shall not present a complaint to an employment tribunal under a jurisdiction to which this section applies if –

    (a)   it concerns a matter in relation to which the requirement in paragraph 6 or 9 of Schedule 2 has been complied with, and
    (b)   less than 28 days have passed since the day on which the requirement was complied with.

(4)   An employee shall not present a complaint to an employment tribunal under a jurisdiction to which this section applies if –

    (a)   it concerns a matter in relation to which the requirement in paragraph 6 or 9 of Schedule 2 has been complied with, and
    (b)   the day on which the requirement was complied with was more than one month after the end of the original time limit for making the complaint.

(5)   In such circumstances as the Secretary of State may specify by regulations, an employment tribunal may direct that subsection (4) shall not apply in relation to a particular matter.

(6)   An employment tribunal shall be prevented from considering a complaint presented in breach of subsections (2) to (4), but only if –

    (a)   the breach is apparent to the tribunal from the information supplied to it by the employee in connection with the bringing of the proceedings, or
    (b)   the tribunal is satisfied of the breach as a result of his employer raising the issue of compliance with those provisions in accordance with regulations under section 7 of the Employment Tribunals Act 1996 (c. 17) (employment tribunal procedure regulations).

(7) The Secretary of State may for the purposes of this section by regulations –

    (a) make provision about the application of the procedures set out in Part 2 of Schedule 2;

    (b) make provision about what constitutes compliance with paragraph 6 or 9 of that Schedule;

    (c) make provision about circumstances in which a person is to be treated as having complied with paragraph 6 or 9 of that Schedule;

    (d) make provision for paragraph 6 or 9 of that Schedule to have effect in such circumstances as may be specified by the regulations with such modifications as may be so specified.

(8) The Secretary of State may by order –

    (a) amend, repeal or replace any of subsections (2) to (4);

    (b) amend Schedule 4;

    (c) make provision for this section to apply, with or without modifications, as if –

        (i) any individual of a description specified in the order who would not otherwise be an employee for the purposes of this section were an employee for those purposes, and

        (ii) a person of a description specified in the order were, in the case of any such individual, the individual's employer for those purposes.

(9) Before making an order under subsection (8)(a), the Secretary of State must consult the Advisory, Conciliation and Arbitration Service.

(10) In its application to orders under subsection (8)(a), section 51(1)(b) includes power to amend this section.

33. Consequential adjustment of time limits

(1) The Secretary of State may, in relation to a jurisdiction listed in Schedule 3 or 4, by regulations make provision about the time limit for beginning proceedings in respect of a claim concerning a matter to which a statutory procedure applies.

(2) Regulations under this section may, in particular –

    (a) make provision extending, or authorising the extension of, the time for beginning proceedings,

    (b) make provision about the exercise of a discretion to extend the time for beginning proceedings, or

    (c) make provision treating proceedings begun out of time as begun within time.

*****

SCHEDULE 2
STATUTORY DISPUTE RESOLUTION PROCEDURES

PART 1
DISMISSAL AND DISCIPLINARY PROCEDURES

CHAPTER 1
STANDARD PROCEDURE

Step 1: statement of grounds for action and invitation to meeting

1 (1) The employer must set out in writing the employee's alleged conduct or characteristics, or other circumstances, which lead him to contemplate dismissing or taking disciplinary action against the employee.
   (2) The employer must send the statement or a copy of it to the employee and invite the employee to attend a meeting to discuss the matter.

Step 2: meeting

2 (1) The meeting must take place before action is taken, except in the case where the disciplinary action consists of suspension.
   (2) The meeting must not take place unless –

   (a) the employer has informed the employee what the basis was for including in the statement under paragraph 1(1) the ground or grounds given in it, and
   (b) the employee has had a reasonable opportunity to consider his response to that information.

   (3) The employee must take all reasonable steps to attend the meeting.
   (4) After the meeting, the employer must inform the employee of his decision and notify him of the right to appeal against the decision if he is not satisfied with it.

Step 3: appeal

3 (1) If the employee does wish to appeal, he must inform the employer.
   (2) If the employee informs the employer of his wish to appeal, the employer must invite him to attend a further meeting.
   (3) The employee must take all reasonable steps to attend the meeting.
   (4) The appeal meeting need not take place before the dismissal or disciplinary action takes effect.
   (5) After the appeal meeting, the employer must inform the employee of his final decision.

CHAPTER 2
MODIFIED PROCEDURE

Step 1: statement of grounds for action

4 The employer must –

   (a) set out in writing –

      (i) the employee's alleged misconduct which has led to the dismissal,

      (ii) what the basis was for thinking at the time of the dismissal that the employee was guilty of the alleged misconduct, and

      (iii) the employee's right to appeal against dismissal, and

  (b) send the statement or a copy of it to the employee.

Step 2: appeal

5   (1) If the employee does wish to appeal, he must inform the employer.

    (2) If the employee informs the employer of his wish to appeal, the employer must invite him to attend a meeting.

    (3) The employee must take all reasonable steps to attend the meeting.

    (4) After the appeal meeting, the employer must inform the employee of his final decision.

PART 2
GRIEVANCE PROCEDURES

CHAPTER 1
STANDARD PROCEDURE

Step 1: statement of grievance

6   The employee must set out the grievance in writing and send the statement or a copy of it to the employer.

Step 2: meeting

7   (1) The employer must invite the employee to attend a meeting to discuss the grievance.

    (2) The meeting must not take place unless –

      (a) the employee has informed the employer what the basis for the grievance was when he made the statement under paragraph 6, and

      (b) the employer has had a reasonable opportunity to consider his response to that information.

    (3) The employee must take all reasonable steps to attend the meeting.

    (4) After the meeting, the employer must inform the employee of his decision as to his response to the grievance and notify him of the right to appeal against the decision if he is not satisfied with it.

Step 3: appeal

8   (1) If the employee does wish to appeal, he must inform the employer.

    (2) If the employee informs the employer of his wish to appeal, the employer must invite him to attend a further meeting.

    (3) The employee must take all reasonable steps to attend the meeting.

    (4) After the appeal meeting, the employer must inform the employee of his final decision.

CHAPTER 2
MODIFIED PROCEDURE

Step 1: statement of grievance

9   The employee must –

   (a) set out in writing –

      (i)   the grievance, and
      (ii) the basis for it, and

   (b) send the statement or a copy of it to the employer.

Step 2: response

10   The employer must set out his response in writing and send the statement or a copy of it to the employee.

PART 3
GENERAL REQUIREMENTS

Introductory

11   The following requirements apply to each of the procedures set out above (so far as applicable).

Timetable

12   Each step and action under the procedure must be taken without unreasonable delay.

Meetings

13   (1) Timing and location of meetings must be reasonable.
     (2) Meetings must be conducted in a manner that enables both employer and employee to explain their cases.
     (3) In the case of appeal meetings which are not the first meeting, the employer should, as far as is reasonably practicable, be represented by a more senior manager than attended the first meeting (unless the most senior manager attended that meeting).

PART 4
SUPPLEMENTARY

Status of meetings

14   A meeting held for the purposes of this Schedule is a hearing for the purposes of section 13(4) and (5) of the Employment Relations Act 1999 (c. 26) (definition of 'disciplinary hearing' and 'grievance hearing' in relation to the right to be accompanied under section 10 of that Act).

Scope of grievance procedures

15   (1) The procedures set out in Part 2 are only applicable to matters raised by an employee with his employer as a grievance.

(2) Accordingly, those procedures are only applicable to the kind of disclosure dealt with in Part 4A of the Employment Rights Act 1996 (c. 18) (protected disclosures of information) if information is disclosed by an employee to his employer in circumstances where –

(a) the information relates to a matter which the employee could raise as a grievance with his employer, and

(b) it is the intention of the employee that the disclosure should constitute the raising of the matter with his employer as a grievance.

SCHEDULE 3
TRIBUNAL JURISDICTIONS TO WHICH SECTION 31 APPLIES

Section 2 of the Equal Pay Act 1970 (c. 41) (equality clauses)

Section 63 of the Sex Discrimination Act 1975 (c. 65) (discrimination in the employment field)

Section 54 of the Race Relations Act 1976 (c. 74) (discrimination in the employment field)

Section 145A of the Trade Union and Labour Relations (Consolidation) Act 1992 (inducements relating to union membership or activities)

Section 145B of that Act (inducements relating to collective bargaining)

Section 146 of that Act (detriment in relation to union membership and activities)

Paragraph 156 of Schedule A1 to that Act (detriment in relation to union recognition rights)

Section 17A of the Disability Discrimination Act 1995 (c. 50) (discrimination in the employment field)

Section 23 of the Employment Rights Act 1996 (c. 18) (unauthorised deductions and payments)

Section 48 of that Act (detriment in employment)

Section 111 of that Act (unfair dismissal)

Section 163 of that Act (redundancy payments)

Section 24 of the National Minimum Wage Act 1998 (c. 39) (detriment in relation to national minimum wage)

The Employment Tribunal Extension of Jurisdiction (England and Wales) Order 1994 (S.I. 1994/1623) (breach of employment contract and termination)

The Employment Tribunal Extension of Jurisdiction (Scotland) Order 1994 (S.I. 1994/1624) (corresponding provision for Scotland)

Regulation 30 of the Working Time Regulations 1998 (S.I. 1998/1833) (breach of regulations)

Regulation 32 of the Transnational Information and Consultation of Employees Regulations 1999 (S.I. 1999/3323) (detriment relating to European Works Councils)

Regulation 28 of the Employment Equality (Sexual Orientation) Regulations 2003 (discrimination in the employment field)

Regulation 28 of the Employment Equality (Religion or Belief) Regulations 2003 (discrimination in the employment field)

Regulation 45 of the European Public Limited-Liability Company Regulations 2004 (S.I. 2004/2326) (detriment in employment)

Regulation 33 of the Information and Consultation of Employees Regulations 2004 (S.I. 2004/3426) (detriment in employment)

Paragraph 8 of the Schedule to the Occupational and Personal Pension Schemes (Consultation by Employers and Miscellaneous Amendment) Regulations 2006 (S.I. 2006/349) (detriment in employment)

Regulation 36 of the Employment Equality (Age) Regulations 2006 (discrimination in the employment field)

Regulation 34 of the European Cooperative Society (Involvement of Employees) Regulations 2006 (detriment in relation to involvement in a European Cooperative Society)

Regulation 51 of the Companies (Cross-Border Mergers) Regulations 2007 (detriment in relation to special negotiating body or employee participation)

SCHEDULE 4
TRIBUNAL JURISDICTIONS TO WHICH SECTION 32 APPLIES

Section 2 of the Equal Pay Act 1970 (c. 41) (equality clauses)

Section 63 of the Sex Discrimination Act 1975 (c. 65) (discrimination in the employment field)

Section 54 of the Race Relations Act 1976 (c. 74) (discrimination in the employment field)

Section 145A of the Trade Union and Labour Relations (Consolidation) Act 1992 (inducements relating to union membership or activities)

Section 145B of that Act (inducements relating to collective bargaining)

Section 146 of that Act (detriment in relation to union membership and activities)

Paragraph 156 of Schedule A1 to that Act (detriment in relation to union recognition rights)

Section 17A of the Disability Discrimination Act 1995 (c. 50) (discrimination in the employment field)

Section 23 of the Employment Rights Act 1996 (c. 18) (unauthorised deductions and payments)

Section 48 of that Act (detriment in employment)

Section 111 of that Act (unfair dismissal)

Section 163 of that Act (redundancy payments)

Section 24 of the National Minimum Wage Act 1998 (c. 39) (detriment in relation to national minimum wage)

Regulation 30 of the Working Time Regulations 1998 (S.I. 1998/1833) (breach of regulations)

Regulation 32 of the Transnational Information and Consultation of Employees Regulations 1999 (S.I. 1999/3323) (detriment relating to European Works Councils)

Regulation 28 of the Employment Equality (Sexual Orientation) Regulations 2003 (discrimination in the employment field)

Regulation 28 of the Employment Equality (Religion or Belief) Regulations 2003 (discrimination in the employment field)

Regulation 45 of the European Public Limited-Liability Company Regulations 2004 (S.I. 2004/2326) (detriment in employment)

Regulation 33 of the Information and Consultation of Employees Regulations 2004 (S.I. 2004/3426) (detriment in employment)

Paragraph 8 of the Schedule to the Occupational and Personal Pension Schemes (Consultation by Employers and Miscellaneous Amendment) Regulations 2006 (S.I. 2006/349) (detriment in employment)

Regulation 36 of the Employment Equality (Age) Regulations 2006 (discrimination in the employment field)

Regulation 34 of the European Cooperative Society (Involvement of Employees) Regulations 2006 (detriment in relation to involvement in a European Cooperative Society)

Regulation 51 of the Companies (Cross-Border Mergers) Regulations 2007 (detriment in relation to special negotiating body or employee participation)

Employment Tribunals (Constitution and Rules of Procedure) Regulations 2004, SI 2004/1861, Sched.1

SCHEDULE 1
THE EMPLOYMENT TRIBUNALS RULES OF PROCEDURE

Regulation 16

How to bring a claim

1. **Starting a claim**

    (1) A claim shall be brought before an employment tribunal by the claimant presenting to an Employment Tribunal Office the details of the claim in writing. Those details must include all the relevant required information (subject to paragraph (5) of this rule and to rule 53 (Employment Agencies Act 1973)).

    (2) The claim may only be presented to an Employment Tribunal Office in England and Wales if it relates to English and Welsh proceedings (defined in regulation 19(1)). The claim may only be presented to an Employment Tribunal Office in Scotland if it relates to Scottish proceedings (defined in regulation 19(2)).

    (3) Unless it is a claim in proceedings described in regulation 14(3), a claim which is presented on or after 1st October 2005 must be presented on a claim form which has been prescribed by the Secretary of State in accordance with regulation 14.

    (4) Subject to paragraph (5) and to rule 53, the required information in relation to the claim is –

    (a) each claimant's name;
    (b) each claimant's address;
    (c) the name of each person against whom the claim is made ('the respondent');
    (d) each respondent's address;
    (e) details of the claim;
    (f) whether or not the claimant is or was an employee of the respondent;
    (g) whether or not the claim includes a complaint that the respondent has dismissed the claimant or has contemplated doing so;
    (h) whether or not the claimant has raised the subject matter of the claim with the respondent in writing at least 28 days prior to presenting the claim to an Employment Tribunal Office;
    (i) if the claimant has not done as described in (h), why he has not done so.

    (5) In the following circumstances the required information identified below is not required to be provided in relation to that claim –

(a) if the claimant is not or was not an employee of the respondent, the information in paragraphs (4)(g) to (i) is not required;

(b) if the claimant was an employee of the respondent and the claim consists only of a complaint that the respondent has dismissed the claimant or has contemplated doing so, the information in paragraphs (4)(h) and (i) is not required;

(c) if the claimant was an employee of the respondent and the claim does not relate to the claimant being dismissed or a contemplated dismissal by the respondent, and the claimant has raised the subject matter of the claim with the respondent as described in paragraph (4)(h), the information in paragraph (4)(i) is not required.

(6) References in this rule to being dismissed or a dismissal by the respondent do not include references to constructive dismissal.

(7) Two or more claimants may present their claims in the same document if their claims arise out of the same set of facts.

(8) When section 32 of the Employment Act applies to the claim or part of one and a chairman considers in accordance with subsection (6) of section 32 that there has been a breach of subsections (2) to (4) of that section, neither a chairman nor a tribunal shall consider the substance of the claim (or the relevant part of it) until such time as those subsections have been complied with in relation to the claim or the relevant part of it.

Acceptance of claim procedure

2. What the tribunal does after receiving the claim

(1) On receiving the claim the Secretary shall consider whether the claim or part of it should be accepted in accordance with rule 3. If a claim or part of one is not accepted the tribunal shall not proceed to deal with any part which has not been accepted (unless it is accepted at a later date). If no part of a claim is accepted the claim shall not be copied to the respondent.

(2) If the Secretary accepts the claim or part of it, he shall –

(a) send a copy of the claim to each respondent and record in writing the date on which it was sent;

(b) inform the parties in writing of the case number of the claim (which must from then on be referred to in all correspondence relating to the claim) and the address to which notices and other communications to the Employment Tribunal Office must be sent;

(c) inform the respondent in writing about how to present a response to the claim, the time limit for doing so, what may happen if a response is not entered within the time limit and that the respondent has a right to receive a copy of any judgment disposing of the claim;

(d) when any enactment relevant to the claim provides for conciliation, notify the parties that the services of a conciliation officer are available to them;

(e) when rule 22 (fixed period for conciliation) applies, notify the parties of the date on which the conciliation officer's duty to conciliate ends and that after that date the services of a conciliation officer shall be available to them only in limited circumstances; and

(f) if only part of the claim has been accepted, inform the claimant and any respondent which parts of the claim have not been accepted and that the tribunal shall not proceed to deal with those parts unless they are accepted at a later date.

3. When the claim will not be accepted by the Secretary

(1) When a claim is required by rule 1(3) to be presented using a prescribed form, but the prescribed form has not been used, the Secretary shall not accept the claim and shall return it to the claimant with an explanation of why the claim has been rejected and provide a prescribed claim form.

(2) The Secretary shall not accept the claim (or a relevant part of one) if it is clear to him that one or more of the following circumstances applies –

    (a) the claim does not include all the relevant required information;

    (b) the tribunal does not have power to consider the claim (or that relevant part of it); or

    (c) section 32 of the Employment Act (complaints about grievances) applies to the claim or part of it and the claim has been presented to the tribunal in breach of subsections (2) to (4) of section 32.

(3) If the Secretary decides not to accept a claim or part of one for any of the reasons in paragraph (2), he shall refer the claim together with a statement of his reasons for not accepting it to a chairman. The chairman shall decide in accordance with the criteria in paragraph (2) whether the claim or part of it should be accepted and allowed to proceed.

(4) If the chairman decides that the claim or part of one should be accepted he shall inform the Secretary in writing and the Secretary shall accept the relevant part of the claim and then proceed to deal with it in accordance with rule 2(2).

(5) If the chairman decides that the claim or part of it should not be accepted he shall record his decision together with the reasons for it in writing in a document signed by him. The Secretary shall as soon as is reasonably practicable inform the claimant of that decision and the reasons for it in writing together with information on how that decision may be reviewed or appealed.

(6) Where a claim or part of one has been presented to the tribunal in breach of subsections (2) to (4) of section 32 of the Employment Act, the Secretary shall notify the claimant of the time limit which applies to the claim or the part of it concerned and shall inform the claimant of the consequences of not complying with section 32 of that Act.

(7) Except for the purposes of paragraph (6) and (8) or any appeal to the Employment Appeal Tribunal, where a chairman has decided that a claim or part of one should not be accepted such a claim (or the relevant part of it) is to be treated as if it had not been received by the Secretary on that occasion.

(8) Any decision by a chairman not to accept a claim or part of one may be reviewed in accordance with rules 34 to 36. If the result of such review is that any parts of the claim should have been accepted, then paragraph (7) shall not apply to the relevant parts of that claim and the Secretary shall then accept such parts and proceed to deal with it as described in rule 2(2).

(9) A decision to accept or not to accept a claim or part of one shall not bind any future tribunal or chairman where any of the issues listed in paragraph (2) fall to be determined later in the proceedings.

(10) Except in rule 34 (review of other judgments and decisions), all references to a claim in the remainder of these rules are to be read as references to only the part of the claim which has been accepted.

Response

4. Responding to the claim

(1)   If the respondent wishes to respond to the claim made against him he must present his response to the Employment Tribunal Office within 28 days of the date on which he was sent a copy of the claim. The response must include all the relevant required information. The time limit for the respondent to present his response may be extended in accordance with paragraph (4).

(2)   Unless it is a response in proceedings described in regulation 14(3), any response presented on or after 1st October 2005 must be on a response form prescribed by the Secretary of State pursuant to regulation 14.

(3)   The required information in relation to the response is –

(a)   the respondent's full name;
(b)   the respondent's address;
(c)   whether or not the respondent wishes to resist the claim in whole or in part; and
(d)   if the respondent wishes to so resist, on what grounds.

(4)   The respondent may apply under rule 11 for an extension of the time limit within which he is to present his response. The application must be presented to the Employment Tribunal Office within 28 days of the date on which the respondent was sent a copy of the claim (unless the application is made under rule 33(1)) and must explain why the respondent cannot comply with the time limit. Subject to rule 33, the chairman shall only extend the time within which a response may be presented if he is satisfied that it is just and equitable to do so.

(5)   A single document may include the response to more than one claim if the relief claimed arises out of the same set of facts, provided that in respect of each of the claims to which the single response relates –

(a)   the respondent intends to resist all the claims and the grounds for doing so are the same in relation to each claim; or
(b)   the respondent does not intend to resist any of the claims.

(6)   A single document may include the response of more than one respondent to a single claim provided that –

(a)   each respondent intends to resist the claim and the grounds for doing so are the same for each respondent; or
(b)   none of the respondents intends to resist the claim.

Acceptance of response procedure

5. What the tribunal does after receiving the response

(1)   On receiving the response the Secretary shall consider whether the response should be accepted in accordance with rule 6. If the response is not accepted it shall be returned to the respondent and (subject to paragraphs (5) and (6) of rule 6) the claim shall be dealt with as if no response to the claim had been presented.

(2)   If the Secretary accepts the response he shall send a copy of it to all other parties and record in writing the date on which he does so.

6. When the response will not be accepted by the Secretary

(1)   Where a response is required to be presented using a prescribed form by rule 4(2), but the prescribed form has not been used, the Secretary shall not accept

the response and shall return it to the respondent with an explanation of why the response has been rejected and provide a prescribed response form.

(2) The Secretary shall not accept the response if it is clear to him that any of the following circumstances apply –

    (a) the response does not include all the required information (defined in rule 4(3));

    (b) the response has not been presented within the relevant time limit.

(3) If the Secretary decides not to accept a response for either of the reasons in paragraph (2), he shall refer the response together with a statement of his reasons for not accepting the response to a chairman. The chairman shall decide in accordance with the criteria in paragraph (2) whether the response should be accepted.

(4) If the chairman decides that the response should be accepted he shall inform the Secretary in writing and the Secretary shall accept the response and then deal with it in accordance with rule 5(2).

(5) If the chairman decides that the response should not be accepted he shall record his decision together with the reasons for it in writing in a document signed by him. The Secretary shall inform both the claimant and the respondent of that decision and the reasons for it. The Secretary shall also inform the respondent of the consequences for the respondent of that decision and how it may be reviewed or appealed.

(6) Any decision by a chairman not to accept a response may be reviewed in accordance with rules 34 to 36. If the result of such a review is that the response should have been accepted, then the Secretary shall accept the response and proceed to deal with the response as described in rule 5(2).

7. Counterclaims

(1) When a respondent wishes to present a claim against the claimant ('a counterclaim') in accordance with article 4 of the Employment Tribunals Extension of Jurisdiction (England and Wales) Order 1994, or as the case may be, article 4 of the Employment Tribunals Extension of Jurisdiction (Scotland) Order 1994, he must present the details of his counterclaim to the Employment Tribunal Office in writing. Those details must include –

    (a) the respondent's name;

    (b) the respondent's address;

    (c) the name of each claimant whom the counterclaim is made against;

    (d) the claimant's address;

    (e) details of the counterclaim.

(2) A chairman may in relation to particular proceedings by order made under rule 10(1) establish the procedure which shall be followed by the respondent making the counterclaim and any claimant responding to the counterclaim.

(3) The President may by a practice direction made under regulation 13 make provision for the procedure which is to apply to counterclaims generally.

Consequences of a response not being presented or accepted

8. Default judgments

(1) In any proceedings if the relevant time limit for presenting a response has passed, a chairman may, in the circumstances listed in paragraph (2), issue a

default judgment to determine the claim without a hearing if he considers it appropriate to do so.

(2) Those circumstances are when either –

  (a) no response in those proceedings has been presented to the Employment Tribunal Office within the relevant time limit;

  (b) a response has been so presented, but a decision has been made not to accept the response either by the Secretary under rule 6(1) or by a chairman under rule 6(3), and the Employment Tribunal Office has not received an application under rule 34 to have that decision reviewed; or

  (c) a response has been accepted in those proceedings, but the respondent has stated in the response that he does not intend to resist the claim.

(3) A default judgment may determine liability only or it may determine liability and remedy. If a default judgment determines remedy it shall be such remedy as it appears to the chairman that the claimant is entitled to on the basis of the information before him.

(4) Any default judgment issued by a chairman under this rule shall be recorded in writing and shall be signed by him. The Secretary shall send a copy of that judgment to the parties, to ACAS, and, if the proceedings were referred to the tribunal by a court, to that court. The Secretary shall also inform the parties of their right to have the default judgment reviewed under rule 33. The Secretary shall put a copy of the default judgment on the Register (subject to rule 49 (sexual offences and the Register)).

(5) The claimant or respondent may apply to have the default judgment reviewed in accordance with rule 33.

(6) If the parties settle the proceedings (either by means of a compromise agreement (as defined in rule 23(2)) or through ACAS) before or on the date on which a default judgment in those proceedings is issued, the default judgment shall have no effect.

(7) When paragraph (6) applies, either party may apply under rule 33 to have the default judgment revoked.

9. Taking no further part in the proceedings

A respondent who has not presented a response to a claim or whose response has not been accepted shall not be entitled to take any part in the proceedings except to –

(a) make an application under rule 33 (review of default judgments);

(b) make an application under rule 35 (preliminary consideration of application for review) in respect of rule 34(3)(a), (b) or (e);

(c) be called as a witness by another person; or

(d) be sent a copy of a document or corrected entry in accordance with rule 8(4), 29(2) or 37;

and in these rules the word 'party' or 'respondent' includes a respondent only in relation to his entitlement to take such a part in the proceedings, and in relation to any such part which he takes.

Case management

10. General power to manage proceedings

(1) Subject to the following rules, the chairman may at any time either on the application of a party or on his own initiative make an order in relation to

any matter which appears to him to be appropriate. Such orders may be any of those listed in paragraph (2) or such other orders as he thinks fit. Subject to the following rules, orders may be issued as a result of a chairman considering the papers before him in the absence of the parties, or at a hearing (see regulation 2 for the definition of 'hearing').

(2) Examples of orders which may be made under paragraph (1) are orders –

    (a) as to the manner in which the proceedings are to be conducted, including any time limit to be observed;

    (b) that a party provide additional information;

    (c) requiring the attendance of any person in Great Britain either to give evidence or to produce documents or information;

    (d) requiring any person in Great Britain to disclose documents or information to a party to allow a party to inspect such material as might be ordered by a County Court (or in Scotland, by a sheriff);

    (e) extending any time limit, whether or not expired (subject to rules 4(4), 11(2), 25(5), 30(5), 33(1), 35(1), 38(7) and 42(5) of this Schedule, and to rule 3(4) of Schedule 2);

    (f) requiring the provision of written answers to questions put by the tribunal or chairman;

    (g) that, subject to rule 22(8), a short conciliation period be extended into a standard conciliation period;

    (h) staying (in Scotland, sisting) the whole or part of any proceedings;

    (i) that part of the proceedings be dealt with separately;

    (j) that different claims be considered together;

    (k) that any person who the chairman or tribunal considers may be liable for the remedy claimed should be made a respondent in the proceedings;

    (l) dismissing the claim against a respondent who is no longer directly interested in the claim;

    (m) postponing or adjourning any hearing;

    (n) varying or revoking other orders;

    (o) giving notice to the parties of a pre-hearing review or the Hearing;

    (p) giving notice under rule 19;

    (q) giving leave to amend a claim or response;

    (r) that any person who the chairman or tribunal considers has an interest in the outcome of the proceedings may be joined as a party to the proceedings;

    (s) that a witness statement be prepared or exchanged; or

    (t) as to the use of experts or interpreters in the proceedings.

(3) An order may specify the time at or within which and the place at which any act is required to be done. An order may also impose conditions and it shall inform the parties of the potential consequences of non-compliance set out in rule 13.

(4) When a requirement has been imposed under paragraph (1) the person subject to the requirement may make an application under rule 11 (applications in proceedings) for the order to be varied or revoked.

(5) An order described in paragraph (2)(d) which requires a person other than a party to grant disclosure or inspection of material may be made only when the disclosure sought is necessary in order to dispose fairly of the claim or to save expense.

(6) Any order containing a requirement described in either subparagraph (2)(c) or (d) shall state that under section 7(4) of the Employment Tribunals Act, any person who without reasonable excuse fails to comply with the requirement

shall be liable on summary conviction to a fine, and the document shall also state the amount of the maximum fine.

(7) An order as described in paragraph (2)(j) may be made only if all relevant parties have been given notice that such an order may be made and they have been given the opportunity to make oral or written representations as to why such an order should or should not be made.

(8) Any order made under this rule shall be recorded in writing and signed by the chairman and the Secretary shall inform all parties to the proceedings of any order made as soon as is reasonably practicable.

11. Applications in proceedings

(1) At any stage of the proceedings a party may apply for an order to be issued, varied or revoked or for a case management discussion or pre-hearing review to be held.

(2) An application for an order must be made not less than 10 days before the date of the hearing at which it is to be considered (if any) unless it is not reasonably practicable to do so, or the chairman or tribunal considers it in the interests of justice that shorter notice be allowed. The application must (unless a chairman orders otherwise) be in writing to the Employment Tribunal Office and include the case number for the proceedings and the reasons for the request. If the application is for a case management discussion or a pre-hearing review to be held, it must identify any orders sought.

(3) An application for an order must include an explanation of how the order would assist the tribunal or chairman in dealing with the proceedings efficiently and fairly.

(4) When a party is legally represented in relation to the application (except where the application is for a witness order described in rule 10(2)(c) only), that party or his representative must, at the same time as the application is sent to the Employment Tribunal Office, provide all other parties with the following information in writing –

(a) details of the application and the reasons why it is sought;

(b) notification that any objection to the application must be sent to the Employment Tribunal Office within 7 days of receiving the application, or before the date of the hearing (whichever date is the earlier);

(c) that any objection to the application must be copied to both the Employment Tribunal Office and all other parties;

and the party or his representative must confirm in writing to the Employment Tribunal Office that this rule has been complied with.

(5) Where a party is not legally represented in relation to the application, the Secretary shall inform all other parties of the matters listed in paragraphs (4)(a) to (c).

(6) A chairman may refuse a party's application and if he does so the Secretary shall inform the parties in writing of such refusal unless the application is refused at a hearing.

12. Chairman acting on his own initiative

(1) Subject to paragraph (2) and to rules 10(7) and 18(7), a chairman may make an order on his own initiative with or without hearing the parties or giving them an opportunity to make written or oral representations. He may also decide to hold a case management discussion or pre-hearing review on his own initiative.

(2) Where a chairman makes an order without giving the parties the opportunity to make representations –

    (a) the Secretary must send to the party affected by such order a copy of the order and a statement explaining the right to make an application under paragraph (2)(b); and

    (b) a party affected by the order may apply to have it varied or revoked.

(3) An application under paragraph (2)(b) must (subject to rule 10(2)(e)) be made before the time at which, or the expiry of the period within which, the order was to be complied with. Such an application must (unless a chairman orders otherwise) be made in writing to an Employment Tribunal Office and it must include the reasons for the application. Paragraphs (4) and (5) of rule 11 apply in relation to informing the other parties of the application.

13. Compliance with orders and practice directions

(1) If a party does not comply with an order made under these rules, under rule 8 of Schedule 3, rule 7 of Schedule 4 or a practice direction, a chairman or tribunal –

    (a) may make an order in respect of costs or preparation time under rules 38 to 46; or

    (b) may (subject to paragraph (2) and rule 19) at a pre-hearing review or a Hearing make an order to strike out the whole or part of the claim or, as the case may be, the response and, where appropriate, order that a respondent be debarred from responding to the claim altogether.

(2) An order may also provide that unless the order is complied with, the claim or, as the case may be, the response shall be struck out on the date of non-compliance without further consideration of the proceedings or the need to give notice under rule 19 or hold a pre-hearing review or Hearing.

(3) Chairmen and tribunals shall comply with any practice directions issued under regulation 13.

Different types of hearing

14. Hearings – general

(1) A chairman or a tribunal (depending on the relevant rule) may hold the following types of hearing –

    (a) a case management discussion under rule 17;

    (b) a pre-hearing review under rule 18;

    (c) a Hearing under rule 26; or

    (d) a review hearing under rule 33 or 36.

(2) So far as it appears appropriate to do so, the chairman or tribunal shall seek to avoid formality in his or its proceedings and shall not be bound by any enactment or rule of law relating to the admissibility of evidence in proceedings before the courts.

(3) The chairman or tribunal (as the case may be) shall make such enquiries of persons appearing before him or it and of witnesses as he or it considers appropriate and shall otherwise conduct the hearing in such manner as he or it considers most appropriate for the clarification of the issues and generally for the just handling of the proceedings.

(4) Unless the parties agree to shorter notice, the Secretary shall send notice of any hearing (other than a case management discussion) to every party not less than 14 days before the date fixed for the hearing and shall inform them that they have the opportunity to submit written representations and to advance oral argument. The Secretary shall give the parties reasonable notice before a case management discussion is held.

(5) If a party wishes to submit written representations for consideration at a hearing (other than a case management discussion) he shall present them to the Employment Tribunal Office not less than 7 days before the hearing and shall at the same time send a copy to all other parties.

(6) The tribunal or chairman may, if it or he considers it appropriate, consider representations in writing which have been submitted otherwise than in accordance with paragraph (5).

15. Use of electronic communications

(1) A hearing (other than those mentioned in subparagraphs (c) and (d) of rule 14(1)) may be conducted by use of electronic communications provided that the chairman or tribunal conducting the hearing considers it just and equitable to do so.

(2) Where a hearing is required by these rules to be held in public and it is to be conducted by use of electronic communications in accordance with this rule then, subject to rule 16, it must be held in a place to which the public has access and using equipment so that the public is able to hear all parties to the communication.

16. Hearings which may be held in private

(1) A hearing or part of one may be conducted in private for the purpose of hearing from any person evidence or representations which in the opinion of the tribunal or chairman is likely to consist of information –

(a) which he could not disclose without contravening a prohibition imposed by or by virtue of any enactment;

(b) which has been communicated to him in confidence, or which he has otherwise obtained in consequence of the confidence placed in him by another person; or

(c) the disclosure of which would, for reasons other than its effect on negotiations with respect to any of the matters mentioned in section 178(2) of TULR(C)A, cause substantial injury to any undertaking of his or any undertaking in which he works.

(2) Where a tribunal or chairman decides to hold a hearing or part of one in private, it or he shall give reasons for doing so. A member of the Council on Tribunals (in Scotland, a member of the Council on Tribunals or its Scottish Committee) shall be entitled to attend any Hearing or pre-hearing review taking place in private in his capacity as a member.

Case management discussions

17. Conduct of case management discussions

(1) Case management discussions are interim hearings and may deal with matters of procedure and management of the proceedings and they shall

be held in private. Case management discussions shall be conducted by a chairman.

(2) Any determination of a person's civil rights or obligations shall not be dealt with in a case management discussion. The matters listed in rule 10(2) are examples of matters which may be dealt with at case management discussions. Orders and judgments listed in rule 18(7) may not be made at a case management discussion.

Pre-hearing reviews

18. Conduct of pre-hearing reviews

(1) Pre-hearing reviews are interim hearings and shall be conducted by a chairman unless the circumstances in paragraph (3) are applicable. Subject to rule 16, they shall take place in public.

(2) At a pre-hearing review the chairman may carry out a preliminary consideration of the proceedings and he may –

  (a) determine any interim or preliminary matter relating to the proceedings;

  (b) issue any order in accordance with rule 10 or do anything else which may be done at a case management discussion;

  (c) order that a deposit be paid in accordance with rule 20 without hearing evidence;

  (d) consider any oral or written representations or evidence;

  (e) deal with an application for interim relief made under section 161 of TULR(C)A or section 128 of the Employment Rights Act.

(3) Pre-hearing reviews shall be conducted by a tribunal composed in accordance with section 4(1) and (2) of the Employment Tribunals Act if –

  (a) a party has made a request in writing not less than 10 days before the date on which the pre-hearing review is due to take place that the pre-hearing review be conducted by a tribunal instead of a chairman; and

  (b) a chairman considers that one or more substantive issues of fact are likely to be determined at the pre-hearing review, that it would be desirable for the pre-hearing review to be conducted by a tribunal and he has issued an order that the pre-hearing review be conducted by a tribunal.

(4) If an order is made under paragraph (3), any reference to a chairman in relation to a pre-hearing review shall be read as a reference to a tribunal.

(5) Notwithstanding the preliminary or interim nature of a pre-hearing review, at a pre-hearing review the chairman may give judgment on any preliminary issue of substance relating to the proceedings. Judgments or orders made at a pre-hearing review may result in the proceedings being struck out or dismissed or otherwise determined with the result that a Hearing is no longer necessary in those proceedings.

(6) Before a judgment or order listed in paragraph (7) is made, notice must be given in accordance with rule 19. The judgments or orders listed in paragraph (7) must be made at a pre-hearing review or a Hearing if one of the parties has so requested. If no such request has been made such judgments or orders may be made in the absence of the parties.

(7) Subject to paragraph (6), a chairman or tribunal may make a judgment or order –

(a)   as to the entitlement of any party to bring or contest particular proceedings;

(b)   striking out or amending all or part of any claim or response on the grounds that it is scandalous, or vexatious or has no reasonable prospect of success;

(c)   striking out any claim or response (or part of one) on the grounds that the manner in which the proceedings have been conducted by or on behalf of the claimant or the respondent (as the case may be) has been scandalous, unreasonable or vexatious;

(d)   striking out a claim which has not been actively pursued;

(e)   striking out a claim or response (or part of one) for non-compliance with an order or practice direction;

(f)   striking out a claim where the chairman or tribunal considers that it is no longer possible to have a fair Hearing in those proceedings;

(g)   making a restricted reporting order (subject to rule 50).

(8)   A claim or response or any part of one may be struck out under these rules only on the grounds stated in sub-paragraphs (7)(b) to (f).

(9)   If at a pre-hearing review a requirement to pay a deposit under rule 20 has been considered, the chairman who conducted that pre-hearing review shall not be a member of the tribunal at the Hearing in relation to those proceedings.

19. Notice requirements

(1)   Before a chairman or a tribunal makes a judgment or order described in rule 18(7), except where the order is one described in rule 13(2) or it is a temporary restricted reporting order made in accordance with rule 50, the Secretary shall send notice to the party against whom it is proposed that the order or judgment should be made. The notice shall inform him of the order or judgment to be considered and give him the opportunity to give reasons why the order or judgment should not be made. This paragraph shall not be taken to require the Secretary to send such notice to that party if that party has been given an opportunity to give reasons orally to the chairman or the tribunal as to why the order should not be made.

(2)   Where a notice required by paragraph (1) is sent in relation to an order to strike out a claim which has not been actively pursued, unless the contrary is proved, the notice shall be treated as if it were received by the addressee if it has been sent to the address specified in the claim as the address to which notices are to be sent (or to any subsequent replacement for that address which has been notified to the Employment Tribunal Office).

Payment of a deposit

20. Requirement to pay a deposit in order to continue with proceedings

(1)   At a pre-hearing review if a chairman considers that the contentions put forward by any party in relation to a matter required to be determined by a tribunal have little reasonable prospect of success, the chairman may make an order against that party requiring the party to pay a deposit of an amount not exceeding £500 as a condition of being permitted to continue to take part in the proceedings relating to that matter.

(2)   No order shall be made under this rule unless the chairman has taken reasonable steps to ascertain the ability of the party against whom it is proposed to

make the order to comply with such an order, and has taken account of any information so ascertained in determining the amount of the deposit.

(3) An order made under this rule, and the chairman's grounds for making such an order, shall be recorded in a document signed by the chairman. A copy of that document shall be sent to each of the parties and shall be accompanied by a note explaining that if the party against whom the order is made persists in making those contentions relating to the matter to which the order relates, he may have an award of costs or preparation time made against him and could lose his deposit.

(4) If a party against whom an order has been made does not pay the amount specified in the order to the Secretary either –

(a) within the period of 21 days of the day on which the document recording the making of the order is sent to him; or

(b) within such further period, not exceeding 14 days, as the chairman may allow in the light of representations made by that party within the period of 21 days;

a chairman shall strike out the claim or response of that party or, as the case may be, the part of it to which the order relates.

(5) The deposit paid by a party under an order made under this rule shall be refunded to him in full except where rule 47 applies.

Conciliation

21. Documents to be sent to conciliators

In proceedings brought under the provisions of any enactment providing for conciliation, the Secretary shall send copies of all documents, orders, judgments, written reasons and notices to an ACAS conciliation officer except where the Secretary and ACAS have agreed otherwise.

22. Fixed period for conciliation

(1) This rule and rules 23 and 24 apply to all proceedings before a tribunal which are brought under any enactment which provides for conciliation except national security proceedings and proceedings which include a claim made under one or more of the following enactments –

(a) the Equal Pay Act, section 2(1);
(b) the Sex Discrimination Act, Part II, section 63;
(c) the Race Relations Act, Part II, section 54;
(d) the Disability Discrimination Act, Part II, section 17A or 25(8);
(e) the Employment Equality (Sexual Orientation) Regulations 2003;
(f) the Employment Equality (Religion or Belief) Regulations 2003;
(g) Employment Rights Act, sections 47B, 103A and 105(6A); and
(h) the Employment Equality (Age) Regulations 2006.

(2) In all proceedings to which this rule applies there shall be a conciliation period to give a time limited opportunity for the parties to reach an ACAS conciliated settlement (the 'conciliation period'). In proceedings in which there is more than one respondent there shall be a conciliation period in relation to each respondent.

(3) In any proceedings to which this rule applies a Hearing shall not take place during a conciliation period and where the time and place of a Hearing has been fixed to take place during a conciliation period, such Hearing shall be

postponed until after the end of any conciliation period. The fixing of the time and place for the Hearing may take place during a conciliation period. Pre-hearing reviews and case management discussions may take place during a conciliation period.

(4) In relation to each respondent the conciliation period commences on the day following the date on which the Secretary sends a copy of the claim to that respondent. The duration of the conciliation period shall be determined in accordance with the following paragraphs and rule 23.

(5) In any proceedings which consist of claims under any of the following enactments (but no other enactments) the conciliation period is seven weeks (the 'short conciliation period') –

(a) Employment Tribunals Act, section 3 (breach of contract);
(b) the following provisions of the Employment Rights Act –

  (i) sections 13 to 27 (failure to pay wages or an unauthorised deduction of wages);
  (ii) section 28 (right to a guarantee payment);
  (iii) section 50 (right to time off for public duties);
  (iv) section 52 (right to time off to look for work or arrange training);
  (v) section 53 (right to remuneration for time off under section 52);
  (vi) section 55 (right to time off for ante-natal care);
  (vii) section 56 (right to remuneration for time off under section 55);
  (viii) section 64 (failure to pay remuneration whilst suspended for medical reasons);
  (ix) section 68 (right to remuneration whilst suspended on maternity grounds);
  (x) sections 163 or 164 (failure to pay a redundancy payment);

(c) the following provisions of TULR(C)A –

  (i) section 68 (right not to suffer deduction of unauthorised subscriptions)
  (ii) section 168 (time off for carrying out trade union duties);
  (iii) section 169 (payment for time off under section 168);
  (iv) section 170 (time off for trade union activities);
  (v) section 192 (failure to pay remuneration under a protective award);

(d) regulation 15(10) of the Transfer of Undertakings (Protection of Employment) Regulations 2006 (failure to pay compensation following failure to inform or consult);
(e) regulations 13, 14(2) or 16(1) of the Working Time Regulations 1998 (right to paid annual leave).

(6) In all other proceedings to which this rule applies the conciliation period is thirteen weeks (the 'standard conciliation period').

(7) In proceedings to which the standard conciliation period applies, that period shall be extended by a period of a further two weeks if ACAS notifies the Secretary in writing that all of the following circumstances apply before the expiry of the standard conciliation period –

(a) all parties to the proceedings agree to the extension of any relevant conciliation period;
(b) a proposal for settling the proceedings has been made by a party and is under consideration by the other parties to the proceedings; and
(c) ACAS considers it probable that the proceedings will be settled during the further extended conciliation period.

(8)   A short conciliation period in any proceedings may, if that period has not already ended, be extended into a standard conciliation period if a chairman considers on the basis of the complexity of the proceedings that a standard conciliation period would be more appropriate. Where a chairman makes an order extending the conciliation period in such circumstances, the Secretary shall inform the parties to the proceedings and ACAS in writing as soon as is reasonably practicable.

23. Early termination of conciliation period

(1)   Should one of the following circumstances arise during a conciliation period (be it short or standard) which relates to a particular respondent (referred to in this rule as the relevant respondent), that conciliation period shall terminate early on the relevant date specified (and if more than one circumstance or date listed below is applicable to any conciliation period, that conciliation period shall terminate on the earliest of those dates) –

   (a)   where a default judgment is issued against the relevant respondent which determines both liability and remedy, the date on which the default judgment is signed;
   (b)   where a default judgment is issued against the relevant respondent which determines liability only, the date which is 14 days after the date on which the default judgment is signed;
   (c)   where either the claim or the response entered by the relevant respondent is struck out, the date on which the judgment to strike out is signed;
   (d)   where the claim is withdrawn, the date of receipt by the Employment Tribunal Office of the notice of withdrawal;
   (e)   where the claimant or the relevant respondent has informed ACAS in writing that they do not wish to proceed with attempting to conciliate in relation to those proceedings, the date on which ACAS sends notice of such circumstances to the parties and to the Employment Tribunal Office;
   (f)   where the claimant and the relevant respondent have reached a settlement by way of a compromise agreement (including a compromise agreement to refer proceedings to arbitration), the date on which the Employment Tribunal Office receives notice from both of those parties to that effect;
   (g)   where the claimant and the relevant respondent have reached a settlement through a conciliation officer (including a settlement to refer the proceedings to arbitration), the date of the settlement;
   (h)   where no response presented by the relevant respondent has been accepted in the proceedings and no default judgment has been issued against that respondent, the date which is 14 days after the expiry of the time limit for presenting the response to the Secretary.

(2)   Where a chairman or tribunal makes an order which re-establishes the relevant respondent's right to respond to the claim (for example, revoking a default judgment) and when that order is made, the conciliation period in relation to that respondent has terminated early under paragraph (1) or has otherwise expired, the chairman or tribunal may order that a further conciliation period shall apply in relation to that respondent if they consider it appropriate to do so.

(3)   When an order is made under paragraph (2), the further conciliation period commences on the date of that order and the duration of that period shall be

determined in accordance with paragraphs (5) to (8) of rule 22 and paragraph (1) of this rule as if the earlier conciliation period in relation to that respondent had not taken place.

24. Effect of staying or sisting proceedings on the conciliation period

Where during a conciliation period an order is made to stay (or in Scotland, sist) the proceedings, that order has the effect of suspending any conciliation period in those proceedings. Any unexpired portion of a conciliation period takes effect from the date on which the stay comes to an end (or in Scotland, the sist is recalled) and continues for the duration of the unexpired portion of that conciliation period or two weeks (whichever is the greater).

Withdrawal of proceedings

25. Right to withdraw proceedings

(1) A claimant may withdraw all or part of his claim at any time – this may be done either orally at a hearing or in writing in accordance with paragraph (2).

(2) To withdraw a claim or part of one in writing the claimant must inform the Employment Tribunal Office of the claim or the parts of it which are to be withdrawn. Where there is more than one respondent the notification must specify against which respondents the claim is being withdrawn.

(3) The Secretary shall inform all other parties of the withdrawal. Withdrawal takes effect on the date on which the Employment Tribunal Office (in the case of written notifications) or the tribunal (in the case of oral notification) receives notice of it and where the whole claim is withdrawn, subject to paragraph (4), proceedings are brought to an end against the relevant respondent on that date. Withdrawal does not affect proceedings as to costs, preparation time or wasted costs.

(4) Where a claim has been withdrawn, a respondent may make an application to have the proceedings against him dismissed. Such an application must be made by the respondent in writing to the Employment Tribunal Office within 28 days of the notice of the withdrawal being sent to the respondent. If the respondent's application is granted and the proceedings are dismissed those proceedings cannot be continued by the claimant (unless the decision to dismiss is successfully reviewed or appealed).

(5) The time limit in paragraph (4) may be extended by a chairman if he considers it just and equitable to do so.

The Hearing

26. Hearings

(1) A Hearing is held for the purpose of determining outstanding procedural or substantive issues or disposing of the proceedings. In any proceedings there may be more than one Hearing and there may be different categories of Hearing, such as a Hearing on liability, remedies, costs (in Scotland, expenses) or preparation time.

(2) Any Hearing of a claim shall be heard by a tribunal composed in accordance with section 4(1) and (2) of the Employment Tribunals Act.

(3) Any Hearing of a claim shall take place in public, subject to rule 16.

27. What happens at the Hearing

(1)   The President, Vice President or a Regional Chairman shall fix the date, time and place of the Hearing and the Secretary shall send to each party a notice of the Hearing together with information and guidance as to procedure at the Hearing.

(2)   Subject to rule 14(3), at the Hearing a party shall be entitled to give evidence, to call witnesses, to question witnesses and to address the tribunal.

(3)   The tribunal shall require parties and witnesses who attend the Hearing to give their evidence on oath or affirmation.

(4)   The tribunal may exclude from the Hearing any person who is to appear as a witness in the proceedings until such time as they give evidence if it considers it in the interests of justice to do so.

(5)   If a party fails to attend or to be represented (for the purpose of conducting the party's case at the Hearing) at the time and place fixed for the Hearing, the tribunal may dismiss or dispose of the proceedings in the absence of that party or may adjourn the Hearing to a later date.

(6)   If the tribunal wishes to dismiss or dispose of proceedings in the circumstances described in paragraph (5), it shall first consider any information in its possession which has been made available to it by the parties.

(7)   At a Hearing a tribunal may exercise any powers which may be exercised by a chairman under these rules.

Orders, judgments and reasons

28. Orders and judgments

(1)   Chairmen or tribunals may issue the following –

    (a)   a 'judgment', which is a final determination of the proceedings or of a particular issue in those proceedings; it may include an award of compensation, a declaration or recommendation and it may also include orders for costs, preparation time or wasted costs;

    (b)   an 'order', which may be issued in relation to interim matters and it will require a person to do or not to do something.

(2)   If the parties agree in writing upon the terms of any order or judgment a chairman or tribunal may, if he or it thinks fit, make such order or judgment.

(3)   At the end of a hearing the chairman (or, as the case may be, the tribunal) shall either issue any order or judgment orally or shall reserve the judgment or order to be given in writing at a later date.

(4)   Where a tribunal is composed of three persons any order or judgment may be made or issued by a majority; and if a tribunal is composed of two persons only, the chairman has a second or casting vote.

29. Form and content of judgments

(1)   When judgment is reserved a written judgment shall be sent to the parties as soon as practicable. All judgments (whether issued orally or in writing) shall be recorded in writing and signed by the chairman.

(2)   The Secretary shall provide a copy of the judgment to each of the parties and, where the proceedings were referred to the tribunal by a court, to that court. The Secretary shall include guidance to the parties on how the judgment may be reviewed or appealed.

(3)   Where the judgment includes an award of compensation or a determination that one party is required to pay a sum to another (excluding an order for costs, expenses, allowances, preparation time or wasted costs), the document shall also contain a statement of the amount of compensation awarded, or of the sum required to be paid.

30. Reasons

(1)   A tribunal or chairman must give reasons (either oral or written) for any –

    (a)   judgment; or
    (b)   order, if a request for reasons is made before or at the hearing at which the order is made.

(2)   Reasons may be given orally at the time of issuing the judgment or order or they may be reserved to be given in writing at a later date. If reasons are reserved, they shall be signed by the chairman and sent to the parties by the Secretary.

(3)   Where oral reasons have been provided, written reasons shall only be provided –

    (a)   in relation to judgments if requested by one of the parties within the time limit set out in paragraph (5); or
    (b)   in relation to any judgment or order if requested by the Employment Appeal Tribunal at any time.

(4)   When written reasons are provided, the Secretary shall send a copy of the reasons to all parties to the proceedings and record the date on which the reasons were sent. Written reasons shall be signed by the chairman.

(5)   A request for written reasons for a judgment must be made by a party either orally at the hearing (if the judgment is issued at a hearing), or in writing within 14 days of the date on which the judgment was sent to the parties. This time limit may be extended by a chairman where he considers it just and equitable to do so.

(6)   Written reasons for a judgment shall include the following information –

    (a)   the issues which the tribunal or chairman has identified as being relevant to the claim;
    (b)   if some identified issues were not determined, what those issues were and why they were not determined;
    (c)   findings of fact relevant to the issues which have been determined;
    (d)   a concise statement of the applicable law;
    (e)   how the relevant findings of fact and applicable law have been applied in order to determine the issues; and
    (f)   where the judgment includes an award of compensation or a determination that one party make a payment to the other, a table showing how the amount or sum has been calculated or a description of the manner in which it has been calculated.

31. Absence of chairman

Where it is not possible for a judgment, order or reasons to be signed by the chairman due to death, incapacity or absence –

(a)   if the chairman has dealt with the proceedings alone the document shall be signed by the Regional Chairman, Vice President or President when it is practicable for him to do so; and

(b) if the proceedings have been dealt with by a tribunal composed of two or three persons, the document shall be signed by the other person or persons;

and any person who signs the document shall certify that the chairman is unable to sign.

32. The Register

(1) Subject to rule 49, the Secretary shall enter a copy of the following documents in the Register –

(a) any judgment (including any costs, expenses, preparation time or wasted costs order); and

(b) any written reasons provided in accordance with rule 30 in relation to any judgment.

(2) Written reasons for judgments shall be omitted from the Register in any case in which evidence has been heard in private and the tribunal or chairman so orders. In such a case the Secretary shall send the reasons to each of the parties and where there are proceedings before a superior court relating to the judgment in question, he shall send the reasons to that court, together with a copy of the entry in the Register of the judgment to which the reasons relate.

Power to review judgments and decisions

33. Review of default judgments

(1) A party may apply to have a default judgment against or in favour of him reviewed. An application must be made in writing and presented to the Employment Tribunal Office within 14 days of the date on which the default judgment was sent to the parties. The 14 day time limit may be extended by a chairman if he considers that it is just and equitable to do so.

(2) The application must state the reasons why the default judgment should be varied or revoked. When it is the respondent applying to have the default judgment reviewed, the application must include with it the respondent's proposed response to the claim, an application for an extension of the time limit for presenting the response and an explanation of why rules 4(1) and (4) were not complied with.

(3) A review of a default judgment shall be conducted by a chairman in public. Notice of the hearing and a copy of the application shall be sent by the Secretary to all other parties.

(4) The chairman may –

(a) refuse the application for a review;

(b) vary the default judgment;

(c) revoke all or part of the default judgment;

(d) confirm the default judgment;

and all parties to the proceedings shall be informed by the Secretary in writing of the chairman's judgment on the application.

(5) A default judgment must be revoked if the whole of the claim was satisfied before the judgment was issued or if rule 8(6) applies. A chairman may revoke or vary all or part of a default judgment if the respondent has a reasonable prospect of successfully responding to the claim or part of it.

(6)   In considering the application for a review of a default judgment the chairman must have regard to whether there was good reason for the response not having been presented within the applicable time limit.

(7)   If the chairman decides that the default judgment should be varied or revoked and that the respondent should be allowed to respond to the claim the Secretary shall accept the response and proceed in accordance with rule 5(2).

34. Review of other judgments and decisions

(1)   Parties may apply to have certain judgments and decisions made by a tribunal or a chairman reviewed under rules 34 to 36. Those judgments and decisions are –

    (a)   a decision not to accept a claim, response or counterclaim;

    (b)   a judgment (other than a default judgment but including an order for costs, expenses, preparation time or wasted costs); and

    (c)   a decision made under rule 6(3) of Schedule 4;

and references to 'decision' in rules 34 to 37 are references to the above judgments and decisions only. Other decisions or orders may not be reviewed under these rules.

(2)   In relation to a decision not to accept a claim or response, only the party against whom the decision is made may apply to have the decision reviewed.

(3)   Subject to paragraph (4), decisions may be reviewed on the following grounds only –

    (a)   the decision was wrongly made as a result of an administrative error;

    (b)   a party did not receive notice of the proceedings leading to the decision;

    (c)   the decision was made in the absence of a party;

    (d)   new evidence has become available since the conclusion of the hearing to which the decision relates, provided that its existence could not have been reasonably known of or foreseen at that time; or

    (e)   the interests of justice require such a review.

(4)   A decision not to accept a claim or response may only be reviewed on the grounds listed in paragraphs (3)(a) and (e).

(5)   A tribunal or chairman may on its or his own initiative review a decision made by it or him on the grounds listed in paragraphs (3) or (4).

35. Preliminary consideration of application for review

(1)   An application under rule 34 to have a decision reviewed must be made to the Employment Tribunal Office within 14 days of the date on which the decision was sent to the parties. The 14 day time limit may be extended by a chairman if he considers that it is just and equitable to do so.

(2)   The application must be in writing and must identify the grounds of the application in accordance with rule 34(3), but if the decision to be reviewed was made at a hearing, an application may be made orally at that hearing.

(3)   The application to have a decision reviewed shall be considered (without the need to hold a hearing) by the chairman of the tribunal which made the decision or, if that is not practicable, by –

(a)   a Regional Chairman or the Vice President;

(b)   any chairman nominated by a Regional Chairman or the Vice President; or

(c)   the President;

and that person shall refuse the application if he considers that there are no grounds for the decision to be reviewed under rule 34(3) or there is no reasonable prospect of the decision being varied or revoked.

(4)   If an application for a review is refused after such preliminary consideration the Secretary shall inform the party making the application in writing of the chairman's decision and his reasons for it. If the application for a review is not refused the decision shall be reviewed under rule 36.

36. The review

(1)   When a party has applied for a review and the application has not been refused after the preliminary consideration above, the decision shall be reviewed by the chairman or tribunal who made the original decision. If that is not practicable a different chairman or tribunal (as the case may be) shall be appointed by a Regional Chairman, the Vice President or the President.

(2)   Where no application has been made by a party and the decision is being reviewed on the initiative of the tribunal or chairman, the review must be carried out by the same tribunal or chairman who made the original decision and –

    (a)   a notice must be sent to each of the parties explaining in summary the grounds upon which it is proposed to review the decision and giving them an opportunity to give reasons why there should be no review; and

    (b)   such notice must be sent before the expiry of 14 days from the date on which the original decision was sent to the parties.

(3)   A tribunal or chairman who reviews a decision under paragraph (1) or (2) may confirm, vary or revoke the decision. If the decision is revoked, the tribunal or chairman must order the decision to be taken again. When an order is made that the original decision be taken again, if the original decision was taken by a chairman without a hearing, the new decision may be taken without hearing the parties and if the original decision was taken at a hearing, a new hearing must be held.

37. Correction of judgments, decisions or reasons

(1)   Clerical mistakes in any order, judgment, decision or reasons, or errors arising in those documents from an accidental slip or omission, may at any time be corrected by certificate by the chairman, Regional Chairman, Vice President or President.

(2)   If a document is corrected by certificate under paragraph (1), or if a decision is revoked or varied under rules 33 or 36 or altered in any way by order of a superior court, the Secretary shall alter any entry in the Register which is so affected to conform with the certificate or order and send a copy of any entry so altered to each of the parties and, if the proceedings have been referred to the tribunal by a court, to that court.

(3)   Where a document omitted from the Register under rules 32 or 49 is corrected by certificate under this rule, the Secretary shall send a copy of the
corrected document to the parties; and where there are proceedings before
any superior court relating to the decision or reasons in question, he shall
send a copy to that court together with a copy of the entry in the Register of
the decision, if it has been altered under this rule.

(4)   In Scotland, the references in paragraphs (2) and (3) to superior courts shall
be read as referring to appellate courts.

Costs orders and orders for expenses

38. General power to make costs and expenses orders

(1)   Subject to paragraph (2) and in the circumstances listed in rules 39, 40 and
47 a tribunal or chairman may make an order ('a costs order') that –

(a)   a party ('the paying party') make a payment in respect of the costs
incurred by another party ('the receiving party');

(b)   the paying party pay to the Secretary of State, in whole or in part, any
allowances (other than allowances paid to members of tribunals) paid
by the Secretary of State under section 5(2) or (3) of the Employment
Tribunals Act to any person for the purposes of, or in connection with,
that person's attendance at the tribunal.

(2)   A costs order may be made under rules 39, 40 and 47 only where the receiving party has been legally represented at the Hearing or, in proceedings which
are determined without a Hearing, if the receiving party is legally represented
when the proceedings are determined. If the receiving party has not been so
legally represented a tribunal or chairman may make a preparation time
order (subject to rules 42 to 45). (See rule 46 on the restriction on making a
costs order and a preparation time order in the same proceedings.)

(3)   For the purposes of these rules 'costs' shall mean fees, charges, disbursements or expenses incurred by or on behalf of a party, in relation to the proceedings. In Scotland all references to costs (except when used in the
expression 'wasted costs') or costs orders shall be read as references to
expenses or orders for expenses.

(4)   A costs order may be made against or in favour of a respondent who has not
had a response accepted in the proceedings in relation to the conduct of any
part which he has taken in the proceedings.

(5)   In these rules legally represented means having the assistance of a person
(including where that person is the receiving party's employee) who –

(a)   has a general qualification within the meaning of section 71 of the
Courts and Legal Services Act 1990;

(b)   is an advocate or solicitor in Scotland; or

(c)   is a member of the Bar of Northern Ireland or a solicitor of the
Supreme Court of Northern Ireland.

(6)   Any costs order made under rules 39, 40 or 47 shall be payable by the
paying party and not his representative.

(7)   A party may apply for a costs order to be made at any time during the proceedings. An application may be made at the end of a hearing, or in writing
to the Employment Tribunal Office. An application for costs which is
received by the Employment Tribunal Office later than 28 days from the issuing of the judgment determining the claim shall not be accepted or

considered by a tribunal or chairman unless it or he considers that it is in the interests of justice to do so.

(8) In paragraph (7), the date of issuing of the judgment determining the claim shall be either –

   (a) the date of the Hearing if the judgment was issued orally; or
   (b) if the judgment was reserved, the date on which the written judgment was sent to the parties.

(9) No costs order shall be made unless the Secretary has sent notice to the party against whom the order may be made giving him the opportunity to give reasons why the order should not be made. This paragraph shall not be taken to require the Secretary to send notice to that party if the party has been given an opportunity to give reasons orally to the chairman or tribunal as to why the order should not be made.

(10) Where a tribunal or chairman makes a costs order it or he shall provide written reasons for doing so if a request for written reasons is made within 14 days of the date of the costs order. The Secretary shall send a copy of the written reasons to all parties to the proceedings.

39. When a costs or expenses order must be made

(1) Subject to rule 38(2), a tribunal or chairman must make a costs order against a respondent where in proceedings for unfair dismissal a Hearing has been postponed or adjourned and –

   (a) the claimant has expressed a wish to be reinstated or reengaged which has been communicated to the respondent not less than 7 days before the Hearing; and
   (b) the postponement or adjournment of that Hearing has been caused by the respondent's failure, without a special reason, to adduce reasonable evidence as to the availability of the job from which the claimant was dismissed, or of comparable or suitable employment.

(2) A costs order made under paragraph (1) shall relate to any costs incurred as a result of the postponement or adjournment of the Hearing.

40. When a costs or expenses order may be made

(1) A tribunal or chairman may make a costs order when on the application of a party it has postponed the day or time fixed for or adjourned a Hearing or pre-hearing review. The costs order may be against or, as the case may require, in favour of that party as respects any costs incurred or any allowances paid as a result of the postponement or adjournment.

(2) A tribunal or chairman shall consider making a costs order against a paying party where, in the opinion of the tribunal or chairman (as the case may be), any of the circumstances in paragraph (3) apply. Having so considered, the tribunal or chairman may make a costs order against the paying party if it or he considers it appropriate to do so.

(3) The circumstances referred to in paragraph (2) are where the paying party has in bringing the proceedings, or he or his representative has in conducting the proceedings, acted vexatiously, abusively, disruptively or otherwise unreasonably, or the bringing or conducting of the proceedings by the paying party has been misconceived.

(4)   A tribunal or chairman may make a costs order against a party who has not complied with an order or practice direction.

41. The amount of a costs or expenses order

(1)   The amount of a costs order against the paying party shall be determined in any of the following ways –

    (a)   the tribunal may specify the sum which the paying party must pay to the receiving party, provided that sum does not exceed £10,000;

    (b)   the parties may agree on a sum to be paid by the paying party to the receiving party and if they do so the costs order shall be for the sum so agreed;

    (c)   the tribunal may order the paying party to pay the receiving party the whole or a specified part of the costs of the receiving party with the amount to be paid being determined by way of detailed assessment in a County Court in accordance with the Civil Procedure Rules 1998 or, in Scotland, as taxed according to such part of the table of fees prescribed for proceedings in the sheriff court as shall be directed by the order.

(2)   The tribunal or chairman may have regard to the paying party's ability to pay when considering whether it or he shall make a costs order or how much that order should be.

(3)   For the avoidance of doubt, the amount of a costs order made under paragraphs (1)(b) or (c) may exceed £10,000.

Preparation time orders

42. General power to make preparation time orders

(1)   Subject to paragraph (2) and in the circumstances described in rules 43, 44 and 47 a tribunal or chairman may make an order ('a preparation time order') that a party ('the paying party') make a payment in respect of the preparation time of another party ('the receiving party').

(2)   A preparation time order may be made under rules 43, 44 or 47 only where the receiving party has not been legally represented at a Hearing or, in proceedings which are determined without a Hearing, if the receiving party has not been legally represented when the proceedings are determined. (See: rules 38 to 41 on when a costs order may be made; rule 38(5) for the definition of legally represented; and rule 46 on the restriction on making a costs order and a preparation time order in the same proceedings).

(3)   For the purposes of these rules preparation time shall mean time spent by –

    (a)   the receiving party or his employees carrying out preparatory work directly relating to the proceedings; and

    (b)   the receiving party's legal or other advisers relating to the conduct of the proceedings;

up to but not including time spent at any Hearing.

(4)   A preparation time order may be made against a respondent who has not had a response accepted in the proceedings in relation to the conduct of any part which he has taken in the proceedings.

(5)   A party may apply to the tribunal for a preparation time order to be made at any time during the proceedings. An application may be made at the end of

a hearing or in writing to the Secretary. An application for preparation time which is received by the Employment Tribunal Office later than 28 days from the issuing of the judgment determining the claim shall not be accepted or considered by a tribunal or chairman unless they consider that it is in the interests of justice to do so.

(6) In paragraph (5) the date of issuing of the judgment determining the claim shall be either –

(a) the date of the Hearing if the judgment was issued orally; or,

(b) if the judgment was reserved, the date on which the written judgment was sent to the parties.

(7) No preparation time order shall be made unless the Secretary has sent notice to the party against whom the order may be made giving him the opportunity to give reasons why the order should not be made. This paragraph shall not be taken to require the Secretary to send notice to that party if the party has been given an opportunity to give reasons orally to the chairman or tribunal as to why the order should not be made.

(8) Where a tribunal or chairman makes a preparation time order it or he shall provide written reasons for doing so if a request for written reasons is made within 14 days of the date of the preparation time order. The Secretary shall send a copy of the written reasons to all parties to the proceedings.

43. When a preparation time order must be made

(1) Subject to rule 42(2), a tribunal or chairman must make a preparation time order against a respondent where in proceedings for unfair dismissal a Hearing has been postponed or adjourned and –

(a) the claimant has expressed a wish to be reinstated or reengaged which has been communicated to the respondent not less than 7 days before the Hearing; and

(b) the postponement or adjournment of that Hearing has been caused by the respondent's failure, without a special reason, to adduce reasonable evidence as to the availability of the job from which the claimant was dismissed, or of comparable or suitable employment.

(2) A preparation time order made under paragraph (1) shall relate to any preparation time spent as a result of the postponement or adjournment of the Hearing.

44. When a preparation time order may be made

(1) A tribunal or chairman may make a preparation time order when on the application of a party it has postponed the day or time fixed for or adjourned a Hearing or a pre-hearing review. The preparation time order may be against or, as the case may require, in favour of that party as respects any preparation time spent as a result of the postponement or adjournment.

(2) A tribunal or chairman shall consider making a preparation time order against a party (the paying party) where, in the opinion of the tribunal or the chairman (as the case may be), any of the circumstances in paragraph (3) apply. Having so considered the tribunal or chairman may make a preparation time order against that party if it considers it appropriate to do so.

(3) The circumstances described in paragraph (2) are where the paying party has in bringing the proceedings, or he or his representative has in conducting the proceedings, acted vexatiously, abusively, disruptively or otherwise unreasonably, or the bringing or conducting of the proceedings by the paying party has been misconceived.

(4) A tribunal or chairman may make a preparation time order against a party who has not complied with an order or practice direction.

45. Calculation of a preparation time order

(1) In order to calculate the amount of preparation time the tribunal or chairman shall make an assessment of the number of hours spent on preparation time on the basis of –

(a) information on time spent provided by the receiving party; and

(b) the tribunal or chairman's own assessment of what it or he considers to be a reasonable and proportionate amount of time to spend on such preparatory work and with reference to, for example, matters such as the complexity of the proceedings, the number of witnesses and documentation required.

(2) Once the tribunal or chairman has assessed the number of hours spent on preparation time in accordance with paragraph (1), it or he shall calculate the amount of the award to be paid to the receiving party by applying an hourly rate of £25.00 to that figure (or such other figure calculated in accordance with paragraph (4)). No preparation time order made under these rules may exceed the sum of £10,000.

(3) The tribunal or chairman may have regard to the paying party's ability to pay when considering whether it or he shall make a preparation time order or how much that order should be.

(4) For the year commencing on 6th April 2006, the hourly rate of £25 shall be increased by the sum of £1.00 and for each subsequent year commencing on 6 April, the hourly rate for the previous year shall also be increased by the sum of £1.00.

46. Restriction on making costs or expenses orders and preparation time orders

(1) A tribunal or chairman may not make a preparation time order and a costs order in favour of the same party in the same proceedings. However where a preparation time order is made in favour of a party in proceedings, the tribunal or chairman may make a costs order in favour of another party or in favour of the Secretary of State under rule 38(1)(b) in the same proceedings.

(2) If a tribunal or a chairman wishes to make either a costs order or a preparation time order in proceedings, before the claim has been determined, it or he may make an order that either costs or preparation time be awarded to the receiving party. In such circumstances a tribunal or chairman may decide whether the award should be for costs or preparation time after the proceedings have been determined.

47. Costs, expenses or preparation time orders when a deposit has been taken

(1) When –

(a) a party has been ordered under rule 20 to pay a deposit as a condition of being permitted to continue to participate in proceedings relating to a matter;

(b) in respect of that matter, the tribunal or chairman has found against that party in its or his judgment; and

(c) no award of costs or preparation time has been made against that party arising out of the proceedings on the matter;

the tribunal or chairman shall consider whether to make a costs or preparation time order against that party on the ground that he conducted the proceedings relating to the matter unreasonably in persisting in having the matter determined; but the tribunal or chairman shall not make a costs or preparation time order on that ground unless it has considered the document recording the order under rule 20 and is of the opinion that the grounds which caused the tribunal or chairman to find against the party in its judgment were substantially the same as the grounds recorded in that document for considering that the contentions of the party had little reasonable prospect of success.

(2) When a costs or preparation time order is made against a party who has had an order under rule 20 made against him (whether the award arises out of the proceedings relating to the matter in respect of which the order was made or out of proceedings relating to any other matter considered with that matter), his deposit shall be paid in part or full settlement of the costs or preparation time order –

(a) when an order is made in favour of one party, to that party; and

(b) when orders are made in favour of more than one party, to all of them or any one or more of them as the tribunal or chairman thinks fit, and if to all or more than one, in such proportions as the tribunal or chairman considers appropriate;

and if the amount of the deposit exceeds the amount of the costs or preparation time order, the balance shall be refunded to the party who paid it.

Wasted costs orders against representatives

48. Personal liability of representatives for costs

(1) A tribunal or chairman may make a wasted costs order against a party's representative.

(2) In a wasted costs order the tribunal or chairman may –

(a) disallow, or order the representative of a party to meet the whole or part of any wasted costs of any party, including an order that the representative repay to his client any costs which have already been paid; and

(b) order the representative to pay to the Secretary of State, in whole or in part, any allowances (other than allowances paid to members of tribunals) paid by the Secretary of State under section 5(2) or (3) of the Employment Tribunals Act to any person for the purposes of, or in connection with, that person's attendance at the tribunal by reason of the representative's conduct of the proceedings.

(3) 'Wasted costs' means any costs incurred by a party –

(a) as a result of any improper, unreasonable or negligent act or omission on the part of any representative; or

(b) which, in the light of any such act or omission occurring after they were incurred, the tribunal considers it unreasonable to expect that party to pay.

(4)   In this rule 'representative' means a party's legal or other representative or any employee of such representative, but it does not include a representative who is not acting in pursuit of profit with regard to those proceedings. A person is considered to be acting in pursuit of profit if he is acting on a conditional fee arrangement.

(5)   A wasted costs order may be made in favour of a party whether or not that party is legally represented and such an order may also be made in favour of a representative's own client. A wasted costs order may not be made against a representative where that representative is an employee of a party.

(6)   Before making a wasted costs order, the tribunal or chairman shall give the representative a reasonable opportunity to make oral or written representations as to reasons why such an order should not be made. The tribunal or chairman may also have regard to the representative's ability to pay when considering whether it shall make a wasted costs order or how much that order should be.

(7)   When a tribunal or chairman makes a wasted costs order, it must specify in the order the amount to be disallowed or paid.

(8)   The Secretary shall inform the representative's client in writing –

(a)   of any proceedings under this rule; or
(b)   of any order made under this rule against the party's representative.

(9)   Where a tribunal or chairman makes a wasted costs order it or he shall provide written reasons for doing so if a request is made for written reasons within 14 days of the date of the wasted costs order. This 14 day time limit may not be extended under rule 10. The Secretary shall send a copy of the written reasons to all parties to the proceedings.

Powers in relation to specific types of proceedings

49. Sexual offences and the Register

In any proceedings appearing to involve allegations of the commission of a sexual offence the tribunal, the chairman or the Secretary shall omit from the Register, or delete from the Register or any judgment, document or record of the proceedings, which is available to the public, any identifying matter which is likely to lead members of the public to identify any person affected by or making such an allegation.

50. Restricted reporting orders

(1)   A restricted reporting order may be made in the following types of proceedings –

(a)   any case which involves allegations of sexual misconduct;
(b)   a complaint under section 17A or 25(8) of the Disability Discrimination Act in which evidence of a personal nature is likely to be heard by the tribunal or a chairman.

(2)   A party (or where a complaint is made under the Disability Discrimination Act, the complainant) may apply for a restricted reporting order (either temporary or full) in writing to the Employment Tribunal Office, or orally at a hearing, or the tribunal or chairman may make the order on its or his own initiative without any application having been made.

(3)   A chairman or tribunal may make a temporary restricted reporting order without holding a hearing or sending a copy of the application to other parties.

(4) Where a temporary restricted reporting order has been made the Secretary shall inform all parties to the proceedings in writing as soon as possible of –

(a) the fact that the order has been made; and

(b) their right to apply to have the temporary restricted reporting order revoked or converted into a full restricted reporting order within 14 days of the temporary order having been made.

(5) If no application under paragraph (4)(b) is made within the 14 days, the temporary restricted reporting order shall lapse and cease to have any effect on the fifteenth day after the order was made. If such an application is made the temporary restricted reporting order shall continue to have effect until the pre-hearing review or Hearing at which the application is considered.

(6) All parties must be given an opportunity to advance oral argument at a pre-hearing review or a Hearing before a tribunal or chairman decides whether or not to make a full restricted reporting order (whether or not there was previously a temporary restricted reporting order in the proceedings).

(7) Any person may make an application to the chairman or tribunal to have a right to make representations before a full restricted reporting order is made. The chairman or tribunal shall allow such representations to be made where he or it considers that the applicant has a legitimate interest in whether or not the order is made.

(8) Where a tribunal or chairman makes a restricted reporting order –

(a) it shall specify in the order the persons who may not be identified;

(b) a full order shall remain in force until both liability and remedy have been determined in the proceedings unless it is revoked earlier; and

(c) the Secretary shall ensure that a notice of the fact that a restricted reporting order has been made in relation to those proceedings is displayed on the notice board of the employment tribunal with any list of the proceedings taking place before the employment tribunal, and on the door of the room in which the proceedings affected by the order are taking place.

(9) Where a restricted reporting order has been made under this rule and that complaint is being dealt with together with any other proceedings, the tribunal or chairman may order that the restricted reporting order applies also in relation to those other proceedings or a part of them.

(10) A tribunal or chairman may revoke a restricted reporting order at any time.

(11) For the purposes of this rule liability and remedy are determined in the proceedings on the date recorded as being the date on which the judgment disposing of the claim was sent to the parties, and references to a restricted reporting order include references to both a temporary and a full restricted reporting order.

51. Proceedings involving the National Insurance Fund

The Secretary of State shall be entitled to appear as if she were a party and be heard at any hearing in relation to proceedings which may involve a payment out of the National Insurance Fund, and in that event she shall be treated for the purposes of these rules as if she were a party.

52. Collective agreements

Where a claim includes a complaint under section 6(4A) of the Sex Discrimination Act 1986 relating to a term of a collective agreement, the following persons, whether or not identified in the claim, shall be regarded as the persons against whom a remedy is claimed and shall be treated as respondents for the purposes of these rules, that is to say –

(a) the claimant's employer (or prospective employer); and
(b) every organisation of employers and organisation of workers, and every association of or representative of such organisations, which, if the terms were to be varied voluntarily, would be likely, in the opinion of a chairman, to negotiate the variation;

provided that such an organisation or association shall not be treated as a respondent if the chairman, having made such enquiries of the claimant and such other enquiries as he thinks fit, is of the opinion that it is not reasonably practicable to identify the organisation or association.

53. Employment Agencies Act 1973

In relation to any claim in respect of an application under section 3C of the Employment Agencies Act 1973 for the variation or revocation of a prohibition order, the Secretary of State shall be treated as the respondent in such proceedings for the purposes of these rules. In relation to such an application the claim does not need to include the name and address of the persons against whom the claim is being made.

54. National security proceedings

(1) A Minister of the Crown (whether or not he is a party to the proceedings) may, if he considers it expedient in the interests of national security, direct a tribunal or chairman by notice to the Secretary to –

(a) conduct proceedings in private for all or part of particular Crown employment proceedings;
(b) exclude the claimant from all or part of particular Crown employment proceedings;
(c) exclude the claimant's representative from all or part of particular Crown employment proceedings;
(d) take steps to conceal the identity of a particular witness in particular Crown employment proceedings.

(2) A tribunal or chairman may, if it or he considers it expedient in the interests of national security, by order –

(a) do in relation to particular proceedings before it anything which can be required by direction to be done in relation to particular Crown employment proceedings under paragraph (1);
(b) order any person to whom any document (including any judgment or record of the proceedings) has been provided for the purposes of the proceedings not to disclose any such document or the content thereof –

(i) to any excluded person;
(ii) in any case in which a direction has been given under paragraph (1)(a) or an order has been made under paragraph (2)(a) read with paragraph (1)(a), to any person excluded from all or part of the proceedings by virtue of such direction or order; or
(iii) in any case in which a Minister of the Crown has informed the Secretary in accordance with paragraph (3) that he wishes to

address the tribunal or chairman with a view to an order being made under paragraph (2)(a) read with paragraph (1)(b) or (c), to any person who may be excluded from all or part of the proceedings by virtue of such an order, if an order is made, at any time before the tribunal or chairman decides whether or not to make such an order;

(c) take steps to keep secret all or part of the reasons for its judgment.

The tribunal or chairman (as the case may be) shall keep under review any order it or he has made under this paragraph.

(3) In any proceedings in which a Minister of the Crown considers that it would be appropriate for a tribunal or chairman to make an order as referred to in paragraph (2), he shall (whether or not he is a party to the proceedings) be entitled to appear before and to address the tribunal or chairman thereon. The Minister shall inform the Secretary by notice that he wishes to address the tribunal or chairman and the Secretary shall copy the notice to the parties.

(4) When exercising its or his functions, a tribunal or chairman shall ensure that information is not disclosed contrary to the interests of national security.

55. Dismissals in connection with industrial action

(1) In relation to a complaint under section 111 of the Employment Rights Act 1996 (unfair dismissal: complaints to employment tribunal) that a dismissal is unfair by virtue of section 238A of TULR(C)A (participation in official industrial action) a tribunal or chairman may adjourn the proceedings where civil proceedings have been brought until such time as interim proceedings arising out of the civil proceedings have been concluded.

(2) In this rule –

(a) 'civil proceedings' means legal proceedings brought by any person against another person in which it is to be determined whether an act of that other person, which induced the claimant to commit an act, or each of a series of acts, is by virtue of section 219 of TULR(C)A not actionable in tort or in delict; and

(b) the interim proceedings shall not be regarded as having concluded until all rights of appeal have been exhausted or the time for presenting any appeal in the course of the interim proceedings has expired.

56. Devolution issues

(1) In any proceedings in which a devolution issue within the definition of the term in paragraph 1 of Schedule 6 to the Scotland Act 1998 arises, the Secretary shall as soon as reasonably practicable by notice inform the Advocate General for Scotland and the Lord Advocate thereof (unless they are a party to the proceedings) and shall at the same time –

(a) send a copy of the notice to the parties to the proceedings; and
(b) send the Advocate General for Scotland and the Lord Advocate a copy of the claim and the response.

(2) In any proceedings in which a devolution issue within the definition of the term in paragraph 1 of Schedule 9 to the Government of Wales Act 2006 arises, the Secretary shall as soon as reasonably practicable by notice inform

the Attorney General and the Counsel General to the Welsh Assembly Government thereof (unless they are a party to the proceedings) and shall at the same time –

(a) send a copy of the notice to the parties to the proceedings; and
(b) send the Attorney General and the Counsel General to the Welsh Assembly Government a copy of the claim and the response.

(3) A person to whom notice is given in pursuance of paragraph (1) or (2) may within 14 days of receiving it, by notice to the Secretary, take part as a party in the proceedings, so far as they relate to the devolution issue. The Secretary shall send a copy of the notice to the other parties to the proceedings.

57. Transfer of proceedings between Scotland and England & Wales

(1) The President (England and Wales) or a Regional Chairman may at any time, with the consent of the President (Scotland), order any proceedings in England and Wales to be transferred to an Employment Tribunal Office in Scotland if it appears to him that the proceedings could be (in accordance with regulation 19), and would more conveniently be, determined in an employment tribunal located in Scotland.

(2) The President (Scotland) or the Vice President may at any time, with the consent of the President (England and Wales), order any proceedings in Scotland to be transferred to an Employment Tribunal Office in England and Wales if it appears to him that the proceedings could be (in accordance with regulation 19), and would more conveniently be, determined in an employment tribunal located in England or Wales.

(3) An order under paragraph (1) or (2) may be made by the President, Vice President or Regional Chairman without any application having been made by a party. A party may apply for an order under paragraph (1) or (2) in accordance with rule 11.

(4) Where proceedings have been transferred under this rule, they shall be treated as if in all respects they had been presented to the Secretary by the claimant.

58. References to the European Court of Justice

Where a tribunal or chairman makes an order referring a question to the European Court of Justice for a preliminary ruling under Article 234 of the Treaty establishing the European Community, the Secretary shall send a copy of the order to the Registrar of that Court.

59. Transfer of proceedings from a court

Where proceedings are referred to a tribunal by a court, these rules shall apply to them as if the proceedings had been sent to the Secretary by the claimant.

General provisions

60. Powers

(1) Subject to the provisions of these rules and any practice directions, a tribunal or chairman may regulate its or his own procedure.

(2) At a Hearing, or a pre-hearing review held in accordance with rule 18(3), a tribunal may make any order which a chairman has power to make under these rules, subject to compliance with any relevant notice or other procedural requirements.

(3) Any function of the Secretary may be performed by a person acting with the authority of the Secretary.

61. Notices, etc

(1) Any notice given or document sent under these rules shall (unless a chairman or tribunal orders otherwise) be in writing and may be given or sent –

    (a) by post;
    (b) by fax or other means of electronic communication; or
    (c) by personal delivery.

(2) Where a notice or document has been given or sent in accordance with paragraph (1), that notice or document shall, unless the contrary is proved, be taken to have been received by the party to whom it is addressed –

    (a) in the case of a notice or document given or sent by post, on the day on which the notice or document would be delivered in the ordinary course of post;

    (b) in the case of a notice or document transmitted by fax or other means of electronic communication, on the day on which the notice or document is transmitted;

    (c) in the case of a notice or document delivered in person, on the day on which the notice or document is delivered.

(3) All notices and documents required by these rules to be presented to the Secretary or an Employment Tribunal Office, other than a claim, shall be presented at the Employment Tribunal Office as notified by the Secretary to the parties.

(4) All notices and documents required or authorised by these rules to be sent or given to any person listed below may be sent to or delivered at –

    (a) in the case of a notice or document directed to the Secretary of State in proceedings to which she is not a party and which are brought under section 170 of the Employment Rights Act, the offices of the Redundancy Payments Directorate of the Insolvency Service at PO Box 203, 21 Bloomsbury Street, London WC1B 3QW, or such other office as may be notified by the Secretary of State;

    (b) in the case of any other notice or document directed to the Secretary of State in proceedings to which she is not a party (or in respect of which she is treated as a party for the purposes of these rules by rule 51), the offices of the Department for Business, Enterprise and Regulatory Reform (Employment Relations Directorate) at 1 Victoria Street, London, SW1H 0ET, or such other office as may be notified by the Secretary of State;

    (c) in the case of a notice or document directed to the Attorney General under rule 56, the Attorney General's Chambers, 9 Buckingham Gate, London, SW1E 7JP;

    (d) in the case of a notice or document directed to the Counsel General to the Welsh Assembly Government under rule 56, the Counsel General to the Welsh Assembly Government, Crown Buildings, Cathays Park, Cardiff, CF10 3NQ;

(e)   in the case of a notice or document directed to the Advocate General for Scotland under rule 56, the Office of the Solicitor to the Advocate General for Scotland, Victoria Quay, Edinburgh, EH6 6QQ;

(f)   in the case of a notice or document directed to the Lord Advocate under rule 56, the Legal Secretariat to the Lord Advocate, 25 Chambers Street, Edinburgh, EH1 1LA;

(g)   in the case of a notice or document directed to a court, the office of the clerk of the court;

(h)   in the case of a notice or document directed to a party –

    (i)   the address specified in the claim or response to which notices and documents are to be sent, or in a notice under paragraph (5); or

    (ii)   if no such address has been specified, or if a notice sent to such an address has been returned, to any other known address or place of business in the United Kingdom or, if the party is a corporate body, the body's registered or principal office in the United Kingdom, or, in any case, such address or place outside the United Kingdom as the President, Vice President or a Regional Chairman may allow;

(i)   in the case of a notice or document directed to any person (other than a person specified in the foregoing provisions of this paragraph), his address or place of business in the United Kingdom or, if the person is a corporate body, the body's registered or principal office in the United Kingdom;

and a notice or document sent or given to the authorised representative of a party shall be taken to have been sent or given to that party.

(5)   A party may at any time by notice to the Employment Tribunal Office and to the other party or parties (and, where appropriate, to the appropriate conciliation officer) change the address to which notices and documents are to be sent or transmitted.

(6)   The President, Vice President or a Regional Chairman may order that there shall be substituted service in such manner as he may deem fit in any case he considers appropriate.

(7)   In proceedings which may involve a payment out of the National Insurance Fund, the Secretary shall, where appropriate, send copies of all documents and notices to the Secretary of State whether or not she is a party.

(8)   In proceedings under the Equal Pay Act, the Sex Discrimination Act, the Race Relations Act or the Disability Discrimination Act, copies of every document sent to the parties underrules 29, 30 or 32 shall be sent by the Secretary to the Commission for Equality and Human Rights.

APPENDIX 4

IDS Brief employment law time chart

See pp.291–2 for explanation of abbreviations.

Statutory right/complaint	Qualifying period	Time limit for complaint
Dismissal		
Written reasons for dismissal (ERA, s.92)	1 year (a)	3 months starting with EDT*
Unfair dismissal (ERA, Part X)	1 year	3 months starting with EDT* (l)
UD for a reason connected with medical suspension (ERA, s.108(2))	1 month	3 months starting with EDT*
UD for taking part in official industrial action (TULR(C)A, s.238A)	None	6 months from complainant's date of dismissal* (b)
UD for 'trade union' reasons (TULR(C)A, ss.152 and 153)	None	3 months starting with EDT*
UD by reason of business transfer, or a reason connected with the transfer which is not an ETO reason entailing changes in the workforce (TUPE, reg.7)	1 year	3 months starting with EDT*
UD for a reason connected with pregnancy, childbirth, maternity, maternity leave, parental leave or dependant care leave (ERA, s.99)	None	3 months starting with EDT*
UD for a health and safety reason (ERA, s.100)	None	3 months starting with EDT*
UD of a shop or betting worker for refusing to work on a Sunday (ERA, s.101)	None	3 months starting with EDT*
UD for a reason connected with the Working Time Regulations 1998 (ERA, s.101A)	None	3 months starting with EDT*
UD for performing functions as an occupational pension trustee (ERA, s.102)	None	3 months starting with EDT*
UD for performing functions as an employee representative (ERA, s.103)	None	3 months starting with EDT*
UD related to making a protected disclosure (ERA, s.103A)	None	3 months starting with EDT*

Statutory right/complaint	Qualifying period	Time limit for complaint
UD for asserting a statutory right (ERA, s.104)	None	3 months starting with EDT*
UD related to national minimum wage (ERA, s.104A)	None	3 months starting with EDT*
UD related to status as part-time worker (PTW Regs, reg.7)	None	3 months starting with EDT*
UD related to status as fixed-term employee (FTE Regs, reg.6)	None	3 months starting with EDT*
UD for enforcing right to working family tax credits (ERA, s.104B)	None	3 months starting with EDT*
UD related to a claim for union recognition (TULR(C)A, Sched.A1, para.161)	None	3 months starting with EDT*
UD related to establishment of, or participation in, a European Works Council or information and consultation procedure (TICE Regs, reg.28)	None	3 months starting with EDT*
UD for performing or proposing to perform functions or activities of an information and consultation representative or candidate (ICE Regs, reg.30)	None	3 months starting with EDT*
UD in relation to a request for flexible working (ERA, s.104)	None	3 months starting with EDT*
UD relating to jury service (ERA, s.98B)	None	3 months starting with EDT*
Interim relief pending complaint under ERA, ss.100, 101A, 102, 103, 103A or TULR(C)A, Sched.A1, para.161 (ERA, s.128)	None	7 days immediately following EDT***
Redundancy/business transfers		
Redundancy payment (ERA, Part XI)	2 years (c)	6 months starting with 'relevant date' (d)(I)
Consultation with appropriate representatives over proposed redundancies (TULR(C)A, s.188)	N/A	Either before dismissal or 3 months starting with date on which dismissal takes effect*
Failure to pay remuneration under protective award (TULR(C)A, s.190)	None	3 months starting with last day in respect of which complaint is made*
Failure to consult with appropriate representatives over a business transfer (TUPE, reg.15)	N/A	3 months starting with date of completion of transfer*

Statutory right/complaint	Qualifying period	Time limit for complaint
Failure to comply with a compensation order made under reg.15 (TUPE, reg.15(10))	N/A	3 months starting with date of tribunal's order*
Failure by transferor to notify transferee of relevant information (TUPE, reg.12)	N/A	3 months starting with date of relevant transfer*
Maternity and parental leave		
Right to 26 weeks' ordinary maternity leave (ERA, s.71)	None	N/A
Right to 26 weeks' additional maternity leave (ERA, s.73)	None	N/A
Right to 26 weeks' ordinary adoption leave (ERA, s.75A)	None	N/A
Right to 26 weeks' additional adoption leave (ERA, s.75B)	None	N/A
Right to 2 weeks' paternity leave (ERA, s.80A)	26 weeks' continuous service at 15th week before EWC	N/A
Right to return to the same job or, if that is not practicable, to a suitable alternative job after additional maternity leave or a period of parental leave of more than 4 weeks (MPL Regs, reg.18)	None	N/A
Right to be offered alternative work before maternity suspension (ERA, s.67)	None	3 months starting with first day of suspension*
Right to be paid during maternity suspension (ERA, s.68)	None	3 months starting with day in respect of which the claim is made*
Right to 13 weeks' unpaid parental leave in respect of each child, 18 weeks for parents of disabled children (MPL Regs, regs.13 and 14)	1 year (f)	3 months from when employer refuses right*
Right to return to the same job after a period of parental leave of 4 weeks or less (MPL Regs, reg.18)	None	N/A
Right not to suffer detriment in relation to pregnancy, maternity leave, adoption leave, paternity leave, parental leave, or time off for dependants (ERA, s.47C)	None	3 months starting with date of (last) act or failure to act*

Statutory right/complaint	Qualifying period	Time limit for complaint
Discrimination		
Sex discrimination claim (SDA, Parts I, II and VII)	None	3 months starting with date of act complained of** (g)(l)
Race discrimination claim (RRA, Parts I, II and VIII)	None	3 months starting with date of act complained of** (g)(l)
Disability discrimination claim (DDA, Parts I, II and Sched.3)	None	3 months starting with date of act complained of** (g)(l)
Sex discrimination claim under EC law (Equal Treatment Directive 76/207, Art.5)	None	3 months starting with date of act complained of (h)
Equal pay/value claim under EC law (EC Treaty, Art.141 and Equal Pay Directive 75/117, Art.1)	None	3/6 months starting with termination of employment (h)
Equal pay claim (EqPA)	None	6 months starting with termination of employment (i)
Preliminary complaint by EHRC (m) (SDA, s.73(1)/RRA, s.64(1))	N/A	6 months starting with date of act complained of**
Application by EHRC (m) in connection with discriminatory advertising etc. and/or pressure to discriminate (SDA, s.72(2)(a)/RRA, s.63(2)(a))	N/A	6 months starting when act to which application relates was done**
Religion or belief discrimination claim (EE(RoB) Regs)	None	3 months starting with date of act complained of** (g)(l)
Sexual orientation discrimination claim (EE(SO) Regs)	None	3 months starting with date of act complained of** (g)(l)
Age discrimination claim (EE(Age) Regs)	None	3 months starting with date of act complained of** (g)(l)
Claim of discrimination on the ground of civil partnership status (SDA, s.251)	None	3 months starting with date of act complained of** (g)(l)
Trade unions and union members		
Interim relief pending s.152 complaint (TULR(C)A, s.161)	None	7 days immediately following EDT***
Right not to suffer detriment as a result of being a union member or taking part in union activities (TULR(C)A, s.146)	None	3 months starting with date of (last) act or failure to act* (l)
Unlawful exclusion/expulsion from union (TULR(C)A, s.174)	None	6 months starting with date of exclusion/expulsion*
Application for compensation after successful s.174 complaint (TULR(C)A, s.176)	None	Not earlier than 4 weeks and not later than 6 months from date of ET's decision***

Statutory right/complaint	Qualifying period	Time limit for complaint
Unjustifiable discipline by union (TULR(C)A, ss.64 to 66)	None	3 months starting with date of union's decision****
Application for compensation after successful s.66 complaint (TULR(C)A, s.67)	None	Not earlier than 4 weeks and not later than 6 months from date of ET's decision***
Unauthorised deduction of union subscriptions (TULR(C)A, s.68)	None	3 months starting with date of payment*
Refusal of employment/services of employment agency on grounds related to union membership (TULR(C)A, s.137/s.138)	N/A	3 months starting with date of conduct complained of*
Complaint by trade union over employer's failure to comply with collective bargaining obligations regarding training (TULR(C)A, s.70B)	N/A	3 months starting with the alleged failure*
Complaint about either a wrongful deduction of contributions to a union political fund, or a refusal to deduct union dues	N/A	3 months starting with date of payment of emoluments*
Complaint by a worker about inducements relating to trade union membership or activities, or to collective bargaining (TULR(C)A, ss.145A–B)	N/A	3 months beginning when the offer, or last offer, was made*
Time off		
Right to unpaid time off for public duties (ERA, s.50)	None	3 months from date of failure to give time off*
Right to paid time off to look for work where notice of dismissal by reason of redundancy has been given (ERA, ss.52 and 53)	2 years	3 months starting with day time off should have been allowed*
Right to paid time off for antenatal care (ERA, ss.55 and 56)	None	3 months starting with date of appointment*
Right to unpaid time off to care for dependants (ERA, s.57A)	None	3 months starting with date when refusal occurred*
Right to paid time off for pension scheme trustees (ERA, ss.58 and 59)	None	3 months starting with the date when the failure occurred*
Right to paid time off for employee representatives (ERA, ss.61 and 62)	None	3 months starting with day time off taken or on which time off should have been allowed*

APPENDIX 4

Statutory right/complaint	Qualifying period	Time limit for complaint
Right to paid time off for representatives of employee safety and for candidates standing for election as such a representative (H&S Regs)	None	3 months starting with the date when the failure occurred*
Right to paid time off for safety representatives (SRSC Regs)	None	3 months starting with the date when the failure occurred*
Right to paid time off for information and consultation representatives (ICE Regs, reg.27)	None	3 months starting with the day time off taken or on which time off should have been allowed*
Right to paid time off for union duties (TULR(C)A, ss.168 and 169)	None	3 months starting with the date when the failure occurred*
Right to unpaid time off for union activities (TULR(C)A, s.170)	None	3 months starting with the date when the failure occurred*
Right to time off for study or training (ERA, ss.63A, 63B and 63C)	None	3 months starting with day time off taken or on which time off should have been allowed*

Working Time Regulations 1998

Right to daily rest (reg.10)	None	3 months from date when right should have been permitted* (k)(l)
Right to weekly rest (reg.11)	None	3 months from date when right should have been permitted (or, if rest period extended over more than one day, date when right should have been permitted to begin)* (k)
Right to rest breaks (reg.12)	None	3 months from date when right should have been permitted* (k)
Right to compensatory rest in case where the above regulations are modified or excluded (reg.24)	None	3 months from date when right should have been permitted* (k)
Right to annual leave (reg.13)	None	3 months from date when right should have been permitted (or, if leave extended over more than one day, date when right should have been permitted to begin)* (k)
Right to payment in lieu of holiday on termination of employment (reg.14(2))	None	3 months from date payment should have been made* (k)
Right to pay during annual leave (reg.16(1))	None	3 months from date payment should have been made* (k)

Statutory right/complaint	Qualifying period	Time limit for complaint
Right not to suffer detriment in relation to working time (ERA, s.45A)	None	3 months starting with date of (last) act or failure to act*
Miscellaneous		
Guarantee pay (ERA, ss.28–35)	1 month	3 months starting with day for which payment claimed*
Rights on insolvency of employer (ERA, Part XII)	None (j)	3 months starting with date of communication of Secretary of State's decision*
Itemised pay statement (ERA, ss.812)	None	3 months starting with date on which employment ceased*
Written particulars of employment (ERA, ss.17)	1 month (l)	3 months starting with date on which employment ceased*
Medical suspension pay (ERA, s.64)	1 month	3 months starting with first day of suspension
Unlawful deduction from wages (ERA, Part II)	None	3 months from date of (last) deduction or (last) payment to employer*
Right to be accompanied at a grievance or disciplinary hearing (ERelA, ss.10–15)	None	3 months from date of failure or threat of failure*
Unlawful infringement of human rights by public body (HRA)	None	1 year from date of act complained of*****
Failure to allow access to records relating to national minimum wage (NMWA, ss.9 to 11)	None	3 months after the period of 14 days (or longer if agreed) following receipt of the production notice
Failure to allow access to records relating to national minimum wage (NMWA, ss.19 and 22)	N/A	4 weeks following date of service of notice
Right not to be treated less favourably because of part-time status (PTW Regs, reg.5)	None	3 months from date of less favourable treatment**(g)
Right of part-time worker to receive written statement of reasons for less favourable treatment (PTW Regs, reg.6)		None N/A
Right not to be treated less favourably because of fixed-term status (FTE Regs, reg.3)	N/A	3 months from date of less favourable treatment or detriment to which complaint relates, or, where act is part of a series, the last of them**

Statutory right/complaint	Qualifying period	Time limit for complaint
Right of fixed-term employee to receive written statement of reasons for less favourable treatment (FTE Regs, reg.5)	N/A	N/A
Right of fixed-term employee to be informed by employer of permanent vacancies (FTE Regs, reg.3(6))	N/A	3 months from (last) date on which other individuals, whether or not employees of the employer, were informed of the vacancy**
Right of employee employed under successive fixed-term contracts to be regarded as a permanent employee (FTE Regs, reg.8)	N/A	N/A
Right of employee employed under successive fixed-term contracts to receive written statement that he or she is a permanent employee (FTE Regs, reg.9)	N/A	N/A
Right not to suffer detriment in relation to: health and safety (ERA, s.44); Sunday working (ERA, s.45); jury service (ERA, s.43M); performing functions as a pension trustee (ERA, s.46) or as an employee representative (ERA, s.47); time off for study or training (ERA, s.47A); protected disclosures (ERA, s.47B); dependant care leave (ERA, s.47C); part-time working (PTW Regs, reg.7); right to be accompanied at a grievance or disciplinary hearing (ERelA, s.12); national minimum wage (NMWA, s.23); European Works Councils (TICE Regs, reg.32); or payment of tax credits by the employer (TCA, Sched.3, para.1)	None	3 months starting with date of (last) act or failure to act* (l)
Complaint that Secretary of Sate has not paid a sum in respect of the unpaid pensions contributions of an insolvent employer (Pensions Schemes Act 1993, s.126(2))	None	3 months starting with the date on which the Secretary of State's decision was communicated to the person(s) presenting it*
Contract claim by employee	None	In the employment tribunal, 3 months starting with EDT or if no EDT the last day on which the employee worked.* In the county court or High Court, 6 years from breach of contract

Statutory right/complaint	Qualifying period	Time limit for complaint
Contract claim by employer	None	In the employment tribunal, 6 weeks from receipt of employee's claim.* In the county court or High Court, 6 years from breach of contract

NOTES

(a) There is no qualifying period where a woman is dismissed during pregnancy or during ordinary or additional maternity leave periods (ERA, s.92(4)).

(b) For these purposes 'date of dismissal' means (a) where the employee's contract of employment was terminated by notice, the date on which the employer's notice was given, and (b) in any other case, the EDT – TULR(C)A, s.238(5).

(c) Starting on 18th birthday if the employee started work before that date.

(d) If during those six months the employee gives a written notice to the employer claiming a redundancy payment or refers a redundancy pay claim to a tribunal or submits a claim for unfair dismissal to a tribunal. The time limit may be extended to one year if during the six months immediately following the first six-month period the employee makes a written claim for payment to the employer or refers a redundancy pay claim to a tribunal or presents an unfair dismissal claim to a tribunal and it appears to the tribunal to be just and equitable that the employee should receive a redundancy payment – ERA, s.164. It may also be extended to one year if the employee dies during the six months following the relevant date – ERA, s.176(7).

(e) Unless the claimant was employed under a fixed-term contract for three months or less or a contract for the performance of a specific task which was not expected to last more than three months in which case he or she must have been continuously employed for more than three months in order to qualify.

(f) At the beginning of the 11th week before the expected week of childbirth.

(g) However, an act may be treated as done at the end of a period if it is an act 'extending over' that period (SDA, s.76(6)(b)/RRA, s.68(7)(b)/DDA, Sched.3, para.3(3)(b)) – see *Barclays Bank plc* v. *Kapur & ors* [1991] ICR 208.

(h) There are no expressly stated time limits governing actions under EC law. Time limits will generally be analogous to those under national law, i.e three months under the EC Equal Treatment Directive (No.76/207), and three or six months under Article 141 of the EC Treaty and the EC Equal Pay Directive (No.75/117). In *Biggs* v. *Somerset County Council* [1996] ICR 364 (Brief 559) a part-time employee brought a claim for unfair dismissal compensation relying on *R* v. *Secretary of State for Employment ex parte EOC & anor* [1994] IRLR 176 (Brief 513), in which the House of Lords ruled that the qualifying hours thresholds in UK legislation were contrary to Article 141. The Court of Appeal held that the relevant national time limit of three months began to run against the applicant from the date of her dismissal in the 1970s.

(i) The House of Lords confirmed the legality of the six-month time limit in *Preston & ors* v. *Wolverhampton Healthcare NHS Trust & ors (No.2); Fletcher & ors* v. *Midland Bank plc (No.2)* [2001] ICR 217, except in cases involving the application of the time limit to employees working on a succession of fixed-term contracts.

(j)   No statutory minimum qualifying period, but the rights in question – e.g payment of statutory notice pay – in practice involve a period of qualifying employment.

(k)   In a case where reg.38(2) applies (complaints by members of the armed forces), the time limit is extended from three months to six months (reg.30(2)(a)).

(l)   Where a tribunal jurisdiction is listed in Sched.4 to the Employment Act 2002, and s.32 of that Act applies, reg.15 of the Employment Act 2002 (Dispute Resolution) Regulations 2004, SI 2004/752 operates to extend the normal time limit for bringing a claim for a period of three months beginning with the day after the day on which it would otherwise have happened. The extension applies in two scenarios: where the employee has reasonable grounds for believing that a dismissal or disciplinary procedure, statutory or otherwise, was being followed when the normal time limit expired; or where the employee has lodged a step 1 grievance letter within the normal time limit.

(m)   The work and enforcement powers of the EOC and CRE transferred to the Equality and Human Rights Commission in October 2007.

*   ET can extend time limit where they consider it was 'not reasonably practicable' to present the complaint in time.

**   ET can extend time limit where they consider it 'just and equitable' to do so.

***   No extension of time allowed, except possibly where there has been deliberate fraud by the employer, causing the employee to suffer real injustice in missing the time limit – *Grimes* v. *Sutton London Borough Council* [1973] ICR 240.

**** ET can extend time limit on 'not reasonably practicable' grounds, as above, or where delay was caused by reasonable attempts to pursue internal appeal, etc.

***** Under HRA, s.7(5), the court or tribunal have the discretion to extend the time limit to such longer period as they consider equitable having regard to all the circumstances.

APPENDIX 5

Jurisdiction list

See pp. 291–2 for explanation of abbreviations.

Descriptor	Employment qualifications	Time limits	Originating legislation
Failure to allow time off for trade union duties	Nil	Within 3 months of the date on which the failure occurred	TULR(C)A 1992, ss.168–9
Failure to allow time off for antenatal care	Nil	Within 3 months of the date on which the failure occurred	ERA 1996, ss.55–6
Failure to allow time off to seek work during a redundancy situation	2 years	Within 3 months of the date on which the failure occurred	ERA 1996, ss.52–3
Failure to allow time off for trade union activities	Nil	Within 3 months of the date on which the failure occurred	TULR(C)A 1992, ss.170–1
Failure to allow time off for public duties	Nil	Within 3 months of the date on which the failure occurred	ERA 1996, ss.50 and 51
Unfairly dismissed because of disability	Nil	Within 3 months of the date of termination	DDA 1995, s.4(2)
Suffered other detriment(s) because of disability	Nil	Within 3 months of the date on which the act occurred	DDA 1995, s.4
Suffer discrimination in obtaining employment because of disability	Nil	Within 3 months of the date on which the act occurred	DDA 1995, s.4(1)
Employer fails to make reasonable adjustment to accommodate a disability	Nil	Within 3 months of the date on which the which the failure occurred	DDA 1995, s.6

Descriptor	Employment qualifications	Time limits	Originating legislation
Discrimination or victimisation on grounds of religion or belief	Nil	Within 3 months of the act complained of	EE (Religion or Belief) Regs 2003
Discrimination or victimisation on grounds of sexual orientation	Nil	Within 3 months of the act complained of	EE (Sexual Orientation) Regs 2003
Action short of dismissal to penalise trade union membership	Nil	Within 3 months of the date on which the act occurred	TULR(C)A 1992, s.146
Action short of dismissal to compel trade union membership	Nil	Within 3 months of the date on which the act occurred	TULR(C)A 1992, s.46
Unreasonable exclusion or expulsion from a trade union	Nil	Within 3 months of the date on which the act occurred	TULR(C)A 1992, s.174
Unjustified discipline by a trade union	Nil	Within 3 months of the date on which the act occurred	TULR(C)A 1992, s.66
Suffer discrimination in obtaining employment because of membership or non-membership of a trade union	Nil	Within 3 months of the date on which the act occurred	TULR(C)A 1992, s.137
Suffer discrimination in obtaining the services of an employment agency because of membership or non-membership of a trade union	Nil	Within 3 months of the date on which the act occurred	TULR(C)A 1992, s.138
Application by the Secretary of State for Trade and Industry to prohibit a person from running an Employment Agency	Nil	Nil	DCOA 1994, s.35

Descriptor	Employment qualifications	Time limits	Originating legislation
Failure to provide a written statement of reasons for dismissal or the contents of the statement are disputed	1 year	Within 3 months of the date on which the failure occurred	ERA 1996, ss.92 and 93
Failure to provide a written pay statement or an adequate pay statement	Nil	Within 3 months of the date on which the failure occurred	ERA 1996, ss.10 and 11
Failure to provide a written statement of terms and conditions and any subsequent changes to those terms	Within 2 months after beginning employment	Within 3 months of the date on which the failure occurred (no powers to extend)	ERA 1996, ss.1 and 4
Failure to provide a guarantee payment	1 month	Within 3 months of the day for which the employer has not made a guaranteed payment	ERA 1996, s.28
Failure to pay remuneration whilst suspended for medical reasons	1 month	Within 3 months of the day for which the payment is first claimed	ERA 1996, s.64
Application by an employee, their representative or trade union for a protective award as a result of an employer's failure to consult over a redundancy situation	Nil	Within 3 months of the effective date of termination	TULR(C)A 1992, s.189
Application by an employee that an employer has failed to pay a protected award as ordered by a tribunal	Nil	Within 3 months of the date of the award	TULR(C)A 1992, s.192
Failure to provide equal pay for equal value work	Nil	If employment has ceased, within 6 months	EPA 1970, s.2(1)

Descriptor	Employment qualifications	Time limits	Originating legislation
Failure of the employer to consult with an employee representative or trade union about a proposed transfer of an undertaking	Nil	Within 3 months of the relevant transfer being completed	TUPE 1981, regs.10, 10a and 11(1)
Failure of an employer to comply with an award by a tribunal following a finding that the employer had previously failed to consult about a proposed transfer of an undertaking	Nil	Within 3 months of the date of compensation order	TUPE 1981, reg.11(5)
Unfair dismissal for claiming under the flexible working regulations	Nil	Within 3 months of the act complained of	FWR 2002, reg.16(3)
Suffer a detriment for claiming under the flexible working regulations	Nil	Within 3 months of the act complained of	FWR 2002, reg.14(2) and (4)
Breach of procedure of the flexible working regulations	Nil	Within 3 months of the act complained of	FWR 2002, reg.6
Suffered less favourable treatment and/or dismissal as a fixed-term employee, than a full-time employee	Nil	Within 3 months of the alleged infringement, the date of less favourable treatment/detriment or the last of them	FTE 2002, reg.7
Appeal against an enforcement notice imposed by the HSE Inspector relating to notification of a hazardous substance	Nil	Within 21 days of the date of the notice	NESE 1994, reg.6 or HSWA 1974, s.24(2)

Descriptor	Employment qualifications	Time limits	Originating legislation
Appeal against an improvement or prohibition notice imposed by the HSE or Environmental Health Inspector, or by the Environment Agency	Nil	Within 21 days of the date of the notice	HSWA 1974, s.24 or COMAH 1999, s.18
Failure to allow a Safety Representative time off to carry out duties or undertake training	Nil	Within 3 months of the act complained of	HSCE 1996, reg.7 or SRSC 1977, reg.4(2)
Failure to pay a Safety Representative for time off to carry out duties or undertake training	Nil	Within 3 months of the act complained of	SRSC 1977, reg.4(2)
Failure by the Secretary of State for Trade and Industry to make an insolvency payment in lieu of wages and/or redundancy	Nil	Within 3 months of the refusal, or if the amount is disputed, the date of payment	ERA 1996, s.182
Appeal against the levy assessment of an Industrial Training Board	Nil	Set by the relevant board	Relevant Industrial Training Levy Order – either Construction Board or Engineering Construction Board
Failure to allow access to records or some other detriment whilst exercising rights under the NMWA 1998, or an appeal against an HMRC enforcement notice	Nil	3 months and 14 days from the act/omission relied upon (for records claims only)	NMWA 1998, s.10
		3 months and 14 days from the act/omission relied upon (for records claims only)	NMWA 1998, s.22
		Within 3 months of the act complained of	NMWA 1998, s.23

Descriptor	Employment qualifications	Time limits	Originating legislation
Loss of office as a result of the reorganisation of a statutory body	As applicable	As applicable	Miscellaneous statutes
Appeal against a non-discrimination notice issued by either the CRE or DRC or EOC	Nil	Within 6 weeks of the notice being served	DRC 1999, Sched.3 or RRA 1976, s.59 or SDA 1975, s.68
Failure of the employer to consult with an employee representative or trade union about a proposed contracting out of a pension scheme	Nil	None	SSPA 1975
Suffered a detriment and/or dismissal because of exercising rights under PIDA 1998	Nil	Within 3 months of the act complained of	PIDA 1998, s.3
Suffered a detriment and/or dismissal because of requesting or taking parental leave	Nil	Within 3 months of the act complained of	ERelA 1999, ss.76 and 80, Sched.4; MPL 1999, regs.13–16; PAL 2002, ss.28–9; see also MPL 2002
Suffered less favourable treatment and/or dismissal as a part-time employee, than a full-time employee	Nil	Within 3 months of the act complained of	PTW 2002, regs.5–8
Failure to pay a redundancy payment	2 years from 18th birthday	An employee should make a written request to the employer or tribunal within 6 months of the date of termination	ERA 1996, ss.163–4

Descriptor	Employment qualifications	Time limits	Originating legislation
Failure of the Secretary of State for Trade and Industry to pay a redundancy payment following an application to the National Insurance Fund	2 years from 18th birthday	An employee should make a written request to the employer or tribunal within 6 months of the date of termination	ERA 1996, ss.163–4
Race discrimination	Nil	Within 3 months of the act complained of	RRA 1976, ss.54 and 64
Unfairly dismissed because of refusing to work on a Sunday	Nil	Within 3 months of the date of termination or the last day of employment (whichever is applicable)	STA 1994, Sched.4(7)
Suffered detriment(s) because of refusing to work on a Sunday	Nil	Within 3 months of the act complained of	STA 1994, Sched.4(10)
Unfairly dismissed because of refusing to work on a Sunday (betting employee)	Nil	Within 3 months of the date of termination or the last day of employment	ERA 1996, s.101
Suffered detriment(s) because of refusing to work on a Sunday (betting employee)	Nil	Within 3 months of the date of detriment	ERA 1996, s.45
Sex discrimination	Nil	Within 3 months of the act complained of but there is no limit on pension claims	SDA 1975, ss.6 and 10
Failure to allow time off in order to assist a dependant	Nil	Within 3 months of the act complained of	ERA 1996, s.57A
Failure of the employer to prevent unauthorised or excessive deductions in the form of union subscriptions	Nil	Within 3 months of the deduction	TURER 1993, s.15(68)

Descriptor	Employment qualifications	Time limits	Originating legislation
Failure to provide written reasons for dismissal to an employee who is pregnant or on maternity leave	Nil	Within 3 months of the date of termination	ERA 1996, s.92(4)
Failure to pay remuneration whilst suspended from work for health and safety reasons whilst pregnant or on maternity leave	Nil	Within 3 months of the first date of suspension	ERA 1996, s.66
Unfairly dismissed/made redundant for health and safety reasons	Nil	Within 3 months of the date of termination	ERA 1996, ss.100 and 136
Application for interim relief by a health and safety representative, employee representative or pension trustee following dismissal	Nil	Within 7 days of the date of termination (no power to extend time limit)	ERA 1996, s.128
Suffer detriment(s) for other reasons	Nil	Within 3 months of the date of termination or the date of the act complained of	ERA 1996, ss.44–47, 58–63; or ERelA 1999, s.23
Unfair dismissal after exercising or claiming a statutory right	Nil	Within 3 months of the date of termination	ERA 1996, s.104
Failure to allow an employee to be accompanied at a disciplinary/grievance hearing	Nil	Within 3 months of the date of failure or threat of failure	ERelA 1999, ss.10–15
Application for a declaration that the inclusion of discriminatory terms/rules within certain agreements or rules causes the aforesaid to be invalid	Nil	None	TURER 1993, s.32

Descriptor	Employment qualifications	Time limits	Originating legislation
Breach of contract	Nil	Within 3 months of the date of termination or the last day of employment	ETA 1996, s.3
Suffered a detriment and/or dismissal because of exercising rights under the TCA 2002	Nil	Within 3 months of the date of detriment	TCA 2002, s.27 and Sched.1
Unfair dismissal for being, proposing or refusing to be a trade union member, or for involvement in trade union activities	Nil	Within 3 months of the date of termination	TULR(C)A 1992, s.152
Application for interim relief following dismissal for being, proposing or refusing to be a trade union member, or for involvement in trade union activities	Nil	Within 7 days of the date of termination (no power to extend time limit)	TULR(C)A 1992, s.161
Unfair dismissal for not being a trade union member	Nil	Within 3 months of the date of termination	TULR(C)A 1992, s.152
Application for interim relief following dismissal for not being a trade union member	Nil	Within 7 days of the date of termination (no power to extend time limit)	TULR(C)A 1992, s.161
Failure to allow maternity leave	Nil	Within 3 months beginning with the date of the act or failure to act to which the complaint relates	ERA 1996, s.74C (as inserted by ERelA 1999, Sched.4, Part III); also MPL, reg.18 and ERA 1996, s.48
Failure to allow a return to work following maternity leave	Nil	3 months after 29 weeks from intended return	ERA 1996, s.79
Unfair dismissal on grounds of pregnancy, child birth or maternity	Nil	Within 3 months of the date of termination	ERA 1996, s.99

Descriptor	Employment qualifications	Time limits	Originating legislation
Unfair dismissal in connection to a lock out, strike or other industrial action	Nil	Within 6 months of the date of termination	TULR(C)A 1992, s.238a
Unfair dismissal	1 year	Within 3 months of the date of termination	ERA 1996, s.94
Unfair dismissal as a result of a transfer of an undertaking	1 year	Within 3 months of the date of termination	TUPE 1981, reg.8
Failure to pay wages or an unauthorised deduction of wages	Nil	Within 3 months of deduction	ERA 1996, ss.13–27 or CEC 1975, reg.42
Failure to limit weekly or night working time, or to ensure rest breaks or annual leave entitlement	Nil	Within 3 months from the date when the right was refused	WTR 1998, regs.4, 6, 10, 12–17

* Under s.4(2) of the Employment (Industrial) Tribunals Act 1996, a Chairman can sit alone on:

(a) proceedings on an application under ss.161, 165 or 166 of the Trade Union and Labour Relations (Consolidation) Act 1992;

(b) proceedings on a complaint under s.126 of the Pension Schemes Act 1993;

(c) proceedings on a complaint under ss.23 or 188 of the Employment Rights Act 1996 or on an application under ss.128, 131 or 132 of that Act;

(d) proceedings in respect of which an Employment Tribunal has jurisdiction by virtue of s.3 of the Employment (Industrial) Tribunals Act 1996;

(e) proceedings in which the parties have given their written consent to the proceedings being heard in accordance with subsection 2 (whether or not they subsequently withdraw it);

(f) proceedings in which the person bringing the proceedings has given written notice withdrawing the case; and

(h) proceedings in which the person (or, where more than one, each of the persons) against whom the proceedings are brought does not, or has ceased to, contest the case.

Originating Legislation – Abbreviation and Full Title

CEC 1975	Colleges of Education (Compensation) Regulations 1975
COMAH 1999	Control of Major Accident Hazards Regulations 1999
DCOA 1994	Deregulation and Contracting Out Act 1994
DDA 1995	Disability Discrimination Act 1995
DRC 1999	Disability Rights Commission Act 1999
EE (Religion or Belief) Regs 2003	Employment Equality (Religion or Belief) Regulations 2003
EE (Sexual Orientation) Regs 2003	Employment Equality (Sexual Orientation) Regulations 2003
EPA 1970	Equal Pay Act 1970
ERA 1996	Employment Rights Act 1996
ERelA 1999	Employment Relations Act 1999
ETA 1996	Employment (Industrial) Tribunals Act 1996
FTE 2002	Fixed Term Employees (Prevention of Less Favourable Treatment) Regulations 2002
FWR 2002	Flexible Working (Procedural Requirements) Regulations 2002 and Flexible Working (Eligibility, Complaints and Remedies) Regulations 2002
HSCE 1996	Health and Safety Consultation with Employee Regulations 1996
HSWA 1974	Health and Safety at Work Act 1974
MPL 1999	Maternity and Parental Leave Regulations 1999
MPL 2002	Maternity and Parental Leave (Amendment) Regulations 2002
NESE 1994	Notification of Existing Substances (Enforcement) Regulations 1994
NMWA 1998	National Minimum Wage Act 1998
PAL 2002	Paternity and Adoption Leave Regulations 2002
PIDA 1998	Public Interest Disclosure Act 1998
PTW 2000	Part Time Worker (Prevention of Less Favourable Treatment) Regulations 2000
RRA 1976	Race Relations Act 1976
SDA 1975	Sex Discrimination Act 1975
SRSC 1977	Safety Representatives and Safety Committees Regulations 1977
SSPA 1975	Social Security Pensions Act 1975

STA 1994*	Sunday Trading Act 1994**
TCA 2002	Tax Credits Act 2002
TULR(C)A 1992	Trade Union and Labour Relations (Consolidation) Act 1992
TUPE 1981	Transfer of Undertakings (Protection of Employment) Regulations 1981
TURER 1993	Trade Union Reform and Employment Rights Act 1993
WTR 1998	Working Time Regulations 1998

Art. = (Article) **Par** = (Part) **reg.** = (regulation) **Sched.** = (Schedule) **s.** = (section)

** **Please note – the Sunday Trading Act 1994 does not apply in Scotland**

Revised by Operational Policy – April 2003

APPENDIX 6

Forms ET1 and ET3

Claim to an Employment Tribunal

Please read the **guidance notes** and the notes on this page carefully **before** filling in this form.

By law, your claim **must** be on an approved form provided by the Employment Tribunals Service and you must provide the information marked with ✻ and, if it is relevant, the information marked with ● (see 'Information needed before a claim can be accepted').

You may find it helpful to take advice **before** filling in the form, particularly if your claim involves discrimination.

How to fill in this form

All claimants **must** fill in **sections 1, 2 and 3**. You then only need to fill in those sections of the form that apply to your case. For example:

For **unpaid wages**, fill in **sections 4 and 8**.

For **unfair dismissal**, fill in **sections 4 and 5**.

For **discrimination**, fill in **sections 4 and 6**.

For a **redundancy payment**, fill in **sections 4 and 7**.

For **unfair dismissal** and **discrimination**, fill in **sections 4, 5 and 6**.

For **unfair dismissal** and **unpaid wages**, fill in **sections 4, 5 and 8**.

Fill in **section 10** only if there is some information you wish to draw to the tribunal's attention and **section 12** only if you have appointed a representative to act on your behalf in dealing with your claim.

If this claim is one of a number of claims arising out of the same or similar circumstances, you can obtain a Multiple Claim Form from the ETS Public Enquiry Line on 08457 959775 or from www.employmenttribunals.gov.uk. Alternatively you can give the names and addresses of additional claimants on a separate sheet or sheets of paper. If you do this you must make it clear that the relevant required information for all the additional claimants is the same as stated in the main claim.

Please make sure that all the information you give is as accurate as possible.

Where there are tick boxes, please tick the one that applies.

Please write clearly in black ink using CAPITAL LETTERS.

If you fax the form, do not send a copy in the post.

1 Your details

1.1 Title: Mr Mrs Miss Ms Other

1.2* First name (or names):

1.3* Surname or family name:

1.4 Date of birth (date/month/year): Are you: male? female?

1.5* Address: Number or Name

Street

+ Town/City

County

Postcode

1.6 Phone number (**where we can contact you during normal working hours**):

1.7 How would you prefer us to communicate with you? E-mail Post Fax
(Please tick only one box)

E-mail address:

@

Fax number:

2 Respondent's details

2.1* Give the name of your employer or the organisation you are claiming against.

2.2* Address: Number or Name

Street

Town/City

+ County

Postcode

Phone number:

2.3 If you worked at an address different from the one you have given at 2.2, please give the full address and postcode.

Postcode

Phone number:

2.4● If your complaint is against more than one respondent please give the names, addresses and postcodes of additional respondents.

3 Action before making a claim

3.1* Are you, or were you, an employee of the respondent?   Yes   No
If 'Yes', please now go straight to section 3.3.

3.2 Are you, or were you, a worker providing services to the respondent?   Yes   No
If 'Yes', please now go straight to section 4.
If 'No', please now go straight to section 6.

3.3● Is your claim, or part of it, about a dismissal by the respondent?   Yes   No
If 'No', please now go straight to section 3.5.
If your claim is about constructive dismissal, i.e. you resigned because of something
your employer did or failed to do which made you feel you could no longer continue to
work for them, tick the box here and the 'Yes' box in section 3.4.

3.4● Is your claim about anything else, in addition to the dismissal?   Yes   No
If 'No', please now go straight to section 4.
If 'Yes', please answer questions 3.5 to 3.7 about the
non-dismissal aspects of your claim.

3.5● Have you put your complaint(s) in writing to the respondent?

   Yes   Please give the date you put it to them in writing.

   No

If 'No', please now go straight to section 3.7.

3.6● Did you allow at least 28 days between the date you put your   Yes   No
complaint in writing to the respondent and the date you sent us this claim?
If 'Yes', please now go straight to section 4.

3.7● Please explain why you did not put your complaint in writing to the respondent or,
if you did, why you did not allow at least 28 days before sending us your claim.
(In most cases, it is a legal requirement to take these procedural steps. Your claim
will not be accepted unless you give a valid reason why you did not have to meet
the requirement in your case. If you are not sure, you may want to get legal advice.)

295

4 Employment details

4.1 Please give the following information if possible.

When did your employment start?

When did or will it end?

Is your employment continuing?   Yes   No

4.2 Please say what job you do or did.

4.3 How many hours do or did you work each week?   hours each week

4.4 How much are or were you paid?

Pay before tax   £   ,   .00   Hourly

Normal take-home pay (including   £   ,   .00   Weekly

overtime, commission, bonuses and so on)   Monthly

                                                                           Yearly

4.5 If your employment has ended, did you work   Yes   No
(or were you paid for) a period of notice?

If 'Yes', how many weeks or months did   weeks   months
you work or were you paid for?

5 Unfair dismissal or constructive dismissal

Please fill in this section only if you believe you have been unfairly or constructively dismissed.

5.1 If you were dismissed by your employer, you should explain why you think your dismissal
was unfair. If you resigned because of something your employer did or failed to do which
made you feel you could no longer continue to work for them (constructive dismissal)
you should explain what happened.

5 Unfair dismissal or constructive dismissal continued

5.1 continued

5.2 Were you in your employer's pension scheme? Yes No

5.3 If you received any other benefits from your employer, please give details.

5.4 Since leaving your employment have you got another job? Yes No
If 'No', please now go straight to section 5.7.

5.5 Please say when you started (or will start) work.

5.6 Please say how much you are now earning (or will earn). £   ,   .00 each

5.7 Please tick the box to say what you want if your case is successful:

a To get your old job back and compensation (reinstatement)

b To get another job with the same employer and compensation (re-engagement)

c Compensation only

6 Discrimination

Please fill in this section only if you believe you have been discriminated against.

6.1 Please tick the box or boxes to indicate what discrimination (including victimisation) you are complaining about:

Sex (including equal pay) ☐   Race ☐

Disability ☐   Religion or belief ☐

Sexual orientation ☐

6.2 Please describe the incidents which you believe amounted to discrimination, the dates of these incidents and the people involved.

7 Redundancy payments

Please fill in this section only if you believe you are owed a redundancy payment.

7.1 ● Please explain why you believe you are entitled to this payment and set out the steps you have taken to get it.

8 Other payments you are owed

Please fill in this section only if you believe you are owed other payments.

8.1 ● Please tick the box or boxes to indicate that money is owed to you for:

unpaid wages?

holiday pay?

notice pay?

other unpaid amounts?

8.2 How much are you claiming? £ , .00

Is this: before tax? after tax?

8.3 ● Please explain why you believe you are entitled to this payment. If you have specified an amount, please set out how you have worked this out.

9 Other complaints

Please fill in this section only if you believe you have a complaint that is not covered elsewhere.

9.1 Please explain what you are complaining about and why.
Please include any relevant dates.

10 Other information

10.1 Please do not send a covering letter with this form.
You should add any extra information you want us to know here.

11 Disability

11.1 Please tick this box if you consider yourself to have a disability   Yes   No
If 'Yes', please say what this disability is and tell us what assistance, if any, you will need as your claim progresses through the system.

12 Your representative

Please fill in this section only if you have appointed a representative. If you do fill this section in, we will in future only send correspondence to your representative and not to you.

12.1 Representative's name:

12.2 Name of the representative's organisation:

12.3 Address:
    Number or Name
    Street
+   Town/City
    County
    Postcode

12.4 Phone number:

12.5 Reference:

12.6 How would you prefer us to communicate with them? (Please tick only one box)   Post   Fax   E-mail
    Fax number:
    E-mail address:
    @

13 Multiple cases

13.1 To your knowledge, is your claim one of a number of claims arising from the same or similar circumstances?   Yes   No

Please sign and date here

Signature: Date:

ET1 v02 008   8   ET1 v02 008

APPENDIX 6

Additional space for notes.

Equal Opportunities Monitoring Form

You are not obliged to fill in this section but, if you do so, it will enable us to monitor our processes and ensure that we provide equality of opportunity to all. The information you give here will be treated in strict confidence and this page will not form part of your case. It will be used only for monitoring and research purposes without identifying you.

1. What is your country of birth?

England   Wales

Scotland

Northern Ireland

Republic of Ireland

Elsewhere, *please write in the present name of the country*

2. What is your ethnic group?
Choose ONE section from A to E, then ✓ the appropriate box to indicate your cultural background.

A White

British   Irish

Any other White background *please write in*

B Mixed

White and Black Caribbean

White and Black African

White and Asian

Any other Mixed background *please write in*

C Asian or Asian British

Indian   Pakistani

Bangladeshi

Any other Asian background *please write in*

D: Black or Black British

Caribbean   African

Any other Black background *please write in*

E Chinese or other ethnic group

Chinese

Any other, *please write in*

3. What is your religion?
✓ box only

None

Christian (including Church of England, Catholic, Protestant and all other Christian denominations)

Buddhist

Hindu

Jewish

Muslim

Sikh

Any other religion, *please write in*

Case number:

1 Name of respondent company or organisation

1.1* Name of your organisation:

Contact name:

1.2* Address   Number or Name

                   Street

                   Town/City

+   County

                   Postcode

1.3 Phone number:

1.4 How would you prefer us to   E-mail   Post   Fax
communicate with you? (Please tick only one box)
E-mail address:

@

Fax number:

1.5 What does this organisation mainly make or do?

1.6 How many people does this organisation employ in Great Britain?

1.7 Does this organisation have more than one site in Great Britain?   Yes   No

1.8 If 'Yes', how many people are employed at the place where the
claimant worked?

2 Action before a claim

2.1 Is, or was, the claimant an employee?   Yes   No
If 'Yes', please now go straight to section 2.3.

2.2 Is, or was, the claimant a worker providing services to you?   Yes   No
If 'Yes', please now go straight to section 3.
If 'No', please now go straight to section 5.

2.3 If the claim, or part of it, is about a dismissal,   Yes   No
do you agree that the claimant was dismissed?
If 'Yes', please now go straight to section 2.6.

2.4 If the claim includes something **other than** dismissal,   Yes   No
does it relate to an action you took on
grounds of the claimant's conduct or capability?
If 'Yes', please now go straight to section 2.6.

2.5 Has the substance of this claim been raised by the claimant   Yes   No
in writing under a grievance procedure?

2.6 If 'Yes', please explain below what stage you have reached in the dismissal and disciplinary
procedure or grievance procedure (whichever is applicable).
If 'No' and the claimant says they have raised a grievance with you in writing, please say
whether you received it and explain why you did not accept this as a grievance.

3 Employment details

3.1 Are the dates of employment given by the claimant correct?   Yes   No
If 'Yes', please now go straight to section 3.3.

3.2 If 'No', please give dates and say why you disagree with the dates given by the claimant.

When their employment started

When their employment ended or will end

Is their employment continuing?   Yes   No

I disagree with the dates for the following reasons.

3.3 Is the claimant's description of their job or job title correct?   Yes   No
If 'Yes', please now go straight to section 3.5.

3.4 If 'No', please give the details you believe to be correct below.

3.5 Is the information given by the claimant correct about being paid for, or working, a period of notice?   Yes   No
If 'Yes', please now go straight to section 3.7.

3.6 If 'No', please give the details you believe to be correct below. If you gave them no notice or didn't pay them instead of letting them work their notice, please explain what happened and why.

3.7 Are the claimant's hours of work correct?   Yes   No
If 'Yes', please now go straight to section 3.9.

3.8 If 'No', please enter the details you believe to be correct.   hours each week

3.9 Are the earnings details given by the claimant correct?   Yes   No
If 'Yes', please now go straight to section 4.

3.10 If 'No', please give the details you believe to be correct below.

Pay before tax   £   ,   .00   Hourly / Weekly

Normal take-home pay (including overtime, commission, bonuses and so on)   £   ,   .00   Monthly / Yearly

305

4 Unfair dismissal or constructive dismissal

4.1 Are the details about pension and other benefits   Yes   No
given by the claimant correct?
If 'Yes', please now go straight to section 5.

4.2 If 'No', please give the details you believe to be correct below.

5 Response

5.1* Do you resist the claim?   Yes   No
If 'No', please now go straight to section 6.

5.2● If 'Yes', please set out in full the grounds on which you resist the claim.

6 Other information

6.1 Please do not send a covering letter with this form. You should add any extra information you want us to know here.

7 Your representative   If you have a representative, please fill in the following.

7.1 Representative's name:

7.2 Name of the representative's organisation:

7.3 Address   Number or Name

Street

+ Town/City

County

Postcode

7.4 Phone number:

7.5 Reference:

7.6 How would you prefer us to communicate with them? (Please tick only one box)   E-mail   Post   Fax

E-mail address:

@

Fax number:

Please sign and date here

Signature: Date:

ET3 v02 004 URN 05/1442   4   ET3 v02 004 URN 05/1442

APPENDIX 7

Useful websites

Advisory Conciliation and Arbitration Service (ACAS)	**www.acas.org.uk**
British and Irish Legal Information Institute	**www.bailii.org**
Citizens Advice Bureaux	**www.citizensadvice.org.uk**
Her Majesty's Courts Service	**www.hmcourts-service.gov.uk/**
Employment Appeal Tribunal	**www.employmentappeals.gov.uk**
Employment Lawyer's Association	**www.elaweb.org.uk**
Employment Tribunal Service	**www.employmenttribunals.gov.uk**
Equality and Human Rights Commission	**www.equalityhumanrights.com**

On 1 October 2007 the three equality commissions – Commission for Racial Equality, Disability Rights Commission and Equal Opportunities Commission – merged into the new Equality and Human Rights Commission

European Commission	**http://europa.eu.int**
European Court of Human Rights	**www.echr.coe.int**
Incorporated Council of Law Reporting	**www.lawreports.co.uk**
Legal Services Commission	**www.legalservices.gov.uk**
Law Centres Federation	**www.lawcentres.org.uk**
Law Society	**www.lawsociety.org.uk**
Office of Public Sector Information	**www.opsi.gov.uk**
Acts of Parliament (since 1988) and SIs (since 1987) (legislation as enacted)	
Statute Law Database	**www.statutelaw.gov.uk**

Index